Perspectives in Neural Computing

T0140544

Springer

London
Berlin
Heidelberg
New York
Barcelona
Hong Kong
Milan
Paris
Singapore
Tokyo

Also in this series:

Gustavo Deco and Dragan Obradovic
An Information-Theoretic Approach to Neural Computing
0-387-94666-7

Achilleas Zapranis and Apostolos-Paul Refenes
Principles of Neural Model Identification, Selection and Adequacy
1-85233-139-9

Walter J. Freeman
Neurodynamics: An Exploration in Mesoscopic Brain Dynamics
1-85233-616-1

H. Malmgren, M Borga and L. Niklasson (Eds)
Artificial Neural Networks in Medicine and Biology
1-85233-289-1

Mark Girolami
Advances in Independent Component Analysis
1-85233-263-8

Robert M. French and Jacques P. Sougné (Eds)
Connectionist Models of Learning, Development and Evolution
1-85233-354-5

Artur S. d'Avila Garcez, Krysia B. Broda and Dov M. Gabbay
Neural-Symbolic Learning Systems
1-85233-512-2

Roberto Tagliaferri and Maria Marinaro
Neural Nets – WIRN VIETRI-01
1-85233-505-X

Related Title

Robert Hecht-Nielsen and Thomas McKenna (Eds)
Computational Models for Neuroscience: Human Cortical Information
Processing
1-85233-593-9

Preface

This is a book about the methods developed by our research team, over a period of 10 years, for predicting financial market returns.

The work began in late 1991, at a time when one of us (Jimmy Shadbolt) had just completed a rewrite of the software used at Econostat by the economics team for medium-term trend prediction of economic indicators. Looking for a new project, it was suggested that we look at non-linear modelling of financial markets, and that a good place to start might be with neural networks.

One small caveat should be added before we start: we use the terms "prediction" and "prediction model" throughout the book, although, with only such a small amount of information being extracted about future performance, can we really claim to be building predictors at all? Some might say that the future of markets, especially one month ahead, is too dim to perceive. We think we can claim to "predict" for two reasons. Firstly we do indeed predict a few per cent of future values of certain assets in terms of past values of certain indicators, as shown by our track record. Secondly, we use standard and in-house prediction methods that are purely quantitative. We allow no subjective view to alter what the models tell us. Thus we are doing prediction, even if the problem is very hard. So while we could throughout the book talk about "getting a better view of the future" or some such euphemism, we would not be correctly describing what it is we are actually doing. We are indeed getting a better view of the future, by using prediction methods.

The initial results looked very promising, and we soon had a small team working on one-month-ahead bond prediction. Late in 1992 we were given funds to manage on the basis of those predictions. Over the nine years since then we have continuously managed funds and consistently outperformed our benchmark (the Salomon Index). The team came to be known as the *NewQuant* Team, and the product the *NewQuant* Product. References are made throughout the book to both as *NewQuant*.

The contributors to this book have all contributed directly to our work, either as researchers in our team or as consultants on specific aspects.

We would like to thank them heartily for their efforts.

Others who have contributed to our work (but not the book) in more or less chronological order are Paul Refenes, Magali Azema-Barak and Ugur Bilge (who got us up to date with neural networks), John Coyne (who worked with genetic algorithms for input selection and developed our first network integration models), Drago Indjic (who developed, amongst other things, a method that turned out to be the same as Leo Breiman's Bagging), Dario Romare (linear modelling and wavelets), Pano Vergis (PCA, mutual information) and David Chippington (our software backup and system admin). On the way, Brian Ripley kicked our butts and forced some very serious analysis of what we were doing.

Some research directions have been examined and abandoned; some of those will probably be revisited when we have solutions to the problems encountered. Some have taken up to a year to deliver the goods and are part of our toolkit today. In all over 50 person years have gone into our research.

The problems encountered along the way are those due to our living on the edge of randomness. Unlike in most other disciplines, the predictability of our data is marginal – the error bounds are almost as wide as the data variance. We cannot make claims of models fitting data with 90% confidence levels; in fact, we hope only to be consistently a few per cent better than random. The ultimate test of whether our models have value comes only from using them to allocate funds in a portfolio, and here we can make claims to success.

The *NewQuant* process must be considered as a whole, from the economics used for initial input selection, through the quantitative data selection, prediction modelling and model combining, to the portfolio optimisation. No individual model is of use on its own: it is only through the whole process that we can derive benefit.

We would like to close by thanking Charles Diamond, the MD of Econostat, for continued support, allowing the work reported here to be performed.

Jimmy Shadbolt
John G. Taylor

Contents

List of Contributors xiii

Part I   Introduction to Prediction in the Financial Markets

1   Introduction to the Financial Markets 3
   1.1   The Financial Markets 3
   1.2   Economics and the Markets 5
   1.3   Financial Markets and Economic Data 6
   1.4   What Are We Predicting? 7
   1.5   The Overall Process 8

2   Univariate and Multivariate Time Series Predictions 11
   2.1   Philosophical Assumptions 11
   2.2   Data Requirements 16
   2.3   Summary 22

3   Evidence of Predictability in Financial Markets 23
   3.1   Overview 23
   3.2   Review of Theoretical Arguments 24
   3.3   Review of Empirical Research 26
   3.4   Predictability Tests 29
   3.5   Beyond Tests for Market Efficiency 32
   3.6   Summary 32

4   Bond Pricing and the Yield Curve 35
   4.1   The Time Value of Money and Discount Factors 35
   4.2   Pricing Bonds 36
   4.3   Bond Yield and the Yield Curve 37
   4.4   Duration and Convexity 38
   4.5   Summary 39

5   Data Selection 41
   5.1   Introduction 41
   5.2   The General Economic Model 42
   5.3   Proxies 42
   5.4   Principal Components 43

5.5   Summary   45

Part II   Theory of Prediction Modelling

6   General Form of Models of Financial Markets   49
    6.1   Introduction   49
    6.2   Cost Functions   49
    6.3   Parameterisation   51
    6.4   Econometric Models   52
    6.5   Summary   53

7   Overfitting, Generalisation and Regularisation   55
    7.1   Overfitting and Generalisation   55
    7.2   Early Stopping   56
    7.3   Information Criteria   57
    7.4   Regularisation   57
    7.5   Weight Decay   58
    7.6   Forgetting   58
    7.7   Summary   59

8   The Bootstrap, Bagging and Ensembles   61
    8.1   Introduction   61
    8.2   The Bias–Variance Trade-Off   61
    8.3   The Bootstrap   62
    8.4   Bagging   63
    8.5   Bootstrap with Noise   65
    8.6   Decorrelated Models   66
    8.7   Ensembles in Financial Market Prediction   67

9   Linear Models   69
    9.1   Introduction   69
    9.2   Review of Linear Forecasting Methods   70
    9.3   Moving Average/Smoothing Methods   70
    9.4   ARMA, ARIMA and Time Series Regression Models . .   72
    9.5   Cointegration and Error Correction Models   73
    9.6   Ridge Regression   74
    9.7   State Space Models   75
    9.8   Summary   76

10 Input Selection   77
    10.1   Introduction   77
    10.2   Input Selection   77
    10.3   Mutual Information   81
    10.4   Summary   83

Part III Theory of Specific Prediction Models

11 Neural Networks 87
11.1 What Are Neural Networks? 87
11.2 The Living Neuron 89
11.3 The Artificial or Formal Neuron 89
11.4 Neural Network Architectures 90
11.5 Neural Network Training Rules 92
11.6 Further Comments on Neural Networks 93

12 Learning Trading Strategies for Imperfect Markets 95
12.1 Introduction 95
12.2 Trading Predictability 96
12.3 Modelling Trading Strategies 98
12.4 Experimental Design and Simulation Experiments . . 101
12.5 Summary 108

13 Dynamical Systems Perspective and Embedding 109
13.1 Introduction 109
13.2 Practical Problems 112
13.3 Characterising and Measuring Complexity 113
13.4 SVD Smoothing 114
13.5 Summary 115

14 Vector Machines 117
14.1 Introduction 117
14.2 Support Vector Machines 117
14.3 Relevance Vector Machines 118
14.4 Optimising the Hyperparameters for Regression 120
14.5 Optimising the Hyperparameters for Classification . . 120
14.6 Summary 121

15 Bayesian Methods and Evidence 123
15.1 Bayesian Methods 123
15.2 A Bayesian View of Probability 123
15.3 Hypothesis Testing 125
15.4 The Bayesian Evidence Ratio 127
15.5 Conclusions 130

Part IV Prediction Model Applications

16 Yield Curve Modelling 133
16.1 Yield Curve Modelling 133
16.2 Yield Curve Data 133
16.3 Yield Curve Parameterisation 135
16.4 Predicting the Yield Curve 140
16.5 Conclusion 142

17 Predicting Bonds Using the Linear Relevance Vector
Machine 145
   17.1 Introduction 145
   17.2 The RVM as a Predictor 146
   17.3 Input Variable Selection 148
   17.4 Summary and Conclusions 154

18 Artificial Neural Networks 157
   18.1 Introduction 157
   18.2 Artificial Neural Networks 157
   18.3 Models 163
   18.4 Summary 165

19 Adaptive Lag Networks 167
   19.1 The Problem 167
   19.2 Adaptive Lag Networks 167
   19.3 Training the Adaptive Lag Network 169
   19.4 Test Results 170
   19.5 Modelling 171
   19.6 Summary and Conclusions 174

20 Network Integration 175
   20.1 Making Predictions with Network Ensembles 175
   20.2 The Network Integrator 177
   20.3 The Random Vector Functional Link (RVFL) 178
   20.4 Summary 179

21 Cointegration 181
   21.1 Introduction 181
   21.2 Construction of Statistical Mispricings 183
   21.3 Conditional Statistical Arbitrage Strategies 184
   21.4 Application of Cointegration-Based Methodology
       to FTSE 100 Stocks 185
   21.5 Empirical Results of Conditional Statistical Arbitrage
       Models 185
   21.6 Summary 191

22 Joint Optimisation in Statistical Arbitrage Trading 193
   22.1 Introduction 193
   22.2 Statistical Mispricing 194
   22.3 Controlling the Properties of the Forecasting Model . . 195
   22.4 Modelling the Trading Strategy 196
   22.5 Joint Optimisation 197
   22.6 Empirical Experiments 197
   22.7 Summary 201

23 Univariate Modelling 203
    23.1   Introduction 203
    23.2   Nearest Neighbours 203
    23.3   The Group Method of Data Handling (GMDH) 205
    23.4   The Support Vector Machine (SVM) Predictor
           Model 207
    23.5   The Relevance Vector Machine (RVM) 209

24 Combining Models 211
    24.1   Introduction 211
    24.2   Linear Combiners 212
    24.3   A Temperature-Dependent SOFTMAX Combiner . . . 212
    24.4   The Combiner Algorithm 213
    24.5   Results 216
    24.6   Conclusions 217

Part V   Optimising and Beyond

25 Portfolio Optimisation 221
    25.1   Portfolio Optimisation 221
    25.2   Notation and Terminology 222
    25.3   Scope of Portfolio Optimisation Methods 224
    25.4   Efficient Set Mathematics and the Efficient Frontier . . 225
    25.5   Construction of Optimised Portfolios Using Quadratic
           Programming 229
    25.6   Issues in Practical Portfolio Construction 230
    25.7   What Portfolio Selection Requires 233
    25.8   The Process of Building an Optimised Portfolio . . . 234
    25.9   Example of an Asset Allocation Portfolio 236
    25.10 Alternative Measures of Risk and Methods of
           Optimisation 241
    25.11 Questions about Portfolio Optimisation and
           Discussion 245

26 Multi-Agent Modelling 247
    26.1   Introduction 247
    26.2   The Minority Game 248
    26.3   A General Multi-agent Approach to the Financial
           Markets 249
    26.4   Conclusions 251

27 Financial Prediction Modelling: Summary and Future
    Avenues 253
    27.1   Summary of the Results 253
    27.2   Underlying Aspects of the Approach 255
    27.3   Future Avenues 257

Further Reading **259**

References **261**

Index **269**

List of Contributors

John G. Taylor
Professor of Mathematics
Kings College, London, UK
Director of Research
Econostat New Quant Ltd, Wargrave, UK

Jimmy Shadbolt
Head of Research
Econostat New Quant Ltd, Wargrave, UK

Chris Adcock
Professor of Economics
University of Sheffield
Sheffield, UK

David Attew
Econostat New Quant Ltd, Wargrave, UK

Neil Burgess, PhD
Vice President
Portfolio Products
Institutional Equity Division
Morgan Stanley
London, UK

Neep Hazarika, PhD
Econostat New Quant Ltd, Wargrave, UK

Sebastian Larsson, PhD
Econostat New Quant Ltd, Wargrave, UK

Neville Towers, PhD
Risk Analysis Manager
London Electricity Plc
London, UK

PART I
Introduction to Prediction in the Financial Markets

The book commences, in this first part, with chapters giving a broad description of the markets we will consider and the tools we will use. It has relatively few quantitative formulae, which we will develop more fully in later parts and apply in more detail even later.

We start in Chapter 1 with a very general description of the markets: what assets are to be considered, the factors that may influence them, and how financial and economic indicators are of value in our attempt to predict future values of these various assets.

Chapter 2 inserts a little mathematical meat onto the bare bones of the previous chapter, giving the basic structures of the two fundamentally different approaches to prediction: that of pattern matching (univariate), and of indicator driving of assets (multivariate). We then discuss what inputs might be valuable for constructing such multivariate models.

A crucial question is: are the markets predictable? This question of market efficiency is reviewed in Chapter 3, with the conclusion that predictability is present as a necessary component of the financial markets.

In Chapter 4 we turn to a more detailed discussion of one of the main asset classes we consider in more detail later, that of bonds. Here the dependence on maturity of the bond yield – the yield curve – is discussed in terms of the time value of money, so setting up the structure of the price of a given maturity bond.

The final chapter in this part deals with input variable selection. This is a crucial first step in constructing multivariate models for the assets of interest, but is not at all trivial, due to the large number of possible economic and financial variables to choose from. Various features in of such a selection process are considered here, including data compression by principal component analysis, for example.

1. Introduction to the Financial Markets

John G. Taylor

1.1 The Financial Markets

Some indication of an improving global economic environment and stronger stock market pushed government bonds lower this week. (*Financial Times*, 25/26 August 2001)

The yield curve steepened sharply this week as more gloom descended on the economy and investors bet that the US Federal Reserve might cut interest rates by as much as 50 basis points in November (*Financial Times*, 27/28 October 2001)

How can the economic environment influence the values of various assets such as stocks and bonds? More specifically, how can we use such influences to get a better view of how some asset values will change? Even more preliminarily, what do these quantities such as "yield curve" and "basis points" mean for investors and those, like ourselves, who are trying to project the values of certain financial assets? If we can get a better view of asset values in the near future then we may sell those we expect to fall in price while holding on to those we expect to increase in value or even increase our holding of them. But how long is "the future"? How long ahead can we expect to get a worthwhile view that can be used in this way to make money?

Such a process of buying and selling financial assets is risky. This is particularly so in view of the fall in technology shares during 2001, from when they were heavily overpriced to the present, when a number of dotcom firms have gone bankrupt and even large companies are in financial difficulties, with reduced profitability. Even more risk has been added to the economic environment with the attack on the World Trade Center in New York on 11 September 2001. The subsequent reduction in air travel caused a fall of up to 50% in the share values of some airline companies. Numerous bailouts by governments of their local airlines, such as SwissAir, then occurred. Considerable amounts of personal and corporate investment were wiped out in the process. Clearly, predicting the future is made very much more difficult in the presence of such events, with the possibility of more to come. With increased risk must also come better risk assessment and control as an increasingly important part of financial asset management.

But how did we get here from the earlier days? How did the enormous financial services industry, with its decidedly global features straddling international frontiers, develop from the small beginnings of the local financial asset groups of the 18th and 19th centuries?

Various "quant" groups (a term denoting strong dependence on quantitative analysis), especially our own *NewQuant* team, have developed a number of techniques for prediction in the financial markets. To explain these processes to a wider audience, particularly those coming from Artificial Intelligence, we need to start by giving a brief description of the markets and how they function. We will then proceed to answer the questions raised above and related ones as we move through the book.

We start with money, the root of it all. The power of money grew commensurately with the Industrial Revolution. As this took off, increasingly large sums of money were needed to finance the building of factories, enabling goods to be produced for workers. As part of the growth of wealth new methods had to be introduced to support such financing, with new methods of raising money by temporary borrowing from the wealth-owning classes. Thus shares were issued in companies, which promised to pay to the holder a proportion of the profits of the issuing company as well as ultimate return of the capital. Some of these companies did not survive, but in the creative atmosphere of the Industrial Revolution enough became profitable for a flourishing market of such stocks to be created. These stocks had value in themselves, in terms of future share dividends and the level of company profits, and so began to be traded in their own right. Thus began the Stock Market. Assessments of the risk of stocks was important, and such measures as the price-to-earnings ratio are used in the process. Aggregates of stock prices were assembled, such as we now have in the FTSE 100 or FTSE 250 indices in the UK or the S&P 500 index in the USA, so as to give a measure to the overall rises or falls in the most successful and larger companies.

At the same time, governments were called on to provide an increasing range of benefits for their populaces. Each government had to achieve this by either taxing or borrowing. Thus arose the issuance of government bonds, which promised both a dividend at a certain rate of interest as well as repayment of the capital after a certain number of years (the time to maturity). These bonds were more secure than company stocks, since it was much less likely that a government would go bankrupt than would a company (although the value of a government bond could fall drastically if there was high inflation in the country). Banks, which had been developed as a repository of money and provided mechanisms for safe deposits of money over short periods, also issued their own stocks.

As the financial markets grew in size more complex instruments were also created. In order to reduce the risk of future loss of value, future contracts were devised. These were originally for pork bellies, say to be sold at a guaranteed price six months hence. Buyers of these contracts came forward, seeing an opportunity to make a profit, so allowing the formation of futures markets (first in Chicago), so as to allow "hands off" trading to occur, with the market acting as an unbiased intermediary (but also taking its cut of the proceeds) holding to account the buyer and seller of the contracts. Futures contracts were created in other commodities, and became increasingly important, so leading to a spread of futures markets. Further artificial assets were created to allow for leverage, the process in which an investor does not need to pay for the total cost of a futures contract but must only pay a fraction of that ahead of a final day of reckoning. Thus were created options, in which an option could be taken out on a certain asset, with the option allowing the holder to buy a certain asset at a certain price (related to its present price and expectations of the possibility of it changing) at a certain future point. The option need not be exercised if the asset price fell so that the asset was not valuable enough to the prospective buyer; it would be exercised if the price rose enough above its present price at which the option was purchased. Thus the option buyer was only liable for the option price itself, only a small proportion of the actual asset price. In this way leverage could be obtained, and a smaller amount of outlay could lead to a much larger profit. Option pricing has since become a very important part of financial analysis, and has led to much mathematical development involved with stochastic time series.

1.2   Economics and the Markets

What drives the markets? We have already had some indication of factors achieving this in the quotations at the beginning of the chapter. Thus we have cited the general economic environment, the stock market, and interest rates on government and bank short-term lending. These are important, but there are also other factors that should not be neglected. Thus there will be actual costs of manufacturing commodities, such as cars, washing machines and refrigerators, or of manufacturing tools. These commodity prices will themselves be determined by the prices of the raw material, such as precious metals, used in the commodity manufacturing process. Such metals prices will therefore also be important in determining market profitability and hence stock values. Related raw materials for other goods, such as for chip manufacturing, also need to be considered.

Can we recognise, on economic grounds, the economic key players who can be said to drive the markets? The difficulty in so doing is that we need to take account of effects that are lagged by several months, even up to a year or more. Thus a writer in *The Economist* noted recently:

> There is always a lag of 6–12 months before monetary policy has its main impact, but it traditionally works through lower long term bond yields, higher share prices and a weaker dollar. ("Get a Parachute", *The Economist*, 25 August 2001)

If we take account of such longish lag times then we can expect, from this and many other analyses, that monetary policy (levels of interest rates set by central governments, amounts of money supplied, amounts of bonds issued) will play an important role in stock and bond prices month-on-month. This may not be so evident at a higher frequency, such as day-by-day, since the money transmission mechanisms present in the complex economy impact relatively slowly. This goes through the line of changes that have to be taken up by interest-paying company borrowings, which themselves affect factory prices which then impact on consumers and thence profits. This changes demand and confidence in a stock or in the stock market as a whole, and thereby also causes changes in demand in bonds (usually regarded as a safe haven compared to riskier stocks). As noted in the quotation, these effects are delayed. More rapid response can occur day-on-day owing to monetary decisions, but these have a tendency to be smeared out by the numerous effects of local and global disturbances that appear more as the noise seen in the returns, such as shown in the US bond returns of Fig. 1.1.

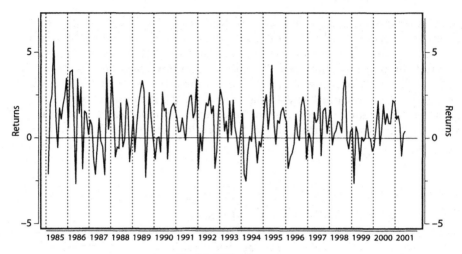

Fig. 1.1 US bond returns.

Thus while we can recognise key players it appears difficult to use them to build *ab initio* models of their effects on market prices. This is to be compounded with market psychology. For investors are strongly swayed by general market sentiment. Thus the rumour "sell – sell – sell" can sweep the markets, driving prices down ever lower; alternatively, and as occurred during the late 1990s, prices can rocket by means of the phenomenon of "irrational exuberance", leading to the "buy – buy – buy" signal swirling around. Both of these effects involve positive feedback – if a lot of traders sell a stock the price will drop, encouraging more to sell. Thus to take account of these psychological effects we must turn to models which include some aspects of these crowd-following features. We will close the book with a brief description of the most recent exciting approach of multi-agent modelling to begin to take some account of these interesting aspects.

1.3   Financial Markets and Economic Data

The data we have available is of two sorts. One is of time series of economic data: for each major country the GDP, money supplies (M1, M2, ...), interest rates, unemployment level, and so on. This data is only collated monthly, if not quarterly. It cannot be obtained with higher frequency since it is difficult to collect and also may not change enormously over the period of a month. It is possible to interpolate between data points so as to produce values every week or even every day. However, the basic problem here is as to what interpolation method is to be used. If we take only the information provided then no new data occurs, and only a constant interpolation is justifiable. Other methods could be employed, such as using a piecewise linear fit, or fitting with a polynomial. But there is no justification for any of these, as we have already noted. Thus if we wish to employ economic data for which we have information, then only a monthly approach can be used.

We meet a discrepancy when we turn to financial data, for that is available at a much higher frequency, often tick-by-tick, but at least daily. We can attempt to correlate market returns with overall changes in the economy. Since some data is available between end of month times, it is more natural, at the higher frequency end, to consider particular stock values as being driven in a more sectorial manner and tied into other higher frequency data relevant to that sector. Thus the price of oil and of relevant commodities may be expected to have the most important effects on the day-to-day values of a particular stock. However, stock indices, which combine a range of stocks across all sectors, cannot expect to be driven only, or even in the main, by such factors. These indices will be responding also to market sentiment (crowd-driven, by rumour and new information mixed together) over the short term. Over the long term we can expect to see the influence of economic variables playing their lagged role. Yet again we cannot expect to be able to deduce specific models of this dependence.

Bond prices are also available at a much higher frequency compared to economic data. What has been said above for stocks can apply to them *mutatis mutandis.*

Finally we must consider exchange rates; they have the highest frequency of all. In the longer term they are clearly affected by economic factors. For example, research at Dresdner Kleinwort Wasserstein has shown that in the last decade movements of the exchange rate of the euro (before 1999 by its constituent currencies) against the dollar have closely reflected the difference between productivity growth in the euro area and the US. This is consistent with our earlier discussion of economic monetary values driving other assets. However, this will not be true in the short term, where dealer psychology is to be expected to play a much stronger, if not totally overwhelming, role.

Behind all this is the question: are the markets predictable at all? This is related to the Efficient Markets Hypothesis: that it is not possible to forecast the return on an asset and that all relevant market information has already been incorporated in its price. This will be discussed more fully in Chapter 3, but suffice it to say here, supported by the quotes on impacts of monetary decisions on bond and asset prices, that the markets do have some degree of predictability. There is still information that has not been incorporated in the price of some assets, and careful search for such fundamentals can lead to valuable forecasts.

We will consider various modelling technologies throughout the book, and in the process indicate that markets are not completely efficient. Increasing uses of forecasting models in the future will undoubtedly tend to make for higher market efficiency. Complete efficiency has not yet arrived, however.

1.4　What Are We Predicting?

Let us summarise the points of the preceding sections

- Economic effects make their evident mark on financial assets over the longer rather than the shorter term (over months rather than days).
- The drivers of changes in financial assets in the shorter term (over days) are difficult to assess, but undoubtedly include changes in market sentiment as well as shorter-term "shocks".

- The most secure financial assets are government bonds rather than company stocks, while among stocks it is preferable to consider stock indices rather than individual stock values themselves.

Contrasting these features leads us to consider as our basic financial assets a portfolio of Government bonds and equity indices. Moreover, we will consider the G7 countries rather than developing countries. This is due to the higher risk of these latter assets.

Taking note of the summary above, if we also wish to use economic fundamentals to help improve our prediction efficiency then we must restrict ourselves to monthly data. Thus our candidate series for prediction (as used in examples in this book) are:

- **Bonds:** US, UK, Germany and France (now becoming the European bond in 2002), Japan, Canada and Australia (instead of Italy).
- **Equity indices:** MSCI (Europe), DAX, TOPIX, S&P500, FTSE100.
- **Fundamentals** used as model inputs: a large range is available, but we use financial advice to reduce them to about 40–80 overall time series. From these we have to search for suitable lagged variables, examining lags of up to 24 months, to pick out from 10 to 50 variable which can encompass the driving force on the target time series.

That is our prediction task. It involves searching through up to 1200 lagged variables to determine suitable fundamentals for our target series, as well as constructing suitable prediction models, combining them for a given market and then designing a portfolio.

We turn to describing more specifically the overall components of this process in the following section.

1.5   The Overall Process

The overall process used by the *NewQuant* team contains components needed in any attack on forecasting of assets. This follows from the nature of the time series being forecast and of the information available from fundamentals, as discussed earlier in this chapter. Thus the following stages have been developed to obtain a final proposal of allocations of assets in a portfolio investing either solely in G7 bonds (and cash) or in both G7 bonds and equity indices:

- **Data analysis,** in which the candidate input series to act as fundamentals are analysed statistically to ensure they possess suitable characteristics to be able to serve the purpose. Those input time series which are unsatisfactory are rejected (usually about a few per cent).
- **Data selection,** where analysis is developed to search through the remaining time series for the most deserving candidates to act as fundamentals in models then to be built.

- **Model building,** where a number of models are constructed on the basis of the previously selected candidate fundamental series, these models being tested to ensure they reach certain levels of forecasting effectiveness.
- **Prediction combining,** in which the various predictions of a given asset made by different model technologies are combined to give a single asset prediction, with a weighting that takes into account the historical success levels of the various model technologies.
- **Portfolio allocation,** involving the allocation of the various assets on the basis of the combined predictions just made for the following month, possibly also taking account of prediction uncertainty (or spread).
- **Advice** sent to clients to act accordingly, with an account of the nature of the results.

This overall process involves a number of stages, each of which is somewhat complex. Thus work has been ongoing on all the stages to continually improve them in the light of new ideas and technology arising from Artificial Intelligence as especially applied to financial forecasting. It is these stages, and related topics, which will be developed throughout the book. It will thus cast light across a number of areas, each of which has been developed to a level of expertise which appears appropriate to attempt to describe in a connected form.

2. Univariate and Multivariate Time Series Predictions

John G. Taylor

2.1 Philosophical Assumptions

2.1.1 Introduction

In this chapter we present the overall framework inside which we develop our quantitative approach to making financial market predictions. This is done by starting with a mathematical formulation of the basic question we face: how do we forecast the future value of a particular asset whose values over a certain period of the past we know? In order to describe the structure of the problem in more quantitative terms we must set out notation for these values, as well of those of other similar assets we also wish to predict at the same time or of economic or other financial data which may be thought to have an influence on the value or values we are trying to predict. We have already set out in the previous chapter reasons why extra variables, the so-called fundamentals, may contain information on the future values of bond or equity prices, so such an approach can have value. Some of the data required may, however, be difficult to obtain or may be of the wrong periodicity. This can happen for economic data in particular, such as overall assessors of the economy of a country, like its GDP, which may only be available quarterly. Thus an alternative is to use only the actual or *target* series itself, the one being predicted. It may be suggested that a given time series of financial data, such as a series of USA bond values, contains all the requisite information in itself. This is reasonable to argue, since in the past all the effects of other economic or financial data on the target series should be observable in the patterns that may arise in successive target values. Thus the way in which these patterns determine future values should be able to be discerned. Such an extreme approach, neglecting all data but the given time series being predicted, is termed *univariate* (it depends only on the values of a single series). On the other hand, the use of information arising from other financial or economic time series (called fundamentals or indicator variables) to make the prediction is termed a *multivariate* approach.

Which of these approaches, the univariate or multivariate, will be most effective cannot necessarily be argued conclusively *ab initio*. There are good arguments in favour of both approaches, some of which we have already mentioned. We tend to support the multivariate approach in principle, since it automatically contains the univariate approach if one includes the target series as an indicator or fundamental. The multivariate approach should also make the prediction problem easier, since it allows the inclusion of financial and economic information in a more explicit form present in the true "drivers" of the target time series, instead of trying to extract and encode this information from patterns contained in the target series alone. However, we have used both approaches in building predictors of various financial assets so as to be able to test which may be better; we present results later in the book comparing and contrasting these methods. Since we have in any case a number of multivariate prediction methods available to us, such as linear and non-linear ones, we automatically face problems of comparing and combining the predictions for a given asset arising from different model technologies. The inclusion of univariate methods in our arsenal should therefore not cause us too much of a problem.

We proceed to present the basic prediction problem in quantitative form for the univariate case before turning to the details of this problem in the multivariate framework. In the following section we consider what data requirements are needed to be imposed before we can expect to obtain good prediction results.

First, then, let us present our basic framework for the prediction problem.

2.1.2   The Basic Prediction Problem

Given a series $\{x(r)\}$ $(r \leq t)$ of values of a quantity x at the times r up to the present time t, we wish to predict the value of $x(t + 1)$ at the next time point. The method which attempts to solve this problem only using the values of $x(r)$ in the past is called *time series analysis*. The corresponding models are called *univariate*, and are of the form:

$$x(t+1) = F(x(r); \quad r \leq t) \tag{2.1}$$

This approach looks at time as a series of discrete steps, with data available at every time step. This step may be a day, a week or a month; economic data can also become available every quarter. We assume here that the time steps are all the same, although we could easily extend our framework to the more general case but do not do so here since it adds too much complexity.

The next question to consider is the set of values of the times r actually entering on the left-hand side of equation (2.1). Not all past values of x will be important in determining future values of x; we are interested in the specific values of r (the lags) at which the values are relevant.

2.1.3   Lags

It is reasonable to suppose that past history becomes less important further into the past. In particular, it is reasonable only to consider values over the past two years. But which particular time points or lags are important on the right-hand side of equation (2.1)? This is one of the basic problems that have to be solved in any attempt to construct a model of the form of equation (2.1). There are numerous indications that earlier values take time to work through the system. For example, "There is always a lag of 6–12 months before monetary policy has its main impact..."

(*The Economist*, 25 August 2001, p. 11). This indicates both that economic effects take some time to affect the prices of assets as well as that a number of lags may be involved in such effects. We assume that no more than the last 24 months data can be relevant today.

Only the values of the target series have so far been discussed. Thus we can now define the basis of our simplest approach.

2.1.4 The Univariate/Time Series Approach

On this assumption equation (2.1) can be rewritten, for purely monthly data, in terms of the vector of past lags for 24 months

$$X(t) = \{x(t), x(t-1), \ldots, x(t-23)\} \tag{2.1a}$$

as

$$x(t+1) = F(X(t)) \tag{2.2}$$

Not all of the values of the components of the vector $X(t)$ of equation (2.1a) may be present. However, we will use all of them presently in order to allow for maximum flexibility. A similar expression to equation (2.2) arises if we are working with higher frequency data with any restricted set of lags, with obvious changes. In either case, we can interpret equation (2.2) as that of a dynamical system moving in a finite dimensional space:

$$X(t) \rightarrow X(t+1) = \Phi(X(t)) \tag{2.3}$$

where the first component of the flow Φ in equation (2.3) is given by the function F of equation (2.1) and the remaining components are purely the identity function.

We need to consider some simple terminology which allows a general description to be given of the nature of the solution to equation (2.3), regarded as the trajectory of the vector $X(t)$ as t increases step by step.

2.1.5 Attractors

The flow equation (2.3) determines a series of points $X(1), X(2), \ldots, X(t), X(t+1), \ldots$ in the space of the vector X. In the case of monthly data this is a 24-dimensional space.

Such flows, with quite general properties, tend to move as time passes to certain sets of points inside which they remain. This means that the trajectory of points $X(t), X(t+1), \ldots$, for large enough t, becomes arbitrarily close to one of:

1. A fixed point where $X(t) = X(t+1)$ for large enough t
2. A closed finite set, for which the motion around the set is periodic, so $X(t+N) = X(t)$ for some N, for large enough t
3. An infinite dimensional so-called "strange attractors", of lower dimension than the whole of the space

In the latter case the motion is said to be "chaotic". This feature has been considered with great excitement by some, who consider the presence of chaos in the

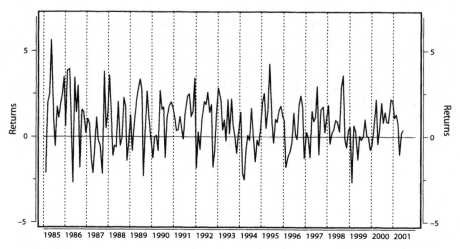

Fig. 2.1 USA bond returns, 1985–present.

dynamics of financial data as proven, so, it has been claimed, leading to the ability to understand various features of the data. In any case, chaos will lead to unpredictability, since one of the important features of chaos is the butterfly effect: that small differences in initial conditions lead to increasingly large differences in two trajectories as time passes. However, the position on chaos in the financial markets is not presently clear; we will return to this question later.

The time series for financial market data is "rough", as shown by the series of Fig. 2.1 for bond returns for the USA over the past 16 years.

The series looks indeed very noisy, and may be shown to have a histogram of distribution of values which is very close to Gaussian. Thus it reasonable to expect that there is considerable "noise" in such series. We turn next to discuss how we can include potential noise into the framework of univariate prediction.

2.1.6   Noise

In addition to the values of a given time series in the past playing a role in determining the future value, as in equations (2.2) or (2.3), there will also be expected to be noise contributions. These arise due to lack of precision in measurements of past values, or from effects brought about in the nature of the dynamics of the system itself. If we denote by $\varepsilon(t)$ a random variable at a given time t belonging to the Gaussian distribution $N(0, \sigma)$, then noise will enter the dynamics of the time series $x(t)$ by the need to include the noise term on the right-hand side of equation (2.2) as

$$x(t+1) = F(X(t), \varepsilon(t)) \qquad (2.4)$$

where the function F in equation (2.4) is an extension of that in equation (2.2).

If equation (2.4) reduces to the trivial case, we have an especially simple noise contribution:

$$x(t+1) = \varepsilon(t) \qquad (2.5)$$

This implies the complete unpredictability of the series; we will discuss this situation and more extensive versions of equation (2.5) in Chapter 3. As noted in the previous chapter (and expanded in Chapter 3), there is expected to be predictability in some assets, so that there is no structure of the form (2.5) or its comparable version as a random walk.

So far we have only considered values of the target series itself as contributing to its future value. To include other information from economic and other financial series we next develop a quantitative framework for the multivariate approach.

2.1.7   The Multivariate/Indicator/Fundamentals Approach

So far we have not introduced any other information than that provided by the given time series itself. However, the quote from *The Economist* given earlier already indicates that other variables can affect financial values, such as the current or past values of the interest rate. Other variables, such as the level of unemployment or the money supply, will be expected, on general economic grounds, to determine the prices of various financial assets. The further information which might help improve accuracy in making predictions of values of a given asset at a given time is termed a set of indicators (or fundamentals). The dependence of the variable $x(t)$ on other variables besides that of values of its own time series in the past is termed the multivariate approach.

Considerable work has been done to develop effective multivariate predictors. However, their use, although possibly of extreme importance, increases the problem already noted for the univariate approach: how are the specific inputs on which a given time series is thought to depend actually determined? This is much harder in the multivariate case. Thus in the univariate case only 24 lags need to be explored. This is an important problem, which we will discuss later, where various methods are developed. Some are specific to the task of input selection but are to be used independently of a particular modelling technology. Other approaches are part of a specific modelling approach itself. However, there are very few modelling technologies which can handle more than a thousand inputs. Thus a general rule of thumb is that input variable selection needs first to be developed on the basis of general statistical methods for a large number (more than a thousand) of potential inputs. Only after winnowing such inputs down to below a hundred in number can input variable selection methods embedded in more specific modelling approaches then be used. These two aspects of lag selection will be developed later in the book.

The general analytic features of the multivariate approach can be expressed by extending equation (2.2) as

$$x(t+1) = F(X(t), Y_1(t), \ldots, Y_N(t)) \qquad (2.6)$$

where N is the number of possible indicators on which the value $x(t+1)$ could depend, and the variables $Y_1(t) \ldots Y_N(t)$ have been constructed from their appropriate variable time series as in equation (2.1a).

We will explore both the univariate and the multivariate methods extensively throughout the book.

2.1.8   Smoothing

The raw data to be considered has the appearance of containing considerable noise, as we saw, for example, in Fig. 2.1. It is usual to remove excess noise in such data by smoothing, such as by taking an average over the data for the previous 12 months. This can be done with a suitable weighting function, such as an exponentially decaying contribution for increasing past lag contributions. More generally, a smoothing process is defined as replacing the original series $x(t)$ by the smoothed series $y(t)$ defined as:

$$y(t+1) = \sum_r w(r)x(t-r) \qquad (2.7)$$

If the weights $w(r)$ in equation (2.7) are all equal and non-zero for only a limited range of values of r, then the smoothing is of window form; if the weights decrease exponentially as r increases then the smoothing has a half-life equal to that of the weight decay. Further approaches can be used to smoothing, such as by the use of a polynomial approximation using values in a suitable neighbourhood of the point at issue. We need to consider carefully whether such an approach helps improve the accuracy of prediction. We might expect that too much smoothing could lead to actual loss of information.

As is to be expected, there is considerable controversy about the value of working with smoothed data. It is clear that if a prediction is only to be made over approximately the lifetime of the smoother or the length of its window then such smoothing may help by removing noise that would otherwise obscure underlying trends. If the smoothing uses a much larger window then information may be thereby "airbrushed" out. Thus smoothing should be of value for long-term trend prediction. However, such smoothing will not necessarily help in achieving accurate predictions for only one time step ahead. Any short-term effects, either of univariate or multivariate form, could be removed by such smoothing. It is necessary to investigate this carefully; we will report on this later in the book.

2.2   Data Requirements

2.2.1   Introduction

In general it is not to be expected that economic or financial data which have very different temporal characteristics than those of the target series can be of great help in its prediction. Information which carries a single shock to the markets, such as the occurrence of a war in oil-producing regions, clearly plays a strong role in determining the values of financial assets. Such events may cause brief large movements in the markets worldwide, but they will normally recover within a few weeks (or continue their upward or downward trends). There may well be long-term effects of such events, but they cannot be included in any quantitative prediction modelling, since they are one-off. It is the ongoing contributors to financial asset values that must be considered, and which are available in general. Indeed, it is the available information that the market has been using itself that should be considered in detail, since that is already part of the pricing process (as noted in the efficient market hypothesis discussed briefly in Chapter 1 and further in Chapter 3). Therefore the rises and falls of these data, where relevant, should be going hand-in-hand with changes in the target assets being considered. More jocularly, "series that rise and fall together can predict each other", provided suitable lags occur. But this means that there should be similar statistical features of the target series and the financial assets that are to be regarded as driving these target asset values. If a financial asset is trending heavily upwards but the target series is remaining static, then there is expected to be little value in the trending series for predicting the target asset. If an asset is bursting with volatility, ranging up one day and down the next, swinging all over the map in an unpredictable surge of activity, but the target asset has no such surges of ups and downs, then again this volatile asset should not be considered in the hunt for effective indicators. In other words, we need to screen potential indicators and exclude those which have a very different statistical character from the target series.

We develop this approach – that of input data analysis – in the following subsection. It is important to exclude in this manner those candidate fundamental series which can cause wild swings in a target series and which can thereby be removed immediately from further consideration.

2.2.2   Input Data Analysis

We start by considering various statistical features of a candidate fundamental series. The initial quantities to be analysed are the mean and the variance. In order to know what statistical properties are suitable for prediction purposes we need first to specify those of the target series we wish to predict. In our case we will discuss daily and monthly bond and equity series. For example, the index for the USA bond series over the past 16 years since 1985 is shown in Fig. 2.2.

This clearly is trending during various periods. Thus over most of the period 1985 to the present there is a clear upward trend, but during 1987, 1994, early 1996 and late 1998 to the end of 1999 there are strong downward trends. We remove the trending components by taking the proportional first difference of the index series to lead to the bond series returns, defined from the index $i(t)$ by the formula:

$$r(t) = \frac{(i(t) - i(t-1))}{i(t)} \tag{2.8}$$

The resulting series has already been shown in Fig. 2.1. It has a histogram of values, obtained by creating an approximation to the probability distribution of the series as the number of times a value of the returns takes its value in a given window. This histogram is very close to a normal Gaussian distribution, as shown in Fig. 2.3 and Table 2.1.

Moreover, the series has a relatively constant mean, as measured by a moving twelve-month window, and a relatively constant volatility, again measured over twelve months. Thus we need to consider input time series which have similar properties.

If we look at certain candidate fundamentals it is clear that they do not fit this bill. Thus the German wholesale price indicator (WPI) shown in Fig. 2.4 does not have the right mean stationarity.

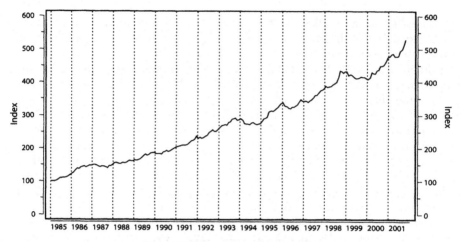

Fig. 2.2 USA bond index, 1985–present.

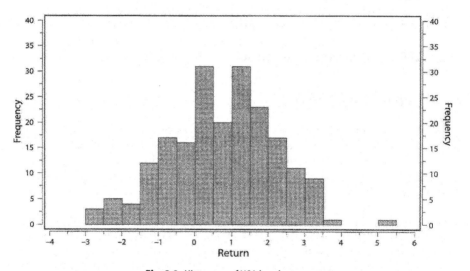

Fig. 2.3 Histogram of USA bond returns.

This is to be compared with, for example, that of the first proportional difference of the commodity price, with a much more stationary mean as evident from the plot in Fig. 2.5.

Another criterion for rejection of a time series is the non-stationarity over time of its variance or standard deviation, as calculated over a twelve-month window. Most series have some such variation, so this is not as strong a criterion as that for relative stationarity of the mean.

A further point to be tested for is the presence of seasonality and other structure in a transformed candidate fundamental time series. Thus a slowly decaying autocorrelation function (ACF) (Fig. 2.6) and partial autocorrelation function (PACF) suggest that residual trends are still present and are strong enough to induce a non-stationary mean, in which case the series should be differenced once

Table 2.1 Statistics of USA bond returns

Sample mean	1.013	SE of Sample mean	0.217
Variance	7.806	Standard Error	2.793
t-statistic	4.659	Significance (mean = 0.0)	0.000
Skewness	0.303	Significance (Sk = 0.0)	0.114
Kurtosis	0.660	Significance (Ku = 0.0)	0.090

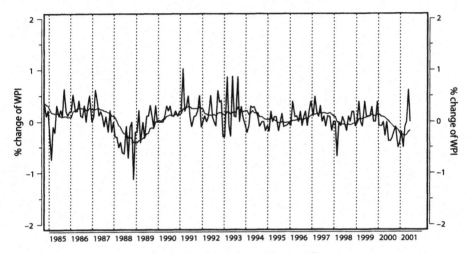

Fig. 2.4 Monthly changes in German WPI.

more and the data analysis repeated on the new series. A sine wave shape in the ACF indicates the presence of a strong deterministic or seasonal component, which may be predicted from the most recent p values of the data, as in an autoregressive process of order p. Similarly, a sine wave shape for the PACF (Fig. 2.7) suggests that present data may be expressed as a linear combination of the present and most recent q values of a random noise process, as a moving average process of order q.

The power spectral density (Fig. 2.8) in the Fourier transform indicates the frequency content of the transformed time series. A non-zero mean is revealed by a peak at zero frequency, a trend by a peak at near-zero frequency, and a seasonal component with period n months by a peak at frequency $12/n$. Similarly, moving average components are revealed by a wavy but smooth spectrum and autoregressive components by sharper waves overlaid on an otherwise flat spectrum. Cumulative spectral estimates as well as smooth parametric estimation are also helpful to discover the detailed statistical components of candidate time series, and have also been used in our analysis.

Let us consider more specifically how the results of such statistical analyses are relevant. Strong structural components may be seen as suspicious. When a linear model is built from a number of input series all spectral components must combine linearly to approximate the spectrum of the target series. As the asset classes which

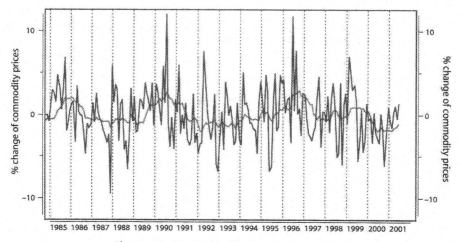

Fig. 2.5 Monthly changes in commodity prices in SDRs.

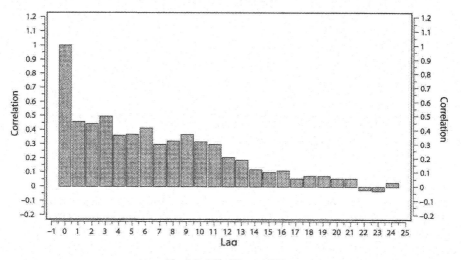

Fig. 2.6 ACF of German WPI.

are being considered need to have flat spectra characteristic of white noise, this is achieved more easily if the spectrum of each series is flat, i.e. if no trends or seasonal or autoregressive moving average components are present. Thus the above techniques of using the ACF, PACF and power spectrum are important to screen out unsuitable series for linear models.

With a non-linear model, such as a neural network, these criteria initially seem less critical. This is because the inherent flexibility of such models makes it easier to combine series with different spectral content and still produce a white noise-like output. However, to remove incorrect characteristics of the target series by combining several input series would require non-trivial non-linear terms. These are coded by higher order non-linearities as arise from product terms between

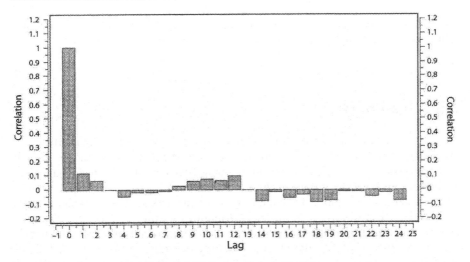

Fig. 2.7 ACF of commodity prices in SDRs.

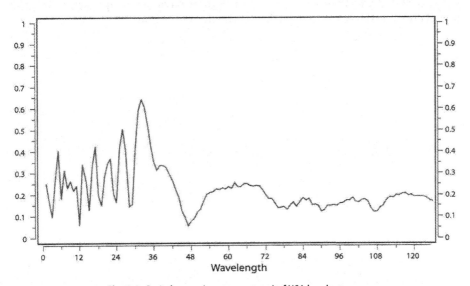

Fig. 2.8 Periodogram (power spectrum) of USA bond returns.

different inputs, without associated higher-order non-linearities in a given input series on its own. Such product contributions are natural in some modelling techniques, such as the GMDH approach to be consider later. However, they are not part of most neural network models that we have used. To avoid a disparity between the input sets used across different modelling technologies we therefore have to remove disparate candidate series at the start using the criterion we have mentioned above: that series only have a white noise spectrum. We have also analysed the outlier structure of input series, although we have not used this as a strong criterion since a few outliers are not bad from a modelling point of view, as they may have a beneficial influence on the model parameters by reducing variance of the estimates.

2.3   Summary

This chapter has illustrated the steps that are advisable in order to guarantee that only market indicators of good quality are considered throughout the model building process. An initial selection is made that complies with an educated economic point of view; this uses economic understanding to ensure that series are not considered that do not make good economic sense as putative fundamentals for bond and stock indices prediction. Transformations are then applied to such series as are economically sensible to ensure that they attain similar statistical structure to the target series being considered. The transformed series are rigorously tested for the presence of any residual components using time and frequency domain techniques, and for validity of the Gaussian assumption of linear regression modelling. Only series that pass these tests satisfactorily go through to the input selection and model creation stages that will be discussed later in the book.

3. Evidence of Predictability in Financial Markets

Neville Towers

For more than a generation, the topic of market efficiency has been of widespread interest and the focus of considerable research. The issue has been hotly debated and primarily tested in the form of two extensively studied theories: the random walk and the efficient market hypothesis. In light of this, we do not intend to provide an exhaustive review of market efficiency or even take a stand on the topic itself, but rather focus on the key findings and arguments that are central to the debate and review the statistical methods that have been used to test and measure efficiency.

3.1 Overview

For over 30 years, researchers have deliberated over the predictive nature of financial markets and proposed theories to explain the underlying mechanism that determines the price dynamics of financial assets. Research has actively focused on searching for predictability in asset returns, with motivation arising from an economic interest in understanding how fluctuations in the economy influence financial markets and also from a practical interest in seeking ways of improving the financial rewards of investing.

Even after this period of much heated debate, no consensus has been reached amongst academics, which conclusively explains the behaviour of asset prices. The dominant (or orthodox) view, however, is epitomised by two related theories known by different forms of the random walk hypothesis of asset prices and the efficient market hypothesis. The former theory assumes that prices are completely stochastic in nature, while the latter theory implies that profit opportunities do not exist in perfectly efficient markets. In essence, both of these theories imply that in well-functioning markets, prices are unpredictable and fully reflect all available information. A more practical but weaker version of the hypothesis is that prices only reflect available information up to the point where profits from acting on the information exceeds the marginal trading costs. This implies that in a rational market, where appropriate information is freely available and correctly interpreted, that prices should not deviate from fundamental economic and market information. In the last ten years, however, theoretical arguments and empirical research have seriously questioned these two theories, but there is still no general agreement over the validity of both the random walk and the efficient market hypotheses. In the next two sections we present an overview of the main controversies over the efficient market hypothesis and the existence of systematically profitable trading strategies, on the basis of theoretical arguments and empirical research. We include arguments for and against these theories, and provide a concise review of the most compelling empirical research.

3.2   Review of Theoretical Arguments

The first application of the random walk hypothesis to financial markets was based on the assumption that randomness in asset prices was due to large groups of investors continuously seeking ways of increasing wealth (Samuelson, 1965). In this view, it was believed that the movement of market prices was a direct response to unanticipated market-sensitive information. This led to the concept of the "efficient market" (Fama *et al.*, 1969), where asset prices rapidly react to new information so that any opportunities for systematically profitable trading are eliminated. At first glance these two related theories seem to adequately explain the functioning of financial markets and provide an elegant link to the microscopic processes found in physics and other natural sciences. However, this unified framework for understanding the dynamics of financial markets has been questioned by a number of authors.

Some of the most notable theoretical arguments against the efficient market hypothesis were put forward by Grossman (1976) and Grossman and Stiglitz (1980). They argued that perfectly efficient markets could only exist if there was no cost to acquiring information. If there were a cost to information collection, then there would be no economic justification to this activity as current prices would already incorporate all current information. Furthermore, in these circumstances there would be little reason to trade, as no excess profits could be made and so even small trading costs would cause financial markets to degenerate and eventually collapse!

To defend the efficient market hypothesis, it was suggested that financial markets must contain inefficient traders, described as noise traders, who speculate on spurious information and trade, not based on new market information, but for other reasons; for example, due to liquidity requirements (Black, 1986). It was proposed that non-information-based trades must lose on average, and therefore provide sufficient profitable opportunities for information-based investors to counterbalance the costs of trading and collecting information. However, this argument fails to explain why trading on the basis of liquidity requirements in efficient markets should necessarily be inherently economically inefficient.

It appears that the main reason for the heated debate amongst financial economists is the idealised nature of the efficient market hypothesis, which means that in practice it cannot be proved or refuted. Researchers have attempted take account of other factors, such as trading conditions, information structure and dividends, but these have the effect of turning the original theory into a conditional or joint hypothesis which requires much more empirical evidence to reject or accept.

Unanswered questions over the original efficient market hypothesis have led to the development of a number of revised theories. One of the most notable is the *Relative Efficient Market Hypothesis*, which states that "the efficient markets hypothesis should be linked with bounded rationality so markets are only efficient and unpredictable with respect to existing available information and not all possible sources of information" (White, 1988). This modification allows the potential for new information to be exploited to generate excess profits and overcomes the costs associated with acquiring information without seriously conflicting with the original efficient markets hypothesis.

A more recent version of the relative efficient market hypothesis states that "it is not possible to systematically earn excess profits without some sort of competitive advantage (e.g. superior technology, proprietary information, advanced methodology) over other market participants" (Lo and MacKinlay, 1999). In this work, it is argued that the functioning of financial markets is analogous to the trading of new products in other industries where patents provide a time frame for generating excess profits before other market participants are permitted to copy the innovation. Although, in general, new products in financial markets are not patentable, there is still a lag time before other market participants are able to identify new forms of competitive advantage that lead to profitable trading strategies. It is considered that this has the effect of making financial markets *relatively efficient*, while the potential rewards associated with further innovation provide sufficient motivation for the development of new forms of competitive advantage. This suggests that some of the technological advances offered by sophisticated modelling techniques that are currently only available to specialist market participants have the potential to generate excess profits.

Furthermore, this definition implies that the dynamics of financial markets will evolve through time as competitive advantages become more widely available to other market participants. In this case, it is likely that the widespread acceptance of any competitive advantage would result in a decline in the associated profits. This would inevitably result in market dynamics moving towards randomness with respect to an old form of competitive advantage. This form of market evolution seems to match the general perception that trading "old" riskless arbitrage strategies will now only offer marginal trading potential.

Another important implication of this form of the relative efficient market hypothesis is that financial markets *must* have some degree of predictable behaviour to allow further innovation that is not just a result of market inefficiency or irrational investors. This is aptly described by Lo and Mackinlay (1999), who say that "predictability is the oil that lubricates the gears of capitalism". If this theory is correct then some degree of predictability is essential to financial markets and that market participants must continuously upgrade and improve research and technological capabilities to remain competitive.

3.3   Review of Empirical Research

After the random walk and efficient market hypotheses were presented in the 1960s, empirical research began to try to establish the validity of these theories and so test the viability of typical trading strategies. A vast literature has accumulated over the last 30 years, and we present an overview of the most notable empirical studies that have attempted to test for predictability and profitability in financial markets. The random walk hypothesis implies that no statistical regularities should exist in well-functioning financial markets. To test the Efficient Markets Theory (EMT) specific information sets are analysed, which has resulted in three forms of the EMT: weak, semi-strong and strong. The weak form of EMT considers information solely from historical prices, the semi-strong form considers all publicly available information and the strong form considers all private and publicly available information.

Most empirical tests have concentrated on the weak form of EMT and these fall into two categories. The first conducts statistical tests on historical data to identify significant patterns and the second examines technical trading rules to determine whether they generate abnormal returns after trading costs. In one sense, these studies are extremely prohibitive given the external forces that are commonly believed to influence asset prices, but provide a good method of analysing market behaviour.

One particular topic, which was the focus of much initial work, considered analysing the effects of *seasonality* from different days of the week or months of the year for any predictable behaviour. One of the first anomalies of the weak form of EMT was identified as the weekend effect (French, 1980). For example, one study (Gibbons and Hess, 1981) analysed daily closing data from the New York Stock Exchange, and found that Monday's return was significantly lower than other days of the week. A 17-year period (1962–1978) was examined where the annualised Monday return was –33.5%! In a more recent related study, conducted by Harris (1986), the intra-day and day effects from a 14-month period (1981–1983) were examined and found that the effect was primarily due to the difference between Friday close and Monday open.

In a number of other studies, seasonal behaviour was investigated in monthly stock returns. Fama (1991) examined monthly returns over a 50-year period (1941–1991) on the New York Stock Exchange, and discovered that returns in January were substantially higher than returns in other months. The examination of returns showed that returns on small stocks outperformed the monthly average by 5.3%. Another comprehensive study examined a wide range of international equity markets and found the existence of a significant *January effect* in 17 countries (Gultekin and Gultekin, 1983).

In order to explain the January effect, researchers have proposed various explanations, one of the most notable is that tax advantages could produce market anomalies in January (Kato and Shallheim, 1985). However, subsequent work has discounted the tax selling hypothesis by still finding the January effect in some tax-exempt markets (Jones et al., 1987). In other related studies, which analysed trading rules that exploit the January effect, evidence suggests that assets purchased in December and sold at the end of January outperform the market by approximately 8% on average (Reinganum, 1983). The general conclusion from these studies is that the January effect cannot be reconciled with the theoretical concept of an efficient market. It is interesting to note that if a sufficiently large number of investors purchased equities in December to anticipate price rises in January then any price rise should occur earlier. Clever investors would then buy in early December to anticipate these price rises, which in turn would lead to even earlier price rises. In principle, the January effect would then move earlier as investors tried to anticipate price rises, until the effect is eliminated.

Although these and other similar seasonal effects are well known, and conclusively show that returns are systematically dependent on the time of day, the week and even the month of the year, there is little practical evidence that these statistical regularities can and are being exploited for trading. To maintain the efficient market hypothesis, most proposed explanations have suggested that the observed seasonality is due to artefacts in the data or where transactions costs are too high to counteract any benefits from trading these time effects.

In another area of early research, simple tests for predictability were conducted to examine whether past returns could forecast future returns. A number of these studies have examined the first-order autocorrelation between returns over time intervals, ranging from 1 day to 3 months, and over various stock markets (e.g. Fama, 1965; Cootner, 1974). In general, however, results have shown no significant correlations and studies argue that correlations should not be used to examine the efficiency of markets because of the influence of the outlying observations (Fama, 1965; Jennergren and Korsvold, 1975). Other non-parametric tests have been proposed, for example, the Runs Test, which counts the sign of consecutive returns; however, in empirical experiments these tests have only found small positive relationships between returns.

In contrast to these negative results, the random walk hypothesis has been tested by comparing *variance estimators* over different time frequencies (Lo and MacKinlay, 1988, 1989). Results from weekly stock returns over a 23-year period (1962–1985) strongly reject the random walk model for various aggregated indices and portfolios. This is primarily attributed to the behaviour of small stocks, and not infrequent trading or time-varying volatilities. They also showed that the Variance Ratio test is a more powerful test of the random walk model than the traditional Dickey–Fuller and Box–Pierce tests.

Other tests for predictability have taken a different view by examining *relative* stock returns by subtracting the related market index from the absolute stock returns. Studies have used the CAPM model or other similar models to examine the correlation of these "excess" returns (e.g. Fama and MacBeth, 1973). Results from these experiments, however, show no significant predictive correlation and so no evidence against the efficient market hypothesis.

Another group of empirical studies advocate searching indirectly for *non-linear relationships* in returns data by developing complex trading rules based on historical price movements. A common example is a breakthrough barrier trading rule (Fama and Blume, 1966; Jennergen and Korsold, 1975). This formulates a trading strategy that sells when the asset price breaks through a lower price barrier and buys when the asset price rises above a upper price barrier. Results have shown some evidence of profitable trading rules, but profits often disappear with practical trading costs. Other more esoteric rules, such as rules for "head and shoulders" patterns and relative strength rules have been devised (Levy, 1967). A number of similar approaches are often advertised and supported by technical traders or chartists, but evidence that trading on the basis on these results can generate excess profits is generally considered inconclusive. However, these forms of investment are similar to empirical research amongst finance academics which has shown some evidence of predictability; recent examples include Brock *et al.* (1992) and LeBaron (1996).

Other studies investigate forms of cyclical behaviour in financial markets with the underlying assumption that predictability can be attributed to periods of under- or overvalue. The belief is that market participants are susceptible to cycles of investor optimism and pessimism which result in asset prices temporarily moving away from their "true" value. These forms of market dynamics have been described by the "stock market overreaction" hypothesis (DeBondt and Thaler, 1985; Delong *et al.*, 1989). The theory implies that asset returns are negatively correlated for some holding period which provides predictability in stock returns. This theory has been tested using the contrarian investment rule, in which stocks that have recently increased in value are sold and stocks that have recently decreased in value are purchased. Results from these studies seems to suggest that stock markets do overreact.

Other studies have examined the cross-autocorrelation structure of securities and empirical findings have shown a lead–lag structure between large capitalisation and small capitalisation stocks producing a source of positive dependence in stock returns (Cohen *et al.*, 1986; Lo and MacKinlay, 1990). However, results may also be due to "thin" or non-synchronous trading between stocks where prices are mistakenly sampled simultaneously. Experiments have been conducted to examine the magnitude of index autocorrelation and cross-correlation generated from models of thin trading. Results show that although some autocorrelation is induced the observed correlation structure would require unrealistically thin markets (Lo and MacKinlay, 1999). For a review of numerous other studies and a thorough examination of empirical research into predictability in asset returns see Campbell *et al.*, 1999).

As an alternative approach, a number of more recent empirical studies have developed time series models using statistical forecasting techniques in an attempt to capture any deterministic component of the underlying dynamics of financial markets. There are a growing number of researchers who indicate that statistical forecasting methods have the potential for models to capture predictability in financial markets, which can then be effectively harnessed to produce profitable trading.

In summary, this section does not attempt to be an exhaustive review of empirical research of tests for market efficiency or predictability. Its purpose is to show that there is considerable and growing evidence that financial markets may not be truly efficient and that some degree of significant predictability may be identified through statistical analysis.

3.4   Predictability Tests

The random walk hypothesis of asset prices can be decomposed into three different versions depending on the strength of the underlying assumptions. The strongest form of the hypothesis assumes that asset returns have independently and identically distributed increments. The assumption of independence implies that increments are uncorrelated and also that non-linear functions of the increments must be uncorrelated. In the case of equities, asset prices are always positive, so this definition requires modification. It is usually assumed that log normal price increments follow a random walk process. If asset prices did follow this hypothesis then it would form an elegant analogy with stochastic processes in the natural world.

However, this model of asset prices is not very realistic when compared with the past behaviour of markets. For example, in the long term, markets adapt and evolve through time as economic, political and structural changes take place. This can be seen by observing the time varying variance (heteroscedasticity) of asset returns. This model of identically distributed increments is too strong an assumption to apply this version of the random walk hypothesis to financial data. We therefore do not consider any tests for this version of the hypothesis.

The second form of the random walk hypothesis assumes that increments are independent but not identically distributed. However, it appears to be extremely difficult to test for independence statistically without assuming identical distributions. Some non-parametric tests have been developed (e.g. rank tests), but these still require some restrictive assumptions about the distribution. The lack of powerful statistical tests for this version of the random walk hypothesis has led to much empirical research to develop "economic" tests of predictability. The aim of these is to indirectly measure predictability by analysing the performance of a simple trading strategy for the predicted asset return.

In general, economic tests of predictability have taken the form of a simple filter rule that is applied to the asset return series. The total return generated from a dynamic trading strategy implemented on the basis of the trading rule is then considered to be a measure of the predictability of the asset returns. Empirical experiments have been conducted to allow for the effects of the market microstructure (dividends, trading costs etc.). The results from initial experiments concluded that such rules do not perform as well as a simple buy-and-hold strategy (Fama, 1965; Fama and Blume, 1966).

However, more recently, similar economic tests have been extended to forecasting models of asset returns. The rule forms a simple trading strategy to provide an "economic" measure of predictability by exploiting the predictive nature of the forecasting model. One simple but plausible strategy buys a fixed amount of the asset if the prediction is positive and sells an equal amount if the prediction is negative. This naïve asset allocation rule was first attributed as the Merton Measure of Market Timing (Merton, 1980) to provide a simple measure of out-of-sample predictability in terms of trading profitability. Recent studies suggest that simple trading rules used in conjunction with a forecasting model of asset returns may be used to outperform a benchmark (e.g. Refenes, 1995).

In other studies, more advanced forms of trading rules have been developed which have formed into a class of investment management known as *technical analysis* and *charting*. The underlying assumption of these trading methods is that historical prices, trading volume and other market statistics exhibit regularities which form patterns such as head and shoulders or support levels that can be profitably exploited to extrapolate future price movements. These can be tested in a similar manner using economic tests to justify the modelling approach.

The third and weakest version of the random walk hypothesis assumes that asset prices may have dependent but uncorrelated increments at all possible leads and lags. This is tested under the null hypothesis that all autocorrelation coefficients are zero. There are a number of simple but powerful tests that have been developed to test this hypothesis and these are reviewed next.

3.4.1   Autocorrelation Test

The most obvious test for this weak form of the random walk hypothesis is to directly test the null hypothesis that the autocorrelation coefficients of the increments (or first differences) are zero. This is achieved by estimating the autocorrelation coefficients and their associated p-values for a given sample.

These sample statistics, however, can sometimes suffer from biases caused by outliers or the estimation of the sample mean. The construction of correlation coefficients requires the measurement of deviations from the mean and a poor estimate can cause a negative bias in the autocorrelation. However, bias-corrected sample autocorrelation coefficients have been presented by Lo and MacKinlay, (1988).

The main deficiency of the autocorrelation test, however, is that it can only detect predictability associated with a particular lag and not test autocorrelation within the entire time series and so are highly sensitive to noise. To compensate for this weakness, other statistics have been developed, sometimes known as "portmanteau" statistics, which are joint tests over the set of individual correlation coefficients. In the next subsections we focus on Q-statistics and the variance ratio test.

3.4.2   Q-Statistic

A more powerful test of the random walk hypothesis is the Q-statistic, initially developed by Box and Pierce (1970). The Q-statistic at lag k is a test statistic for the null hypothesis that there is no autocorrelation up to order k and takes the form:

$$Q_k = T\sum_{i=1}^{k} \rho_i^2 \tag{3.1}$$

where ρ_i is the sample autocorrelation at lag i and k is the number of lags.

The Q-statistic for k lags is defined as the sum of the first k squared autocorrelations, which is asymptotically distributed as a χ^2 distribution with degrees of freedom equal to the number of autocorrelations. The test was further refined for small samples (Ljung and Box, 1979) to account for the number of observations.

The Q-statistic is often used as a test of whether a time series is white noise. It differs from the autocorrelation test by attempting to identify statistically significant predictability by considering the deviations of all autocorrelations from zero. This is a more powerful test, as predictability held within a number of lags may not be identified by examining the correlation at one particular lag.

However, there are practical problems associated with this test. Most notable is the selection of the order of the lag. If you choose too small a lag, the test may not detect serial correlation at high-order lags. However, if you choose too large a lag, the test may have low power, since the significant correlation at one lag may be diluted by insignificant correlations at other lags. For further discussion, see Lyung and Box (1979) and Harvey (1993). As this test does not consider predictability at a specific lag it is often used in conjunction with the autocorrelation test.

This statistic also requires modification when applied to statistical forecasting models. For example, if the series represents the residuals from ARIMA estimation, the appropriate degrees of freedom should be adjusted to represent the number of autocorrelations less the number of AR and MA terms previously estimated.

3.4.3   Variance Ratio Test

A more recent test that is gaining widespread acceptance is known as the Variance Ratio Statistic. For a time-scale τ, which defines the time period between innovations, the variance ratio statistic, $VR(\tau)$, takes the form:

$$VR(\tau) = \frac{Var(r_t(\tau))}{\tau Var(r_t(1))} \tag{3.2}$$

where r_t is the asset return at time τ.

This test exploits the property that the variance of random walk increments must be a linear function of the time interval and result in a ratio close to one. This property has been shown to hold even when applied to the variance of increments that vary through time (Campbell *et al.*, 1999). Extensive studies using the variance ratio test have been completed which provide evidence that stock markets can exhibit non-random walk behaviour (Lo and MacKinlay, 1999; Burgess, 1999).

The variance ratio is directly related to the autocorrelation coefficients and is equivalent to

$$VR(\tau) = 1 + 2\sum_{i=1}^{\tau-1}\left(1 - \frac{i}{\tau}\right)\rho_i \tag{3.3}$$

where ρ_i is the ith-order autocorrelation of the increments of some time series. Equation (3.3) shows that the VR statistic is a weighted combination of the first $\tau - 1$ autocorrelation coefficients.

The test for the random walk hypothesis assumes that the variance ratio of any period must be close to 1. If $VR(\tau)$ is significantly greater than 1 then trending behaviour is detected in the time series. In contrast, if the $VR(\tau)$ is significantly less than 1 then mean reverting behaviour is identified. The variance ratio statistic has been used for predictability tests to distinguish a variety of deviations from random walk behaviour. For example, the variance ratio statistic has also been extended to a multivariate context and used to identify the dynamics of cointegrating time series related to trending and mean reverting behaviour (Burgess, 1999, and Chapter 21 of this book). In this work, empirical studies of FTSE 100 stocks have been found to contain significant evidence of non-random behaviour.

3.5   Beyond Tests for Market Efficiency

So far, we have only considered the investigation of tests for market efficiency in financial markets. In this section we show how predictability tests may be adapted for purposes beyond tests of random walk behaviour to assist the detection of predictability and form the initial part of a methodology to optimise a trading system comprised of forecasting models.

In financial forecasting applications, there are often a wide number of candidate target series which may be modelled at a range of time steps. The large number of potential time series often make the process of model building complex and highly computer-intensive. This problem is compounded by searching for predictability in time series comprised of combinations of assets. Under these conditions the number of candidate time series can grow exponentially within the number of assets. It is then often impractical to construct forecasting models for each possible time series and screening is imposed to filter out series with no detectable predictability.

In the context of trading, the detection of some level of predictability is not the ultimate goal, but rather just one process in the construction of the trading system. This process may be considered as an initial screening stage that selects asset returns with a predictable component from a pool of candidate assets and so suitable for developing statistical forecasting models. Further stages may be developed to optimise models to forecast asset returns and select optimised trading positions.

This conceptual approach has been used by methodologies in financial forecasting that have a large set of candidate target variables. For example, a recent modelling methodology by Burgess (1999) adapts the variance ratio statistic to provide novel tests for predictability for financial asset returns and combinations of assets. He shows how these statistics provide a practical means of identifying potential time series which may be candidate target variables of a forecasting model.

3.6   Summary

Evidence for predictability has emerged against the backdrop of a classical view which strongly upholds the random walk model of asset returns. The empirical evidence for predictability has led to revised theories of the dynamics of financial markets which is encapsulated in the relative efficient market hypothesis. In this view predictability is not only plausible but is a necessary component of financial markets.

If we accept the hypothesis that predictability exists in financial markets, then it seems reasonable to ask how this influences market efficiency. The first point to make is that market inefficiency is not necessarily a consequence or a symptom of market predictability, so predictability may not imply that markets are inefficient. The second is that the properties of predictability (i.e. degree, sources and forecast horizon) can be transient, and so often require sophisticated modelling techniques to capture sufficient predictability for models to be statistically and economically significant, both in-sample and out-of-sample. The final point is that a true test of the significance of a statistical forecasting model requires the incorporation of predictive information into a trading strategy. The performance of the strategy then needs to be tested on out-of-sample or (ideally) real-time data to determine whether trading produces "excess" profits.

The most convincing empirical evidence follows from the underlying assumption that financial markets are dominantly stochastic and only partially deterministic in nature. In addition, the construction of statistical models by identifying interesting linear combinations of stocks and bonds appears to offer the most reliable method of searching for predictable behaviour in financial markets. In general these forecasting models with model parameters, θ, can be described as

$$E[\beta \Delta y_{t+1}] = f(X_t; \theta) \tag{3.4}$$

where X is some vector of explanatory variables, β is the portfolio weights, and Δy is the return from the assets in the portfolio.

In equation (3.4) the explanatory variables depend on the methodology for identifying predictive ability and can represent *ex ante* macroeconomic variables (Lo and MacKinlay, 1995), cointegration residuals (Burgess, 1998), or CAPM residuals (Bentz *et al.*, 1996).

It is worth noting that the topic of predictability in financial markets has wider implications than are discussed within this book. For example, in derivative pricing most models assume that asset returns are unpredictable and that prices are described by drift and volatility processes. If stock returns are predictable then the traditional Black–Scholes equation for pricing options is misspecified, as suggested by Lo and MacKinlay (1999).

4. Bond Pricing and the Yield Curve

Sebastian Larsson

A bond is a simple financial agreement that entitles the holder to a certain set of fixed cash payments in the future. Since all the cash flows are known in advance[1] the price of the bond simply reflects the market place's perception of what constitutes a fair rate of interest.

At first it may seem somewhat circular to price bonds in terms of short rates, as we shall do below, since the latter are in turn inferred from the prices of bonds traded in the market place. However, phrasing the price of a given bond in terms of interest rates gives us a clear picture of how investments in bonds relates to rates of returns of investments in general. In addition, the pricing formula allows us to relate bonds with different maturities and coupons to each other via their underlying interest rate structure.

4.1   The Time Value of Money and Discount Factors

Central to the theory of bond pricing is the concept of the time value of money; that a given amount of cash today is worth more than the same amount made available to us at some future time. In essence, this greater value follows from the fact that if there are non-zero interest rates available to investors, then a smaller value can be invested today to give the required cash payment in the future.

Let us consider for a moment why we expect interest rates to exist, i.e. why we expect to be remunerated for not spending our cash straight away. One contribution to the existence of interest rates is inflation, since if prices are steadily rising we need to be earning interest at at least the same rate in order not to lose spending power. However, although inflation has an effect in setting the level of interest payments, it is not fundamental, since if prices were *not* expected to rise we would still expect to see non-zero interest rates.

---

1   Here and in what follows we assume that all bonds are of investment grade and that the bond issuer can therefore be assumed never to default on payments.

The principal driving force for interest payments is the existence of wealth-producing investment opportunities in the economy. In general, the availability of such opportunities will not be matched with the availability of surplus capital for investment. Conversely, people with available capital are often not able to directly exploit certain investment opportunities. As a result, we have a supply and demand for investment capital which will interact to set interest rates at a level acceptable to both borrowers and lenders.

We quantify the way that the value of cash changes with time by introducing the quantity $b(t,T)$ which is the value at time t of one unit of cash at time T. We refer to these numbers as the *discount factors*, and, as we shall see below, it is also the price at t of a zero-coupon bond with time $T - t$ left to maturity. Thus the value $V(t)$ at time t of two cash flows c_1 and c_2 at times T_1 and T_2 would be written as

$$V(t) = b(t, T_1)c_1 + b(t, T_2)c_2 \tag{4.1}$$

We will often set $t = 0$ to be the present time and we will then simplify our notation by writing $b(T) \equiv b(0,T)$. Armed with the discount factors, calculating the price of any bond becomes relatively straightforward.

4.2   Pricing Bonds

If we can determine the discount factors appropriate for a given bond market, we can also price any specific bond. Since a given bond specifies a sequence of future cash flows, its price is simply the sum of those cash flows discounted to their present value. Thus, the price at time t of a bond $B_c(t)$ with cash flows $c(t)$ is given by

$$B_c(t) = \sum_{j=t}^{T} b(t, j)c(j) \tag{4.2}$$

where the sum runs over all times where $c(t)$ is non-zero between t and the maturity date T of the bond. In general, these cash flows $c(t)$ will consist of a constant coupon, c say, paid at regular intervals, and at time T we have a further contribution due to the redeemed par value of the bond, i.e. $c(T) = c + B_T$, where B_T is the par value. We see that if there is no coupon to be paid, the bond value is simply its discounted par value $B(T) = b(t,T)B_T$, and, conversely, the discount factor is the value of a zero-coupon bond with par value 1.

The bond pricing equation (4.2) is normally written, not in terms of the discount factors directly, but rather in terms of the implied interest rates. The rate of return $i(t,T)$ implied by an investment of $b(t,T)$ at time t with a return of 1 at a time $T - t$ later is given by $b(t,T) = (1 + i(t,T))^{-(T - t)}$ so that

$$B_c(t) = \sum_{j=t}^{T} c(j)[1 + i(t, j)]^{-(j-t)} \tag{4.3}$$

where the rate $i(t,T)$ is the spot rate at time t for the time period $(T - t)$. (Here and in what follows, we are using a discretely compounded interest. The continuously compounded interest $r(t,T)$, which satisfies $b(t,T) = \exp(-r(t,T)(T - t))$ and thus $r(t,T) = \ln(1 + i(t,T))$, has nicer theoretical properties, but is less commonly used in practice.)

Using the expression (4.3) for the bond price given the contributing spot rates, we can easily price any bond provided the spot rates are known. To determine the spot rates we use the pricing equation in reverse. First we examine the market price of bonds which have no coupon payments left before they mature, since in this case we can solve equation (4.3) for the interest rate

$$i(t,T) = \left[\frac{c + B_T}{B_c(t)}\right]^{1/(T-t)} - 1 \qquad (4.4)$$

Once we have the resulting spot rates (usually only available for short times left to maturity) we can then successively extend the inferred short rates to larger and larger maturities by substituting known values for $i(t,T)$ back into the pricing equation. The resulting curve of spot rates at a given time t against the time left to maturity $(T-t)$, is of great practical and theoretical importance, since it shows us directly the returns expected by lenders as a function of the time period of the loan. As we shall see below, this "spot rate curve" is more commonly referred to as the *yield curve*.

4.3 Bond Yield and the Yield Curve

Returning for the moment to the bond pricing equation (4.3), we see that, except for special cases, a single bond is not enough to extract any meaningful information about all the implied rates of return that make up its price. However, we can obtain an estimate for the rate of interest implied by the bond's price by assuming that the spot rate curve is flat, so that

$$B_c(t) = \sum_{j=t}^{T} c(j)[1 + y_c(t)]^{-(j-t)} \qquad (4.5)$$

where $y_c(t) \equiv i(t,T)$ is the *yield to maturity*, or simply yield, of the bond. Since $y_c(t)$ is the only unknown in equation (4.5) we can solve the equation (although we generally have to resort to numerical methods) to obtain the yield for any given bond without reference to the overall interest rate structure of the market. Thus the yield effectively provides an average return represented by the cash flows in a given bond.

We also note that if there are no coupon payments for the particular bond under consideration, the yield is simply the spot rate $i(t,T)$, where T is the time that the bond matures. Thus, the graph of the yield of zero-coupon bonds plotted against the time to maturity (Fig. 4.1) is identical to the spot rate curve, which, for this reason, is most often referred to as the (zero-coupon) yield curve.

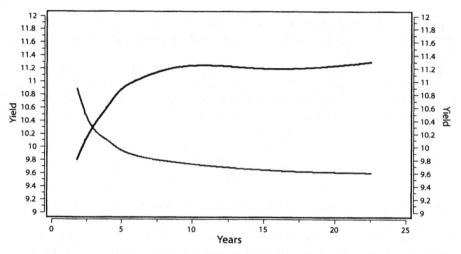

Fig. 4.1 Typical yield curves. When interest rates are expected to fall, the curve will decline.

4.4 Duration and Convexity

Once we have parameterised the price of a bond in terms of its yield it is natural to ask how the price changes for small changes in the yield. We consider the derivative of the bond price with respect to the yield and find that

$$\frac{dB_c(t)}{dy_c(t)} = -\frac{1}{[1 + y_c(t)]} \sum_{j=t}^{T} (j-t)c(j)[1 + y_c(t)]^{-(j-t)} \tag{4.6}$$

where we have assumed that no coupon is due during the infinitesimal period over which the derivative is evaluated. We note that in the zero-coupon case this equation reduces to

$$\frac{dB(t)}{dy(t)} = -\frac{(T-t)}{[1 + y(t)]} B(t) \tag{4.7}$$

and consequently we define the *Macaulay duration* (or just duration) to be the quantity

$$D(t) = \frac{1}{B_c(t)} \sum_{j=t}^{T} (j-t)c(j)[1 + y_c(t)]^{-(j-t)} \tag{4.8}$$

so that, for a coupon-carrying bond, we obtain

$$\frac{dB_c(t)}{dy_c(t)} = -\frac{D(t)}{[1 + y_c(t)]} B_c(t) \tag{4.9}$$

with the duration taking the place of the time left to maturity in the equivalent zero-coupon case. It is sometimes also convenient to introduce the *modified duration* defined by

$$D_m(t) = \frac{D(t)}{[1 + y_c(t)]} \tag{4.10}$$

in terms of which the expression for the rate of change of the bond price with respect to the yield takes on the particularly simple form

$$\frac{dB_c(t)}{dy_c(t)} = -D_m(t)B_c(t) \tag{4.11}$$

Thus, for small changes in the bond yield we obtain

$$\frac{\Delta B_c}{B_c} \approx -D_m(t)\Delta y_c \tag{4.12}$$

showing that, to first order, the bond return is given simply in terms of the modified duration and the change in yield.

The expression (4.12) is just the first term in a Taylor expansion of equation (4.5) about the point $y_c(t)$, and if we include the next higher order we obtain

$$\frac{\Delta B_c}{B_c} \approx \frac{1}{B_c}\frac{dB_c}{dy_c}\Delta y_c + \frac{1}{B_c}\frac{d^2 B_c}{dy_c^2}\frac{(\Delta y_c)^2}{2} \tag{4.13}$$

where we now define the *convexity* C to be the coefficient

$$C \equiv \frac{1}{B_c}\frac{d^2 B_c}{dy^2_c} \tag{4.14}$$

in the second term. If we take the second derivative of the bond pricing equation we can express the convexity as

$$C = \frac{1}{B_c}\frac{1}{[1 + y_c^2]}\sum_{j=t}^{T}(j-t)(j-t-1)c(j)[1 + y_c]^{-(j-t)} \tag{4.15}$$

Both the duration and the convexity find important applications in analysing the risk inherent in holding bonds due to fluctuations in the interest rate structure of the market.

4.5   Summary

In this chapter we have introduced the basic notions used in bond pricing: the time value of money, the coupon, the yield (the average return represented by cash flows in a given bond) and the yield curve (the set of values of the yield for different values of the maturity). The derived notions of duration and convexity were then defined from the yield curve.

Our discussion was mainly qualitative. However, the general concepts are behind many attempts to understand the effects of the markets on bond prices of different maturity values. It is possible to control the risk of a portfolio of bonds by choosing an appropriate range of maturities for the assets held in the portfolio. Thus they could all have longer maturity than average if it is expected that there will be a decrease in interest rates, so that long-term bond values will increase. Conversely, if the expectation is held of an interest rate increase, then bond prices will be expected to fall, with the least fall in short maturity bonds. In this way it is possible to reduce expected risk by changing the average maturity of a portfolio according to the expected values of interest rate differentials. This is why the possibility of predicting the whole of the yield curve has proved of interest to a number of investors. We will consider this possibility later in the book.

5. Data Selection

Jimmy Shadbolt

5.1   Introduction

In earlier chapters we have considered, in general terms, the kind of data we will be interested in for prediction of financial markets. In this chapter we will try to relate this more directly to the specific data used for modelling monthly returns using economic indicators as inputs.

Our initial data selection must come from the use of any prior knowledge that we may have of the markets. In our case, we make use of the expertise, built up over the years, of the company's economists. For 20 years they have been researching the general trends in the economies and markets of the major economies in particular, but also in emerging markets. This involves linear modelling, using smoothed data, and predicting general movements over the periods from 6 to 24 months into the future. Figure 5.1 shows an example of the type of relationship found. The data is

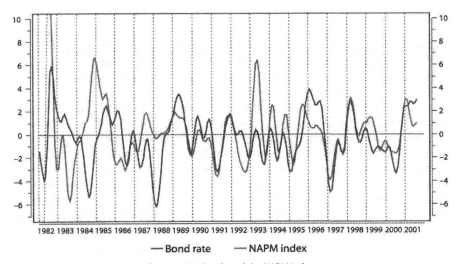

Fig. 5.1 USA bonds and the NAPM index.

smoothed, de-seasonalised and shown in first differenced (% change) terms. It shows the relationship between USA bonds and the NAPM Index.

5.2   The General Economic Model

One important piece of information given to us by the economists is the general form to be expected of a market model. This tells us the kind of data we would expect to need to model, say, the bond or the equity markets.

Bond markets are expected to be driven by a few basic influences: demand and supply, inflation expectations, and capital and currency flows. Demand and supply are measured by data such as interest rates and money supply, inflation by consumer and wholesale price indices, and capital and currency flows by exchange rates, trade balances etc.

Stock markets (the indices, not individual stocks) are driven by traders' views of future profits, expectations of the share of profits that will come back as dividends, and the alternate investments that could be made (one of course being bonds). Certain sectors of the markets will be driven by specific influences, such as the supply and price of raw materials, and these effects will feed through into the market as a whole.

For the purpose of modelling markets we need to ensure that we have data representative of all of these influences available to the models we make.

5.3   Proxies

One problem arising from the discussion above is that we may expect, for example, money supply, global demand or market sentiment to be important in predicting bond returns. For the former we are lucky in that we have data, although unfortunately there is no consensus on exactly how we should be measuring it, leading to a number of data series (M1, M2, money base etc.) all trying to measure the same thing. This problem will be discussed below.

For global demand and market sentiment, however, we have a problem – there is no data. We either have to leave a gap in our model or find data series that can be used as proxies for the missing data. This could, for example, be a series that would be expected to be very sensitive to the missing data and thus contain the same information, albeit in a transformed way, and thus be used in its place. An example would be the use of a proxy for global demand. Figure 5.2 shows a plot of the performance of the Singapore stock market relative to that of the USA plus Europe, together with the performance of non-Japanese bonds. The economic justification for this would be:

Singapore depends on exports and hence is very sensitive to global, mainly USA, demand. Thus rising Singapore stocks anticipates, by a few months, rising commodity prices – which moves closely with global demand. USA and Europe stocks should be viewed only as a deflator for Singapore stocks – the key influence. (Andrew Richardson, Chief Economist, Econostat Ltd)

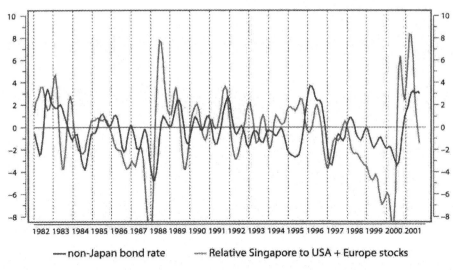

—— non-Japan bond rate   ～～ Relative Singapore to USA + Europe stocks

Fig. 5.2 The influence of a demand proxy on non-Japanese bonds.

A proxy for market sentiment would try to measure the degree of optimism or pessimism amongst traders. In some ways this is reflected in markets being over- or under-priced and approaches such as cointegration could be used to take advantage of the fact that the prices must revert to normality sometime. Another approach is discussed in Chapter 26 (Multi-Agent Systems): the possibility of modelling influences such as market sentiment in the structure of a multi-agent system. Unfortunately, at this stage, this is "under development".

5.4   Principal Components

As mentioned above, we are sometimes in the situation in which we have a number of possible data series all of which, according to our model, are trying to tell us the same thing. The example given was money supply, where we have M1, M2, M3, Money Base, and possibly the Federal Reserves. One way in which to attempt to extract the relevant information is to use *Principal Component Analysis* (PCA).

PCA attempts to reduce the dimensionality of the data at the same time as maximising the amount of information that is retained. In our example we have a five-dimensional data structure (the five money series) and we want to reduce the dimensionality (preferably to one) but not lose information.

If we consider a two-dimensional set of data points, as in Fig. 5.3, we can see that the data is highly correlated and its variance depends equally on both x and y. If we change our coordinates to be x' and y', however, the variance (and hence the information encoded) depends almost entirely on x'. The PCA enables us to define this new direction x' that maximises the variance in that direction.

The first principal component is defined as that direction that encodes the maximum possible variance, The second component is orthogonal to the first and

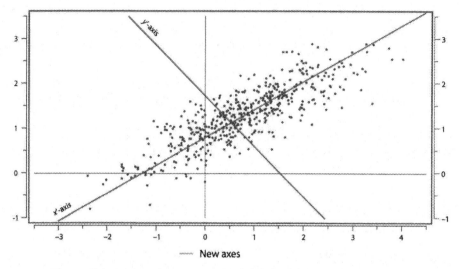

Fig. 5.3 The two principal components, x' and y' of data defined on the x- and y-axes.

encodes as much as possible of the remaining variance. The third component is orthogonal to both of the first two and encodes as much as possible... and so on. To map n-dimensional data without loss of information we need n principal components, but instead of the information being dependent on all the original n dimensions it is now mainly in the first few components.

It turns out that the principal components are the same as the eigenvectors of the variance–covariance matrix and that they are ranked in order of the eigenvalues.

For a detailed discussion of the theory behind the use of PCAs for data reduction see Bishop (1995) and Haykin (1999).

5.4.1   PCA Analysis of USA Money Supply

In Table 5.1 we show the correlations between the various money supply series.

As can be seen, there are very high (anti)correlations between the series, so they should all be giving us very similar information. Table 5.2 shows the results of a principal component analysis of this data.

We can see that the first principal component explains 95.4% of the information in the series, the first two explain 97.0% etc. The weights for the components are given in Table 5.3.

Table 5.1 USA money supply correlations

	Reserves	M1	M2	Money Base	M3
Reserves	1.000				
M1	−0.934	1.000			
M2	−0.924	0.965	1.000		
Money base	0.890	0.970	0.958	1.000	
M3	0.899	0.941	0.995	0.945	1.000

Table 5.2 PCA of USA money supply

	Component				
	1	2	3	4	5
Standard deviation	2.183	0.359	0.279	0.150	0.023
Proportion of variance	0.954	0.026	0.015	0.010	0.005
Cumulative proportion of variance	0.954	0.970	0.985	0.005	1.000

Table 5.3 Principal components weights for USA money supply

	Component				
	1	2	3	4	5
Reserves	0.435	−0.848	0.127	0.270	0.000
M1	0.451	0.000	−0.465	−0.742	0.162
M2	0.454	0.200	0.354	−0.133	−0.782
Money Base	0.447	0.333	−0.575	0.599	0.000
M3	0.448	0.355	0.559	0.000	0.600

We can see that the first principal component gives almost equal weighting to each of the five series. This should not surprise us, as the five different measures are all trying to measure the same thing.

5.5   Summary

We have given a brief review of various aspects of data selection. We started by describing a general economic model, which we suggest is behind the overall behaviour of the markets. However, we do not know the actual form of this model nor the variables on which the assets we are interested in predicting depend. To begin to handle this problem, we considered how we might introduce proxies for these various unknown economic and financial variables in Section 5.3. However, there are still a large number of variables to choose from to act as such proxies. A process of data compression was then introduced – the PCA method – to reduce the number of input time series by rotating them amongst each other in a given economic or financial sector. This allows for a 50% or so reduction in number of such series. Much further data reduction and analysis still remains to be done, however. That is to be considered shortly, after developing next a general mathematical framework for representing our prediction problem.

PART II
Theory of Prediction Modelling

We now deepen our discussion to enable the resulting prediction models to be usefully applied to the assets of interest.

We start this part, in Chapter 6, with a survey of prediction models. These use a set of past values of the asset under consideration, plus others thought to be relevant, to predict the actual value of the asset at the next time step; in our case this is one month ahead. We do not expect to be able to discover a good prediction formula without some hard work. That consists of searching among a range of prediction models to choose an optimal one. To allow sufficient flexibility, we let the prediction model itself depend on a set of free parameters, which will have to be chosen according to some criterion. We consider in Chapter 6 the prediction error itself, so leading to an optimisation problem in parameter choice.

Techniques to avoid various dangers in this optimisation process, such as overfitting past data, are discussed in Chapter 7.

Ways of extending our effective data set, for example, from the few hundred data points presently available (for monthly data, since 1985) are considered in Chapter 8 under the heading of the bootstrap, with its extension to bagging and the use of ensembles.

Linear models are reviewed (including a discussion of state space models) in Chapter 9, as providing a springboard to the larger range of models, especially with a non-linear content, which we will meet in the remainder of the book.

The problem of input selection is basic to our whole modelling process, due to the fact mentioned earlier that there is a plethora of possible inputs to choose from in model construction (above several thousand). Thus we conclude this part of the book with a consideration of how best to reduce the set of inputs to be considered for detailed model building. Various selection methods are described, and their effectiveness briefly considered. However, this cannot be properly assessed until the core model technologies are described and models developed.

6. General Form of Models of Financial Markets

John G Taylor

6.1 Introduction

From our discussion in Chapter 1 we expect on economic grounds that a predictive model for the value of a financial asset (bond or equity index) at one time step in the future, $t + 1$, will have the form

$$x(t+1) = F(Y_1(t), Y_1(t-1), \ldots, Y_2(t), Y_2(t-1), \ldots) \qquad (6.1)$$

where the time series vectors Y_n are economic variables evaluated at earlier times t, $t - 1$, $t - 2$,..., $t - 23$ (where our cut-off at 24 lags is somewhat arbitrary but cannot be expected to be larger with any assurance). In this chapter we will discuss how we proceed in a general manner to construct predictive models in an adaptive manner both to extract the optimal lags to enter in the predictive equation of (6.1) and to give a final assessment of their predictive effectiveness. We will start this process with enumeration of how we can assess such predictions before we then turn to questions of determining the optimal form of such a predictive model. In the following chapter we will discuss various problems associated with this process.

6.2 Cost Functions

In order to assess how effective a predictive model of the form (6.1) is, we must define a suitable cost or error function to use. There is considerable controversy over this, since standard metrics, such as the quadratic error function – the mean square error – is not directly interpretable as a measure of profit made by use of the model (6.1). (See Chapter 12 on Reinforcement Learning for an alternative treatment.) Because of this, a range of metrics have been introduced and tested (Abecasis *et al.*, 1999). The most common of these, however, is the mean square error (MSE) already mentioned:

$$\text{MSE} = \frac{1}{T}\sum_t (x(t) - p(t))^2 \qquad (6.2)$$

where the summation is over the T values of t being considered in the data set, $x(t)$ is the actual target value at time t and $p(t)$ is its prediction at the same time, as given, for example, by equation (6.1). The values of pairs $\{x(t+1); y_1(t), y_1(t-1), y_1(t-2), ..., y_n(t), y_n(t-1), ...\}$ are termed the training data, being used to assess how good the prediction model is by its MSE (6.2). In the next section we will indicate how the MSE may be used to train the prediction model, by modifying a vector of parameters on which the model depends, so as to minimise the cost function (6.2). In this manner it will be justifiable to term the set of pairs $\{x(t+1); y_1(t), ..., y_n(t), ...$ as a training set.

From the MSE we can create its square root, the RMSE. Various extensions can be given to the MSE, for example replacing the squared error term in each summand of equation (6.2) by a different power q, say. The resulting sum is then related to the Lq norm in a corresponding Hilbert sequence space. There is some gain in doing this. It is known that setting $q = 3/2$, for example, leads to a more robust assessment of the error, less liable to effects of outliers. However, we will not consider these in any detail here, especially since they have the defect of not leading to simple expressions for modifying parameters entering in various cases of (6.2), especially for neural networks. (Those interested will find a discussion on robust error measures in Hampel *et al.*, 1986.)

Neither the MSE or RMSE (or the extensions to the Lq spaces mentioned above) are scale free, whereas an industry standard which does possess this scale invariance property is the ARV (average relative variance) formed from the MSE by dividing it by the standard deviation σ of the target series:

$$\text{ARV} = \frac{\text{MSE}}{\sigma} \qquad (6.3)$$

The ARV is a measure of the goodness of the actual predictor (6.1), as given by its MSE, as compared to that of the predictor given by the mean. This can be improved dynamically by replacing the overall standard deviation σ of the target series in equation (6.3) by an MSE calculated on the basis of using the moving average over the previous 12 months as a predictor. If the MSE is also calculated over the same period, then the resulting ARV, denoted ARV$_{12}$, is a dynamically varying assessor of the effectiveness of the model predictor (6.1), compared with the 12 month average, over the previous 12 months (see Chapter 15 on Bayesian Methods and Evidence).

It is also interesting to consider metrics based on the degree of effectiveness in predicting the direction of movement of the next month's value. This is assessed by the directional symmetry metric DS defined as

$$\text{DS} = \frac{100}{T} \sum_t d(t)$$
$$d(t) = 1 \quad \text{if} \quad (x(t) - x(t-1))(p(t) - p(t-1)) > 0 \qquad (6.4)$$
$$d(t) = 0 \quad \text{if} \quad (x(t) - x(t-1))(p(t) - p(t-1)) < 0$$

the summation in equation (6.4) being over the T time values t for which the directional effectiveness is being assessed. Various weightings and related metrics can be defined from equation (6.4), although we do not consider them further here (Abecasis *et al.*, 1999); the directional symmetry metric is regarded by some, however, as closer to the profitability obtainable for a forecasting model than the RSME or ARV. However, we will not consider this in more detail (but see Zapranis and Refenes, 1999).

Modifications can be made to the cost functions above by introducing means or medians as assessors of residuals $\{x(t) - p(t)\}$. Also, it is possible more directly to attempt to introduce an error assessor based on final profit, say of a portfolio. However, these profit-related metrics tend to be data hungry, since they require models with a number of outputs (a prediction for each asset in the portfolio). Since we have only ~200 data points (data for bond markets is generally only available from 1985), we have attempted to simplify our prediction assessment by using mainly the MSE and its related ARV in creating our prediction models. Of course, when portfolios are analysed various metrics associated with profit, such as cumulative return and information ratio, are considered as most crucial. Various approaches using reinforcement based on profit are discussed in Chapter 12.

6.3 Parameterisation

We can now introduce the crucial step in the modelling process, that of bringing in a parameter vector w which allows prediction accuracy to be improved by choosing that value of w for which the prediction cost function is a minimum. Thus we modify the predictor of (6.1) to have the form

$$x(t+1) = F(Y_1(t), Y_1(t-1), \ldots, Y_2(t), Y_2(t-1), \ldots, w) \qquad (6.5)$$

where now the parameter w enters explicitly in the predictor function F on the left-hand side of equation (6.5). This parameter can be regarded as a way of weighting more important lagged variables, the fundamentals, to the detriment of the less important ones. The task we face is thus to determine the value of w that minimises the cost function

$$\text{MSE} = \frac{1}{T}\sum_t (x(t) - F(t,w))^2 \qquad (6.6)$$

where the variables entering into the predictor function F of equation (6.5) have not been inserted explicitly into equation (6.6). Thus we need to minimise the cost function $\text{MSE}(w)$.

We thus arrive at an optimisation formulation of the development of a prediction function (6.5). The difficulty of solving this will depend strongly on the nature of the class of prediction functions being chosen in equation (6.5). Thus for a linear regression expression the parameters w are the regression parameters, and enter linearly in equation (6.5). The cost function (6.6) is therefore quadratic in the parameters w, so leading to an exact expression whose form is well known. However, it is well known that the cost surface defined by (6.6) over the weight parameters w can have local minima which can cause problems determining the true global minimum. Trapping can occur in one or other of these local minima. Various techniques have been suggested to reduce this difficulty (Shepherd, 1996), although they can add considerably to the computational overhead. Later we will consider the simplest approach, that of gradient descent, to determine the global minimum, but using various extra criteria to ensure that there has not been trapping in local minima; these will be discussed in due course. They naturally lead us to consider various questions about avoiding overfitting which is discussed in detail in the next chapter.

6.4   Econometric Models

We introduced, in Section 6.1, a general prediction model for the asset time series $\{x(t)\}$ in terms of a set of assets $\{y_1(t)\}$, $\{y_2(t)\}$,..., using an unknown function F (equation 6.1). Is there anything that can be said about the nature of F or its variables from underlying economic theory? Such knowledge is of crucial importance to allow us to narrow down the input variables; as we have stated before, this is a highly non-trivial problem, with thousands of potential variables available as candidates from the hundreds of financial and economic time series and lags of up to 24 months. There is also the difficulty of the unknown function F. There is considerable mathematical expertise that has been developed on the pricing of various derivatives, such as the Black–Scholes–Merton approach and beyond (Black and Scholes, 1973; Merton, 1973). However, we are more concerned here not with relating risk to future prices of assets (although that is important), but with determining what economic or financial variables determine bond and equity prices. Bond pricing has much discussion in terms of the bond yield curve and its relation to interest rate expectations (see Chapter 4). Yet again, this is an important component of the overall investment process, such as involving maturity calls. However, it also does not help us in refining our basic returns prediction model of equation 6.1.

The natural place to turn for constraining information is economical models of the economy (such as the Treasury model: http://www.warwick.ac.uk/ fac/soc/Economics/MMB/). In general these would argue that a bond return will depend on money supply, interest rates, growth, inflation and possibly other appropriate economic variables. These can be both of the country of the asset and also of other countries with economies correlated with that country. To determine the appropriate model for equation (6.1) a detailed model of the flow of assets in the given economy would then have to be developed. This would involve, for example, delineation of various sectors of the economy, how these affect each other, and so on. Lags would arise from the delays of flow of supply and demand through the economy, from raw materials through to the finished product, and on to the market place, with account taken of inventory levels etc. It can be seen that any such model would be complex, and as far as we know has not been completed at the level of detail we would need to move into equation (6.1).

In summary, we cannot use more than the general common-sense indications from economic and financial ideas that can help refine equation (6.1) of the form:

$$\text{predicted return} = F(\text{capital flows, expected inflation,}$$
$$\text{supply and demand,...}) \qquad (6.7)$$

The form of equation (6.7) requires, in any case, the discovery of proxies for such variables as supply and demand. The determination of appropriate proxies and the functional form of F is as difficult theoretically as the determination of lags entering equation (6.7).

In conclusion, prediction models of the form (6.7) are hard to make specific. We therefore have to resort to information processing techniques to determine the major components of equation (6.7) (inputs, functionality, lags). It is these techniques that are developed throughout this book.

6.5   Summary

We have developed here a general approach to constructing a multivariate prediction model for a given asset by means of minimising, in a suitable manner, a cost function defined by means of the data. Various cost functions were defined, especially the mean square error to be used considerably later. Introducing a parameter vector w into the prediction function (6.1) allows for the cost function to be used explicitly to search for the parameter value which minimises the cost. Various methods can be used to achieve such minimisation, although they have problems. That of overfitting is handled by regularisation, a method leading to powerful variable selection in due course.

7. Overfitting, Generalisation and Regularisation

Jimmy Shadbolt

7.1   Overfitting and Generalisation

In the previous chapter we discussed some problems with the process of learning a prediction function by choosing its parameters as minimising the cost function. However, that assumes that we know how many parameters should be used in the first place. This is related to the process of overfitting, in which any set of data points, for example, can be fitted by a suitably high-order polynomial. Figure 7.1 shows a plot of a signal and measurements made using some noisy method. Minimising the MSE could cause a model to fit these noisy points perfectly.

Fitting the noise will have repercussions when it comes to making predictions – although the model contains the true fitted function, it also has a model of the noise, and will make (useless) predictions of the noise.

To avoid this various methods can be used. In the simplest case we restrict the complexity of the model so that the number of data points being fitted is very much

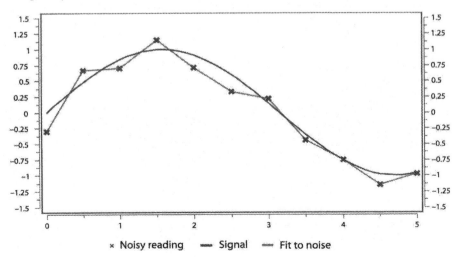

Fig. 7.1 A signal (dark line) and some measured data points (crosses). The grey line shows a fit obtained by minimising the MSE.

larger than the number of free parameters in the model. This would allow us to fit the model with low error bars on the coefficients and hence high confidence in the model. Unfortunately, in the case of, for example, multivariate modelling of bond returns using economic indicators, we have a limited dataset (~200 monthly data points). This is not too much of a problem with linear models, but with neural networks the number of free parameters grows very quickly with the number of hidden neurons, and it is these that give us the means to map non-linear relationships.

If we knew how much noise was in the data we could use this information. We could create a model where the residual matched the noise – although this prompts the question of what part of the signal is the noise.

7.2   Early Stopping

One method for splitting the signal from the noise in the context of an iterative model-fitting procedure is early stopping. This uses a cross-validation technique whereby the data is split into two parts: the first is used to fit the model, while the second is monitored to validate the model. At each stage of the iterative modelling (training in neural network parlance) the MSE of the model will decrease. In the early stages of training we expect the MSE of the validation set to decrease as well as we fit the relationships in the data. During later training, however, we find the model beginning to fit the noise in the data, and in this phase we expect to see the errors in the validation set begin to rise (Fig. 7.2).

We would stop our training at the point where the validation set error is at a minimum.

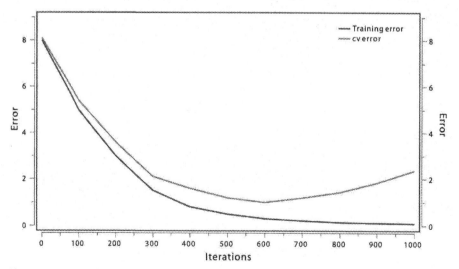

Fig. 7.2 In-sample (dark) and cross-validation (grey) errors during training. For the best generalisation we would stop training when the cross-validation error is at a minimum.

7.3   Information Criteria

Our arguments above for preferring a smaller model can be expressed in the form:

Cost = Training error + complexity term

In the case of the training error being the MSE, this would lead to an equation of the form (Bishop, 1985)

$$C = 2MSE + \frac{2W}{N}\sigma^2 \tag{7.1}$$

where W is the number of parameters in the model, N is the number of data points being fitted and σ is the level of noise in the system (which must be estimated). This gives us a criterion for trading the decrease in MSE against model complexity.

Moody (1992) has generalised this for neural networks using regularisation by introducing an *effective* number of parameters γ.

$$C = 2MSE + \frac{2\gamma}{N}\sigma^2 \tag{7.2}$$

γ is a measure of the number of parameters that have not been "eliminated" by regularisation.

Similar criteria are the AIC (Akaike, 1974), the FIS (final information statistic) (Fogel, 1991) and the NIC (network information criterion) (Murata *et al.*,1994).

7.4   Regularisation

The principle of regularisation is based on Occam's razor – the idea that the best explanation for anything is the simplest. A Bayesian view of the same idea would be that of the *evidence* for a model: a model that can fit lots of data (it has lots of parameters) has lower evidence than a smaller model that fits the same data. The evidence would be inversely related to the ability of a model to fit *any* data with which it was presented. Thus a model with a large number of free parameters is far more flexible than a small model and we would therefore expect it to be able to better fit any data that we presented. This would be irrespective of whether the model had any real meaning. We should therefore use the most restrictive model that will fit the data.

The problem we face, however, is that we do not know in advance precisely what data is relevant, what the forms of the relationships are, or how much noise there is in the system. So how do we formulate the model, and how do we decide which is the best fit (given that the "best" fit to the data is probably fitting the noise)?

Regularisation tackles this problem by starting with an overspecified model (one that has too many free parameters), and allowing the model fitting process to set a number of the parameters to zero, thus removing them from the model. It does this on the basis of some prior belief in the nature of the model.

A simple belief is that for the model to fit noise it requires large derivatives to enable it to fit the spikes in the data. So to prevent fitting the noise we can impose the condition that we will not allow large derivatives. We achieve this by applying a cost function of the form of equation (7.1) (Ripley, 1996):

$$C(w) = \sum_i \|y_i - f(w_i)\|^2 + \lambda \| Pf \|^2 \qquad (7.3)$$

where the first term is the sum of squared errors, and the second term is a penalty on large derivatives of the function. (P is some differential operator on the function f.) λ is a weighting parameter between the terms.

A typical regularisation term is one quadratic in the parameter set w, so it is of the form

$$P(w) = -\frac{1}{2} w^2 \qquad (7.4)$$

The penalty term P corresponds, in the case of a prediction model with additional Gaussian noise, to picking the weight components according to a Gaussian with variance ($1/\lambda$). Thus the larger is λ, the more close to zero will the weights be constrained, as to be expected from the reduced cost they provide in equation (7.2).

For a full discussion of the theory involved in regularisation see Ripley (1996), Bishop (1995) and Girosi *et al.* (1995).

7.5   Weight Decay

The penalty term of equation (7.2) leads to the weight decay methods of neural networks (and also of ridge regression). The iterative training of the weights uses the derivatives of the cost function with respect to the weights:

$$\nabla C = \nabla MSE - \lambda w \qquad (7.5)$$

so that at each training step will will adjust the weights to minimise the MSE, but also decrease (or decay) each weight by a fraction λ of its magnitude.

7.6   Forgetting

Ishikawa has proposed a penalty term of the form:

$$P(w) = -\lambda \sum_{w_i < \theta} |w| \qquad (7.6)$$

He calls this forgetting because the derivative w.r.t. the weights is a constant λ, with sign the opposite of that of the weight. This leads to all weights being driven towards zero by the penalty term, unless, that is, the weights are larger than the threshold θ, in which case they are allowed to grow unhindered. This process leads to a model in which most weights would be forced to zero, but the rest are large, allowing the model to fit very non-linear functions.

7.7 Summary

The topic of this chapter, that of avoiding overfitting and achieving good generalisation on new data sets similar to the old ones, is crucial to our overall process. The problem it presents was discussed at the beginning of this chapter, and then we introduced the method of early stopping in Section 7.2 to attempt to prevent overfitting occurring in any training process that tries to adapt a predictive general model of our assets. A deeper criterion, using an information-theoretic criterion, was then introduced. Another method, that of regularisation, was then defined and shown also to be effective. Further methods of weight decay and of forgetting were also considered. All of these methods are of relevance to applications, and we will later consider some of them in a comparative manner in order to ensure best practice in predictive model building.

8. The Bootstrap, Bagging and Ensembles

Jimmy Shadbolt

8.1 Introduction

Given a set of data and some modelling methodology, how do we achieve the best predictions? In this chapter we consider a number of techniques that, under the right circumstances, allow us to achieve better predictions than simply presenting our methodology with all of the data and accepting its results.

The techniques all derive from using data sampling methods in an attempt to uncover the true distribution of the underlying data generating process from the limited data sample available.

8.2 The Bias–Variance Trade-Off

We begin our analysis by examining the expansion of the expectation for the squared difference between two random variables Y and T (the usual squared error term).

$$
\begin{aligned}
E_x[(Y-T)^2] = & \ E_x[(Y-E_x[Y])^2] + E_x[(T-E_x[T])^2] \\
& - 2E_x[(Y-E_x[Y])(T-E_x[T])] \\
& + (E_x[Y]-E_x[T])^2
\end{aligned}
\tag{8.1}
$$

This is true for any random vectors Y and T with respect to conditional expectation $E_x[]$ for any x. (x is any given information on which the result may depend. In the discussion below it will generally be a data set or a model.)

If we are considering a prediction problem where Y is the prediction and T the target, then the various terms on the right are:

$E_x[(Y-E_x[Y])^2]$	variance in prediction
$E_x[(T-E_x[T])^2]$	variance in target
$2E_x[(Y-E_x[Y])(T-E_x[T])]$	$2 \times$ covariance between predictions and target bias^2

61

$$(E_x[Y] - E_x[T])^2 \qquad\qquad \text{bias}^2$$

The second and third terms are normally considered to be zero on the assumption that the target is known precisely, and thus $T = E_x[T]$. This leads to the normal equation for the bias–variance trade-off:

$$E_x[(Y - T)^2] = (E_x[Y] - E_x[T])^2 + E_x[(Y - E_x[Y])^2] \tag{8.2}$$
$$\text{error} \quad = \quad \text{bias} \quad + \quad \text{variance}$$

It tells us that the error of a model consists of two parts, the bias (the squared difference between the mean of the predictions and the mean of the target), and the variance (the spread of the predictions – confidence in the prediction).

The third (covariance) term in equation (8.1) is the expectation of a product of two random variables conditioned on x. We have (by definition of $P(T|Y,X)$)

$$P(Y, T|X) = P(Y|X)P(T|Y, X) \tag{8.3}$$

If we assume that anything Y may have to tell us about T is contained in the information X has about T (and as Y is a prediction obtained from data in X this should be so), then we can remove Y from the conditioning in $P(T|Y, X)$ and equation (8.3) becomes:

$$P(Y, T|X) = P(Y|X)P(T|X) \tag{8.4}$$

which means that Y and T are conditionally independent, and thus the expectation of their product $E_x[Y]E_x[T]$ is zero (if they are mean zero). In this case we lose the covariance term in (8.1), but keep the noise term on the target:

$$E_x[(Y - T)^2] = (E_x[Y] - E_x[T])^2 + E_x[(Y - E_x[Y])^2] + E_x[(T - E_x[T])^2] \tag{8.5}$$
$$\text{error} \quad = \quad \text{bias} \quad + \quad \text{variance} \quad + \quad \text{noise}$$

The noise on the target derives from the impossibility of knowing (measuring) the target precisely. The noise term then gives the minimum possible error for a model. If the magnitude of the noise is known, then it can be used to detect when overtraining of a model occurs.

8.3   The Bootstrap

Equations for estimates of mean and variance of a sample drawn from a true distribution F with mean μ_F and variance σ_F^2 are:

$$E_F[x] = \frac{1}{N}\sum_{i=1}^{N} x_i = \hat{\mu}_F \tag{8.6}$$

$$E_F[(x - \mu_F)^2] = \frac{1}{(N-1)}\sum_{i=1}^{N}(x_i - \hat{\mu}_F)^2 = \hat{\sigma}_F^2 \tag{8.7}$$

where the "hat" indicates an estimate calculated from our sample, which will tend to the true value as $N \to \infty$.

If we want an estimate of how good an estimate of a mean is (we make a number of estimates of the mean by sampling from the distribution F and want to know the variance of the estimate) we get:

$$E[\bar{x}] = \frac{1}{N} \sum_{i=1}^{N} E_F[x_i] = \hat{\mu}_F \tag{8.8}$$

$$E_F[\sigma_F^2(\bar{x})] = \frac{1}{N} \sum_{i=1}^{N} E_F[\bar{x} - \mu_F] = \frac{\hat{\sigma}_F^2}{N} \tag{8.9}$$

So, by taking a number of samples from a distribution, we can improve the confidence of our estimate of the mean. (A number of samples is the equivalent of a larger sample.)

The question then arises of how to take the samples in a real problem, where we have only a fixed data set that we must use to represent the true distribution. The bootstrap (Efron and Tibshirani, 1993) is a method of generating new samples from our given data to get a better estimate of the full data distribution. If we have a set of data P consisting of n data points, then we create samples ρ by randomly selecting n data points *with replacement* from the full sample. (We select n random numbers between 1 and n, and use them as indices into our full data set. We can therefore select the same index a number of times.) Experimental results indicate that, in general, between 25 and 200 bootstraps should be enough to get stable estimates of coefficients (e.g. correlation, regression) from the data.

8.3.1 Prediction Error Estimation

Each bootstrap sample will select, on average, 63% of the total data samples available (due to some having been selected multiple times). For each data point in the full sample we can calculate an average error from all models fitted to samples that include the point, and a similar error for models fitted to data that did not include the point. The .632 bootstrap (Efron and Tibshirani, 1993) then estimates the true prediction error by adjusting the apparent error rate (calculated from the bootstrap models) with the out-of-sample error:

pe $= 0.368$ apparent error $+ 0.632$ out-of-sample error

8.4 Bagging

Bagging is a similar procedure to the bootstrap, but instead of estimating coefficients and their confidence levels, it applies a bootstrap procedure to improve the prediction confidence of a model.

Given a set of data ρ drawn from P consisting of data pairs $\{x, t\}$ and a predictor $Y(x, \rho)$, where ρ is a sample taken from P, then the aggregated predictor (the averaged predictor over a number of bootstraps) is

$$Y_A(x, P) = E_\rho[Y(x, \rho)] \tag{8.10}$$

The error made by this aggregated predictor is (with a proviso as described below) lower than the expected error from a single predictor, as we will show.

The average error of a single predictor (calculated over all data points in P) is

$$\varepsilon = E_\rho[E_{T,X}[(T-Y(X,\rho))^2]] \tag{8.11}$$

Dropping the (X, ρ) for clarity, we get:

$$\varepsilon = E_\rho[E_{T,X}[(T-Y)^2]]$$

$$= E_\rho E_{T,X}[Y^2] - 2E_\rho E_{T,X}[YT] + E_\rho E_{T,X}[T^2]$$

$$= E_{T,X} E_\rho[Y^2] - 2E_{T,X} E_\rho[YT] + E_{T,X} E_\rho[T^2]$$

$$= E_{T,X} E_\rho[Y^2] - 2E_{T,X}[Y_A T] + E_{T,X} E_\rho[T^2]$$

and by adding and subtracting $E_{T,X}[Y_A^2]$ to the first term, and noting that $Y_A = E_\rho[Y]$

$$= E_{T,X}[E_\rho[Y^2] - E_\rho[Y]^2] + E_{T,X}[Y_A^2] -$$

$$2E_{T,X}[Y_A T] + E_{T,X} E_\rho[T^2]$$

and so

$$\varepsilon = E_{T,X}[E_\rho[Y^2] - E_\rho[Y]^2] + E_{T,X}[(Y_A - T)^2] \tag{8.12}$$

The error of the aggregated predictor is

$$\varepsilon_A = E_{T,X}[(Y_A - T)^2] \tag{8.13}$$

and so

$$\varepsilon = E_{T,X}[E_\rho[Y^2] - E_\rho[Y]^2] + \varepsilon_A$$

As the inequality $E[Z]^2 \leq E[Z^2]$ always holds,

$$\varepsilon \geq \varepsilon_A \tag{8.14}$$

so the aggregated predictor has a lower (or at least no greater) error than a single predictor.

The difference,

$$E_{T,X}[E_\rho[Y^2] - E_\rho[Y]^2]$$

is small if the predictions from different data sets ρ are similar.

The greatest benefit will come when the prediction method is such that the bootstrap samples lead to very divergent predictions. This does not imply that we should choose an unstable modelling procedure rather than one that is able to the handle data (and its noise) to produce stable predictions, rather that if we have a reason to use an unstable modelling procedure (because of its inherent ability to handle the type of data of interest), then we should use bagging/bootstrapping.

The proviso mentioned above is that the method will work provided that the bootstrap actually gives a good estimation of the *true* distribution of the underlying data. If this is not true, then the inequality (8.14) will not hold.

8.5 Bootstrap with Noise

Raviv and Intrator (1999) make use of this relationship in their *bootstrap ensembles with noise* algorithm. They add noise to the bootstrapped data samples to increase the variation in predictions.

If we take the variance term in the error for an ensemble (as in equation 8.2)

$$E[(\bar{Y} - E[\bar{Y}])^2] \tag{8.15}$$

and expand with

$$\bar{Y} = \frac{1}{N} \sum_{i=1}^{N} Y_i(\rho)$$

dropping the (ρ) for clarity, we get

$$
\begin{aligned}
E[(\bar{Y} - E[\bar{Y}])^2] &= E\left[\left(\frac{1}{N}\sum Y_i - E\left[\frac{1}{N}\sum Y_i\right]\right)^2\right] \\
&= E\left[\left(\frac{1}{N}\sum Y_i\right)^2\right] + \left(E\left[\frac{1}{N}\sum Y_i\right]\right)^2 \\
&\quad - 2E\left[\frac{1}{N}\sum Y_i E\left[\frac{1}{N}\sum Y_i\right]\right] \\
&= E\left[\left(\frac{1}{N}\sum Y_i\right)^2\right] - \left(E\left[\frac{1}{N}\sum Y_i\right]\right)^2
\end{aligned}
\tag{8.16}
$$

If we now change the expectations of sums to sums of expectations we obtain

$$
\begin{aligned}
E[(\bar{Y} - E[\bar{Y}])^2] &= \frac{1}{N^2}\sum\{E[Y_i^2] - (E[Y_i])^2\} \\
&\quad + \frac{1}{N^2}\sum_{i \neq j}\{E[Y_i Y_j] - E[Y_i]E[Y_j]\}
\end{aligned}
\tag{8.17}
$$

Equation (8.17) is the covariance matrix between the members of the ensemble. The first term on the right (the variance of the individual predictors) will be increased by adding noise to input data, but at the same time the second term (the covariance between predictors) will decrease due to the uncorrelated noise added to the predictors. The level of noise can be chosen to minimise the sum of these terms.

8.6   Decorrelated Models

Rosen (1996) analyses the effect of correlated neural networks in an ensemble predictor and proposed a method of deliberately creating decorrelated models, thus gaining the benefit of equation (8.4).

He gives the following equation for the expected error of an ensemble (see Ueda and Nakano, 1996), each member of which is trained on the same data set:

$$E_A = E\left[\frac{1}{N}\overline{var}\right] + E\left[\left(1 - \frac{1}{N}\right)\overline{cov}\right] + E[\overline{bias}^2] + \sigma^2 \qquad (8.18)$$

where the averages are over the ensemble. This can be derived from equation (8.1), but we will not give the detail here.

The ensemble averages are:

$$\overline{var} = \frac{1}{N}\sum_{i=1}^{N} var_i$$

$$\overline{cov} = \frac{1}{N(N-1)}\sum_{i,j=1; i \ne j}^{N} cov_{i,j} \qquad (8.19)$$

$$\overline{bias} = \frac{1}{N}\sum_{i=1}^{N} bias_i$$

The variance and bias terms are the same as equations (8.5) and (8.6), and the covariance term is split out in the manner of the second term on the RHS of equation (8.17).

Equation (8.18) tells us that to minimise the ensemble error we must minimise the covariance between the outputs of the ensemble members. Rosen proposes a method for creating decorrelated networks as part of the network training. He adds an extra term to the usual squared error cost function for network j:

$$C_j = \sum_{p=1}^{N}\left[(y_p - \phi_j(x_p))^2 + \sum_{i=1}^{j-1}\lambda d(i,j)P(x_p, y_p, \phi_i, \phi_j)\right] \qquad (8.20)$$

where the $\{x_p, y_p\}$ are the training patterns, λ is a scaling function, d is an indicator function for decorrelation between networks (it determines which pairs (i, j) of networks in the ensemble are to be decorrelated), and P is a correlation penalty function.

$$P(x, y, \phi_i, \phi_j) = (y - \phi_i(x))(y - \phi_j(x)) \qquad (8.21)$$

By deliberately decorrelating the ensemble members, the inequality (8.4) can be maximised, making the best use of bagging.

8.7   Ensembles in Financial Market Prediction

In the real world of financial market prediction we cannot make any assumptions about our true target. We have a target data series that has an unknown noise content (probably large), and the true data mapping is <all data available> leads to <predictable bit of target>. With our leading indicator models all we know (or hope for) is that we can take a restricted set of input data and map it to a prediction that approximates the changes in the market of interest. If we take another set of inputs, we will make a different approximation.

Due to the shortage of monthly data, we use bootstrapping/bagging in all multivariate modelling techniques. We extend this with what amounts (loosely speaking) to a bootstrap from data variables (as apposed to data within the chosen variables), in that we use ensembles of a large number of models each of which selects the relevant input series in its own way. By doing this we should achieve ensembles with low correlation between errors, but high correlation between predictions. (The correlation between predictions giving some measure of confidence in those predictions.)

9. Linear Models

Neville Towers

9.1 Introduction

Given the empirical evidence and theoretical arguments for some degree of predictability in financial markets (see Chapter 3), any departures in asset returns from the random walk model would provide a theoretical basis for a more general form for the expectations of asset returns. Under this assumption the naïve estimate, based purely on statistics of historical data, is replaced by a general estimate conditioned on the most recent past returns and/or fundamental (or market) factors that influence, to some degree, the future behaviour of the financial time series. The unconditional estimates of expected returns and risks, are substituted by statistical time series forecasting models defined by the *conditional mean*, *conditional variance* and *conditional correlation* and, for two time series x and y, take the form:

$$\hat{y}_c = E[y_t | F_{t-\tau}]$$
$$\sigma_c^2 = E[(y_t - \hat{y}_c)^2 | F_{t-\tau}] \tag{9.1}$$
$$\rho_c = E[(y_{t-} \hat{y}_c)(x_{t-} \hat{x}_c) | F_{t-\tau}]$$

where the expectations are conditional on some vector of lagged time series variables, F_{t-1}.

A wide range of forecasting techniques may be applied to the modelling of these statistics which describe the expected distribution of future asset returns. The highly stochastic nature of asset returns and the poor understanding of asset price dynamics has led to the development of ever more complex techniques which attempt to model any non-linear or time varying relationships that may be present in financial markets. Until recently, the search for significant forecasting models has proved elusive, with some empirical studies suggesting possible predictability but offering very little convincing proof. However, in recent years, with researchers combining economic understanding with modelling expertise, explicit empirical research has emerged which is believed to contain concrete evidence that forecasting models can have some degree of predictive power.

9.2   Review of Linear Forecasting Methods

In this section we concisely review statistical modelling techniques for forecasting that range from relatively simple moving average techniques to more complex methods, described by ARIMA (Box and Jenkins, 1970) and time series regression methods, cointegration and error correction models (Granger, 1983), ridge regression (Hoerl and Kennard, 1970a,b) and state space modelling techniques (Harvey, 1989). We discuss the properties, strengths and weaknesses of these competing methods and the selection of forecasting models.

One important underlying assumption of all forecasting methods is the belief that future behaviour is similar or related to the past. If this assumption is violated then the forecasting model is considered to be unreliable and subject to model breakdown. This assumption is normally referred to as stationarity and has been the subject of considerable research in order to maintain the integrity of forecasting models. A comprehensive treatment of issues relating to non-stationarity in investment finance can be found in Harvey (1989). Practical examples can be found in Burgess (1998).

9.3   Moving Average/Smoothing Methods

One of the most pragmatic but commonly used family of methods for forecasting time series are known as the smoothing, or moving average, methods. These have been developed to model the main types of deterministic components (i.e. seasonality, cycles and trends) that may be present in a time series.

For brevity, we focus on the *simple moving average* (SMA) model and the *simple exponential smoothing model* (ESM). The concept is to smooth the sharp variations in the observed time series but allow more recent values to have greater influence on the forecasts than more distant observations. This is achieved by constructing a time-weighted average of past observations. In the case of the simple moving average an equally weighted window of data is used while the weights of the simple exponential smoothing decay exponentially with the number of time periods from the current time step.

The simple moving average model is defined for a time series, y, at time, t, over all future time horizons (denoted by τ), and takes the form:

$$\hat{y}_{t+\tau|t} = \frac{1}{h}\sum_{i=1}^{h} y_{t-i} \tag{9.2}$$

where h controls the window length of the most recent historical observations.

The simple exponential smoothing model is similar but uses a weighted average to increase the importance of the most recent data. It is normally re-expressed so that the future forecasts are equal to the weighted sum of the current observation and the previous forecast and hence takes the form:

$$\hat{y}_{t+\tau|t} = \alpha y_t + (1-\alpha)\hat{y}_t \tag{9.3}$$

where α is the weight decay parameter that controls the relevance of the historical observations.

Both models can also be used for estimating the future variance of the asset return by replacing the last observation with the last observed squared residual. More general smoothing models were developed by Holt (1957) and Winters (1960) to model time series components relating to trends and seasonality by using additional model parameters. Other related methods were suggested by Brown (1963), who used the *discounted least squares* method to emphasise the most recent observations through an exponentially weighted decay function. This method has been extended to consider polynomial models. A review of the development in smoothing methods is provided by Gardner (1985).

The parameters of smoothing models are either pre-specified on the basis of some *a priori* belief in regard to the underlying properties of the time series or selected according to some optimisation criteria that measure forecast accuracy on some test/validation data set. The mean squared error was originally shown to give optimal (one step ahead) forecasts by Muth (1960) when the time series is non-stationary. In general, model parameters are typically selected according to the analysis of a number of metrics of forecast accuracy, as discussed in many texts on statistical forecasting (e.g. Chapter 12 of Diebold, 1998). Smoothing techniques are widely used as forecasting models in many application areas outside of investment finance and have the advantages of being easy to understand, requiring few observations, and having automated parameter selection. The disadvantages of smoothing techniques are due to the simple, univariate nature of the modelling process and the specification of the model parameters. In the next section we progress to more principled modelling techniques.

Surveys of large-scale empirical studies using forecasting methods (Makridakis *et al.*, 1982, 1993, 2000) indicate that simple methods (i.e. exponential smoothing) can perform as well as more complex methods on out-of-sample data. These results are primarily due to the underlying modelling assumptions of model selection that the selected model is the true representation of the process and the time series does not undergo any structural changes. Obviously, in many real applications this occurs, so results favour simple parsimonious models that do not overfit the in-sample data.

In investment finance, moving average/smoothing models are typically used when it is believed that the functioning of markets is slowly changing through time and more emphasis is required on the more recent observations. The conditional mean of a financial time series can be modelled by transforming the price series into a returns series by taking logs of the differences in consecutive prices and then smoothing the returns series. Alternatively, the price series can be smoothed and log differences calculated from the transformed series. The relative efficiency of financial markets and the lack of obvious deterministic components in financial time series limits the advantage of using smoothing models to estimate the future expected return of an individual asset.

9.4   ARMA, ARIMA and Time Series Regression Models

Autoregressive-moving average (ARMA) modelling is a classical methodology for estimating statistical forecasting models. It uses two processes, the autoregressive (AR) terms and the moving average (MA) which describe the lagged values of observed values and forecast errors respectively. These processes are combined to approximate any stochastic time series, where the general equation of the ARMA(p, q) model takes the form:

$$\hat{y}_t = \mu + \sum_{i=1}^{p} \phi y_{t-i} + \sum_{i=1}^{q} \theta \varepsilon_{t-i} \qquad (9.4)$$

where ϕ and θ are the coefficients of the autoregressive and moving average processes respectively, and where p and q denote the number of lagged values of the observed time series and the error terms respectively.

The development of the ARMA process was originally suggested by Yule (1921) and Slutsky (1927) and has formed the basis of a family of forecasting models which has been widely used for modelling economic time series (e.g. Box and Jenkins, 1970). ARMA models have been extended to non-stationary stochastic processes by differencing the time series until it is stationary. This modelling framework was introduced by Box and Jenkins (1970) and is referred to as ARIMA(p, d, q), where d denotes the order of differencing or *integration* within the time series.

In addition to ARIMA models, time series regression models have also been developed to incorporate the effects of exogenous factors that persist over time. Initially, distributed lag models were developed that incorporated lag effects of independent variables into a regression model (see Grilliches, 1967). The finite distributed lag model has the general form:

$$\hat{y}_t = \alpha + \sum_{i=0}^{q} \beta_i x_{t-i} \qquad (9.5)$$

where q is the finite number of time periods in which the independent variable x, has influence and β is the lag coefficient.

These were extended to many types of distributed lag model, including unrestricted finite lag models, polynomial lag models (Almon, 1965) and geometrical lag models. The latter models are designed to control the effects of multicollinearity by imposing some structure on the lagged variables and also benefit from requiring fewer model parameters. These models were a form of mixed autoregressive–regressive model that could recognise any temporal dependence between variables while capturing autocorrelation amongst errors. (For more details of distributed lag models, see Greene (1993).)

ARMA and time series regression models were later combined by the development of *ARMAX models*, introduced by Hatanaka (1975) and Wallis (1977), that incorporate lagged exogenous variables into the autoregressive-moving average process. Further extensions included the development of multivariate ARMA models, with the most common known as the vector autoregressive model or *VAR* model. These models have advantages in not requiring specification of contemporaneous variables as exogenous or independent and have been used to test for causality between variables (Granger, 1969).

The parameters of ARMA models are typically estimated by non-linear least squares estimation (Box and Jenkins, 1970) or maximum likelihood (Newbold, 1974) and these two methods are discussed in most texts on time series modelling. The methodology for selecting between different ARIMA(p, d, q) models is commonly accomplished by model identification procedures developed by Box and Jenkins (1970) using autocorrelation functions (ACF) and partial autocorrelation functions (PACF).

9.5   Cointegration and Error Correction Models

Cointegration is a method for describing the long-run relationship between a group of variables which exhibit an equilibrium relationship with each other. It differs from correlation, the standard measure of linear association between variables, by relaxing the requirement for time series to be jointly covariance stationary and so avoid the loss of information due to differencing. Financial time series (e.g. equity market indices) are particularly good examples of non-stationary variables that may exhibit some long-run relationships between their prices.

The first step in building a cointegration model is to identify a set of time series that are individually non-stationary and of integrated order one, but which drift upwards at roughly the same rate and form a linear combination which is stationary. Intuitively, this implies that the non-stationary component is a common trend and we can use the other time series to detrend a target series rather than differencing. The time series that satisfy this requirement is said to be *cointegrated* and the coefficients are the *cointegrating vector*. In general, the cointegrated time series for some target variable, y_1, takes the form:

$$y_{1,t} = \beta_2 y_{2,t} + \beta_3 y_{3,t} + \beta_4 y_{4,t} + \ldots + \varepsilon_t \qquad (9.6)$$

where $y_2, y_3, \ldots, y_n$ are other cointegrating variables, ε_t is the deviation term and β is the cointegrating vector.

The cointegrating time series can be estimated using standard estimation procedures (e.g. linear regression) and the cointegration hypothesis tested by applying modified versions of standard stationarity tests to the residuals (e.g. Dickey–Fuller) and cointegration regression (Durbin–Watson).

In investment finance, one application is to identify weak form inefficiencies between markets (e.g. Burgess, 1996). In principle, the cointegration perspective is able to detect market inefficiencies or changes in underlying relationships that may otherwise remain undetectable. This is due to cointegration analysis effectively reducing market noise caused by unpredictable events or news information that influences the price of a whole group of assets.

After the cointegrated time series has been specified, a forecasting model of the target time series can be developed by using the residuals from the cointegrating time series. This is known as an *Error Correction Model* (ECM) (Granger, 1983; Engle and Granger, 1987). The model incorporates the deviation term that acts as the error correcting process that forces the asset prices back into some long run equilibrium. The error correction model for a cointegrating time series y_t, with deviations, ε_t, defined from equation (9.6), and lagged variables of the change in the target and cointegrating series, takes the general form:

$$\Delta y_t = \mu + \sum_{i=1}^{p} \theta_i \Delta y_{t-i} + \sum_{k=1}^{n}\sum_{j=1}^{q} \phi_{i,k} \Delta y_{k,t-i} - \gamma \varepsilon_t + e_t \qquad (9.7)$$

where θ and ϕ are the model coefficients, which incorporate the influence of past changes in the time series and γ is the coefficient of the error-correcting process defined from cointegration.

The advantage of this modelling approach is that the long-run relationship (i.e. the common drift) between the time series and the short term dynamics (i.e. the deviation of the time series from the long term trend) can both be taken into account. Error correction models can be constructed using regression analysis (e.g. Granger, 1983; Engle and Granger, 1987; Stock, 1987), or other multivariate methods such as canonical cointegration (Park, 1989), principal components analysis or, where there is more than one cointegrating vector, using vector autoregression (VAR) models (Johansen, 1988).

9.6   Ridge Regression

Standard regression techniques give unbiased estimators of the regression coefficients. This may give rise to a large variance in the estimates from different data samples, and it may be possible to trade off some of this variance by accepting biased estimates of the coefficients. Hoerl and Kennard (1970a,b) developed the technique of ridge regression, which achieves this through a regularisation procedure (see Chapter 7).

The MSE of an estimator $\hat{\beta}$ of β is given by:

$$\begin{aligned} \text{MSE}(\hat{\beta}) &= E(\hat{\beta} - \beta)^2 \\ &= V(\hat{\beta}) + [E(\hat{\beta}) - \beta]^2 \\ &= \text{Var}(\hat{\beta}) + (\text{bias in } \hat{\beta})^2 \end{aligned} \qquad (9.8)$$

(See Chapter 8 for details of the mean–variance trade-off.)

We can therefore allow some bias in the estimator, and for the same MSE have a lower variance and hence higher confidence in the estimator.

Ridge regression minimises a modified error function that penalises large coefficients (in the form of equation 7.3):

$$C = \sum_{i} \left((y_I - \hat{y}_i)^2 + \lambda \sum_{j=1}^{m} w_j^2 \right) \qquad (9.9)$$

This prevents, to some degree, fitting a model to the noise in the system. It also, by forcing some weights to zero, allows the regression to be used as an input selection procedure.

9.7   State Space Models

In the 1960s, state space modelling techniques were initially developed as a recursive method of controlling multi-sensor systems, such as navigation systems to track spacecraft (Kalman, 1960).

The basic notion of the state space model is to represent the components of the time series by a system of equations. The states of the system, described by "state variables", are then determined from the observed time series. In economics, state variables have been developed to represent time series components such as trends, cycles and seasonality (Pagan, 1975; Harvey, 1989), and in investment finance to represent conditional risk factor sensitivities of equity investment management (for a review, see Bentz, 1999).

The advantage of the state space representation is the ability to optimally estimate models using the *Kalman filter*, a powerful estimation algorithm (Kalman, 1960). In economics, this has seen the development of structural models (Harvey, 1989) that are time-invariant models where the observable variables are decomposed into systematic effects (trends, cycles and seasonality) and stochastic components. Other applications of state space models include the development of adaptive models that allow for time-varying or adaptive relationships between variables to be tracked over time (Harvey, 1993). Further details of state space models and the Kalman filter can be found in many textbooks (e.g. Harvey, 1989).

An example of a simple adaptive model is the stochastic coefficient regression model, which can be expressed in state space form by the general system of two equations. The first is referred to as the *observation equation* and the relates the dependent variable y_t to the independent variables x_t through the unobservable state vector, β_t, which represents the model coefficients. The *observation equation*, for all time steps t, takes the form:

$$y_t = \beta_t x_t + \varepsilon_t \qquad (9.10)$$

where ε_t is the unobservable *observation noise* term with variance σ^2.

In general, the elements of β are unobservable, but their time structure is assumed to be known. The evolution of these states is assumed to be a Markov process and described by a *transition equation* that for a random walk model takes the form:

$$\beta_t = \phi \beta_{t-1} + \eta_t \qquad (9.11)$$

where η_t is the *system noise* term with variance q^2. The two noise terms are considered to be uncorrelated Gaussian white noise processes.

The time-varying coefficients β of the stochastic regression are then estimated in the presence of noise using a *Kalman filter*. This is a recursive method that optimally estimates the coefficients at time t based upon the available observations. The assumed levels of observation and system noise are used by the filter to determine how much the variation in the dependent variable y is attributable to the system and how much to observation noise. The filter consists of a system of equations that updates the estimates of the coefficients when new observations are available. The state space formulation of the model allows the estimates of the states to be updated based solely on the last observation and still take into account the entire history of observations. A more general definition of the equations used to update the coefficients is given by Bentz (1999) and the derivation of the Kalman filter by Harvey (1989).

In investment finance, state space models are particularly powerful when they allow for relationships between variables to change through time. In the time-varying regression model a large forecast error may be due to either an unpredictable event or a change in the underlying relationship. The purpose of the Kalman filter is to attribute the innovation to these two sources based upon the relative size of the variances of the noise terms, σ^2 and q^2. Applications of state space models in investment finance can be found in Bentz (1999). Time-varying relationships may also be modelled by modifying standard modelling techniques (e.g. regression) and estimating parameters by time weighting the historical data (e.g. time-weighted least squares regression; Refenes, 1997b).

9.8 Summary

This chapter briefly describes a wide range of linear models which have been used for financial forecasting applications with varying degrees of success. In general, linear models are well understood and so provide a good framework for solving investment finance problems. However, linear models are limited to identifying either fixed or time-varying linear relationships and so cannot detect more general non-linear relationships between variables. In the following chapters we will discuss more general modelling techniques that can identify both linear and non-linear relationships.

10. Input Selection

Jimmy Shadbolt and John G. Taylor

10.1 Introduction

In this chapter we describe a general method for reducing the number of potential inputs to a model. This is required because a number of modelling techniques, especially neural networks, can only use a limited number of inputs because of the parameterisation of the model and the limited number of data points available. We note that a number of techniques (e.g. adaptive lag and linear RVM) have their own selection techniques, and so avoid some of the limitations in the method described below. We also note that before we get to this stage we will have been through a data reduction stage using, for example, the PCA techniques described earlier.

If we are using a regression as our estimator, we can use the technique to actually create a regression model by reducing the number of inputs until we can run a single regression on those remaining.

10.2 Input Selection

Given the general form of a market model $r = f$(growth, inflation, expectation) we have a number n_s of potential data series that could be used as proxies for the different inputs. Each of these inputs is potentially useful at a number n_L of different lags (which is unknown in advance). This leads to $n_s \times n_L$ potential inputs to a model. It we want a model with n_M inputs, we have

$$N = \frac{(n_s \times n_L)!}{(n_s \times n_L - n_M)!\, n_M!}$$

possible groups of inputs. For $n_S = 100$, $n_L = 24$ and $n_M = 10$, this is ~1.7×10^{13}. Obviously we cannot look at all models and must develop some simple method of filtering out irrelevant input series.

A very general procedure can be developed on the basis of bootstrapping and robust statistics to achieve this, as long as we are willing to accept the trade-off that we may reject some inputs that would have been useful in a non-linear model (although we could extend the scheme if we knew in advance the form of the non-linearity). The statistic analysed can be as simple as a correlation coefficient or be any multi-input model that can be quickly estimated. In the case of a multi-input model the requirement is that it will provide a measure of the confidence in the usefulness of each input in the model (in the worst case, we can assume that each input has the same usefulness which is the usefulness of the model).

The modelling procedure used will usually be a robust linear regression (for the sake of speed). This can be ridge regression or a stepwise regression, so that irrelevant inputs can be identified and flagged as having no usefulness. The regression is run a number of times using bootstrap samples to get confidence in its results. After a number of bootstraps the stats on all inputs are compared and some are rejected. The process is then repeated with the remainder.

10.2.1 Example

Results are shown for the case of estimating the coefficients from 12 potential inputs to a model. We use a linear regression of the 12 inputs against our target series, and use a number of bootstrap samples. The estimates of mean and variance for each coefficient over the bootstrap runs are collected.

Both standard confidence and confidence in estimates of robust mean and variance for the 12 inputs are shown in Fig. 10.1.

The plot at the top left shows the means of the estimates of the coefficients over a number of bootstraps. The plot at the top right shows the variance of the estimates of the means. So we see that coefficient 5 has a large estimated mean with very little variance in the estimate, whereas coefficient 4 has very large uncertainty relative to the size of the estimate. The lower plots show similar information for estimates of variance. We can use this information to rank the inputs in order of confidence in their usefulness.

If we have a large number of potential inputs and they cannot all be put into a single model, we take random selections of inputs and repeat the above analysis until we have gathered enough stats on all the inputs to enable a ranking and hence the elimination of some of them. The whole process will then be repeated on those inputs remaining.

10.2.2 Final Selection Procedure

When we are left with few enough inputs that we can use them all in a single model we can modify our procedure. We now use any model that has some built-in method of input relevance detection (stepwise or ridge regression, a regularised model that forces some weights to zero, linear RVM). Using bootstrapped samples, we run the model to estimate coefficients and monitor the results.

Figure 10.2 shows us a plot from the analysis of a number of bootstraps of a 24-input model. In this case the most frequent model size, after the relevance detection procedure has reduced a number of coefficients to zero, would be 7. Figure 10.3 shows the frequency with which each input has been retained in the bootstrapped models. We can use the information to select 7 of our 24 inputs.

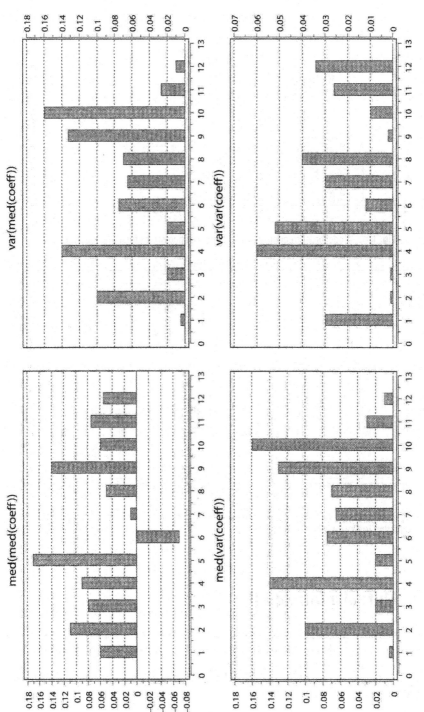

Fig. 10.1 Model coefficients and confidence levels.

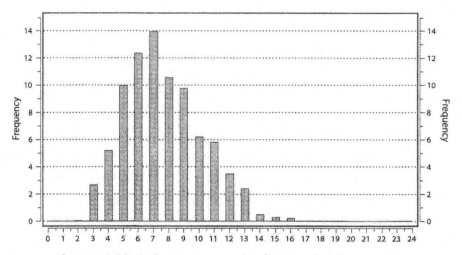

Fig. 10.2 Model order frequency over a number of bootstraps for a 12-input model.

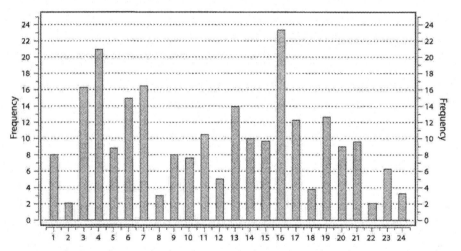

Fig. 10.3 Frequency, over a number of bootstraps, with which each input of a 24-input model is retained by a model weighting irrelevant inputs to zero.

10.3 Mutual Information

As we are wanting to use the inputs selected by the above process in non-linear models, it would make sense to use a non-linear coefficient for the ranking. One such is the Mutual Information coefficient.

The standard measure of information content of a data set is its *entropy H*. This is defined as

$$H(X) = -E_X [\log p(X)] \qquad (10.1)$$

The *joint entropy* measures the amount of information contained in pairs of data series $\{X, Y\}$

$$H(X, Y) = -\sum_{x \in X} \sum_{y \in Y} p(x, y) \log p(x, y) \tag{10.2}$$

The *conditional entropy* measures the amount of information in X dependent on Y:

$$H(X|Y) = \sum_{x \in X} \sum_{y \in Y} p(x, y) \log p(x|y) \tag{10.3}$$

The two series would be independent (there is no information in Y that tells us about X) if

$$H(X|Y) = H(X, Y) \tag{10.4}$$

The *mutual information* between two variables X and Y is given by:

$$I(X; Y) = H(Y) - H(Y|X) = H(X) + H(Y) - H(X, Y)$$

$$= \sum_{x \in X} \sum_{y \in Y} \left(p(x, y) \log \frac{p(x, y)}{p(x) p(y)} \right) \tag{10.5}$$

To apply this approach to the problem of variable selection in time series in a non-parametric manner, we proceed by developing the lagged mutual information between two time series $\{x(t)\}$, $\{y(t)\}$. Using formula (10.5), this quantity is the mutual information between the set of values $\{x(t)\}$ and the corresponding lagged values $\{y(t - \tau)\}$:

$$I(x, y, \tau) = \sum_{t=1}^{N} \sum_{x \in X, y \in Y} \left(p(x(t), y(t - \tau)) \log \frac{p(x(t), y(t - \tau))}{p(x(t)) p(y(t - \tau))} \right) \tag{10.6}$$

In order to calculate this quantity for a given pair of time series we have to obtain estimates of the separate and joint probabilities $p(x)$, $p(y)$, $p(x(*), y(* - \tau))$ (where $*$ denotes a running variable) that enter in equation (10.6). This can be achieved by discretising the space of variables x and y, for example by a set of intervals each of length δ and covering the relevant axis. Then the probabilities of interest are calculated by counting the relative number of values of $x(t)$, $y(t)$ or pairs $\{x(t), y(t - \tau)\}$ as the value of the time variable t runs over the set of possible values of time for the data sets. The value of δ chosen for this approximation cannot made be too small for a relatively small data set, since if it were then some boxes would be uninhabited. On the other hand, if δ is chosen too large, then the approximation to the mutual information will not be good enough. There is thus a happy medium, obtained by running calculations at various values of δ and choosing the value giving minimum effect of noise contributions.

This and related computational questions are discussed more fully in the paper of Fraser and Swinney (1986). They applied the approach for the different problem of determining the embedding dimension of a given time series (discussed more fully in Chapter 13). This they accomplished by determining the lag for which the lagged mutual self-information (obtained from equation (10.6) by replacing y by x) is minimal. Here we use that lag (or set of lags if there are more than one) that give a local maximum of the lagged mutual information between the time series $\{x(t)\}$ and

$\{y(t)\}$. We assume that such a lag value provides, for a given target time series $\{x(t)\}$, a suitably lagged indicator series $\{y(t - \tau)\}$. We performed an initial calculation of the threshold at which mutual information becomes significant by taking the time series for x and y to be random series with the same variances as the ones being studied. In this way a threshold of about 4.4 was obtained for the lagged MI, this being chosen as two standard deviations of the mean in the set of lagged MI values for the stochastic benchmarking series.

The above approach gives a parameter and model free approach to input variable selection since at no time is there any assumption of either a prediction model involved in the calculation nor any parameters that need to be optimised, except the lag itself. It is also possible to calculate, in such a non-parametric and model-free manner, possible higher order lagged contributions in terms of the higher order lagged mutual information $I(x, y, z, \tau, \tau')$. This is defined by an obvious extension of equation (10.6), with the new time series $\{z(t)\}$ being evaluated at lag τ' with respect to the time t in the time series $\{x(t)\}$. We have not tried to determine this higher order MI, since we have too few data points to enable a reasonable approximation to be obtained of the necessary higher order probabilities $p(x(t), y(t - \tau), z(t - \tau'))$ in three dimensions by the discretisation method we used for the above pair of time series. We also note that MI is a non-linear approximation to the correlation coefficient between the two series, based on a linear regression model (Fraser and Swinney, 1986).

Figures 10.4 and 10.5 show typical plots of mutual information against time. (Note that the time axis is scaled as $t = 2\text{lag} + 3$.)

Figure 10.4 shows that there is significant mutual information between consumer sentiment and USA bond returns at a lag of 4. Figure 10.5 shows both short-term (2–4 months) and long-term (11–12 months) mutual information between World money reserves and USA bonds.

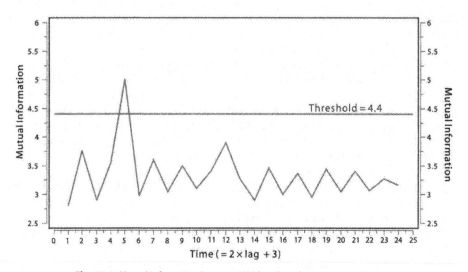

Fig. 10.4 Mutual information between USA bonds and consumer sentiment.

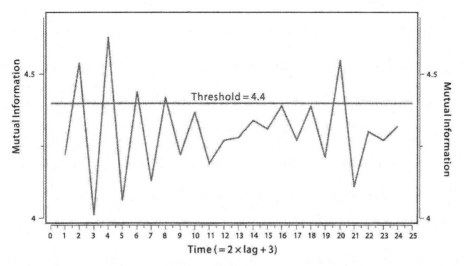

Fig. 10.5 Mutual information between USA bonds and world money reserves.

10.4 Summary

In this chapter we have begun to face up to the hard problem of selecting the relevant inputs from among the large number of putative ones, to build multivariate predictor models for bonds and other assets. This was done on the basis of a linear regression technique, using bootstrap methods to achieve robustness. An example of the application of this approach was given. The method was extended to a non-parametric approach, that of the calculation of the mutual information between a target series and a putative input series. Again this was shown to give useful results. We will apply these and other more model-specific selection techniques later in the book.

PART III
Theory of Specific Prediction Models

At the end of Part II, in Chapter 10, we developed a general method of input selection, especially based on linear modelling technologies. Various selection methods were described for reducing the number of inputs used for modelling. In Part III we look at how we use these inputs.

The core modelling technologies are developed initially in Chapter 11, which contains an introduction to neural networks. The neural network approach has become part of the standard toolkit of information processing, and is basic to our attack on financial prediction. Chapter 11 contains a description of the source of the technology, the living neuron, and a simplified version of it used in our work, as well as a range of architectures of networks and criteria for choosing connection strengths between neurons in such networks.

Learning more specifically by reinforcement is then developed in Chapter 12, the reward/penalty used arising more directly from profitability. This is applied to a simulated example model, but will be used in a later chapter on real data.

The nature of the underlying dynamics of the markets is discussed in Chapter 13, with the notions of embedding and dynamical dimension being defined. Practical problems in extracting these from financial time series are also considered in this chapter.

Another modelling approach, that of vector machines, is introduced in Chapter 14. The general kernel method involved in mapping the input vector into a larger dimension space is discussed and more specifically the support vector and relevance vector machines are described and compared.

Finally, assessment of the effectiveness of models is then developed in Chapter 15, using a Bayesian perspective. A specific quantity is then introduced. This is the Bayesian evidence ratio, so defined as to allow quantification of the effectiveness of a given model in comparison with a specific benchmark. Considerable use is made of this quantification in terms of specific models later in the book.

11. Neural Networks

John G. Taylor

11.1 What Are Neural Networks?

Neural networks, as a discipline, studies the information processing capabilities of networks – "neural networks" – of simple processors which are in some way like the living neurons of the brain. It uses a distributed representation of the information stored in the network, so leading to robustness against damage and corresponding fault tolerance. Training is a very important component of neural networks. By this process there is modification of the strengths with which one neuron affects another – the so-called connection weights – during exposure to an appropriate environment as opposed to programming in the required responses of the network to inputs from the environment. This feature is very important, since a neural network can thereby be trained to give a desired response to a set of inputs even though there are no explicit rules for this response to be achieved.

There are currently an enormous number of applications of neural networks to industrial applications, including control of various types of industrial plants (such as steel plants); pattern recognition (such as the Iris scan system based on retinal feature extraction, or fingerprint recognition); prediction in business (such as of energy demand); to risk control (such as in credit card risk control or to determine insider trading patterns); and many other areas. Other information processing approaches have also advanced as part of a general improvement in artificial information processing methods, such as genetic algorithms, fuzzy set methods and wavelet analyses. Thus artificial neural systems are to be seen as only one component in a toolbox of methods being applied to hard information processing problems. As such, the same approach is being used here: we have already considered various problems of financial prediction as part of the overall process, and we will see that neural network methods fit into the overall process as only one step. Moreover, there are other prediction methods that can be used, so even at that step of making the crucial predictions they can be augmented by other technologies to improve results.

We describe in this section the basics of neural networks, leaving to later sections to describe in more detail how neural systems can be used to make specific predictions in the bond/equity milieu. We start with a brief description of the living neuron before turning to a model artificial neuron, and then discuss various architectures available to neural networks. We conclude with a discussion of learning rules.

11.2 The Living Neuron

We show in Fig. 11.1 a picture of a typical living neuron. In this figure the cell is shown as composed of a cell body, with outgrowths termed dendrites which receive

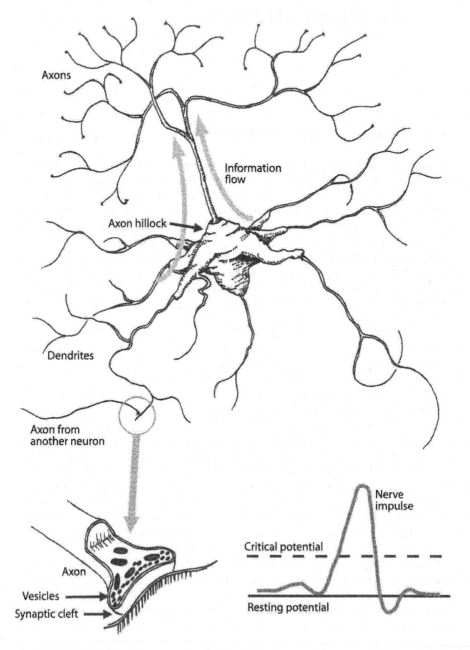

Fig. 11.1 The biological prototype neuron (see text for details). (Drawing of neuron copyright Anne E. Watt.)

the outputs of other cells. These outputs themselves are sent along each of the axons of the other cells, each of these also being an outgrowth from the cell body of its associated cell. At the ending of each axon, where it apposes onto the dendrite or cell body of the next cell, there is a small gap called the synapse. There electrical activity is transferred to chemical form and thereby sent across the synaptic gap to influence the next cell. The effects of these pre-synaptic influences are thus transferred back into chemical form. They are then summed, as membrane potentials, to contribute to the total membrane potential on the cell. Some of these effects are positive or excitatory, making the neuron more likely to respond to the input, whilst others are inhibitory or negative, causing the neuron to be less likely to give any output.

11.3 The Artificial or Formal Neuron

A neuron is a decision unit. It fires, or equivalently transmits, an electrical signal from the beginning of its axon, this travelling without decrement down the length of the axon and along its possibly several branches. This firing occurs if the potential V at the axon ending is above a critical threshold value V_{crit}, which is of the order of 15 mV. This living neuron can be modelled most simply as a pure decision unit. To introduce the mathematics of such an artificial neuron we introduce some notation:

1. Output from the ith neuron is denoted y_i.
2. The connection weight from the ith neuron to the jth neuron is denoted w_{ji}.
3. Net activity on the neuron is

$$a_j = \sum_i w_{ji} y_i - s_i + I_j$$

where a simple linear summation is assumed in determining the activity entering the jth neuron. In the above formula, the quantity s_i is a threshold term (which in the living system is about 15 mV, as noted above), and the quantity I_j is the input current onto the jth neuron from some external source, such as a visual input, and thus arises from outside the network of neurons indexed by i, j.

4. The system is closed by defining the dependence of the output of the jth neuron on its activity defined in 3 above. This is taken to depend solely on the activity a_j in the form $y_j = f(a_j)$, where $f()$ is taken to be a sigmoidal function of its variable, with the general requirements

$$f(-\infty) = 0; \quad f(+\infty) = 1$$

This can be chosen to be a thermodynamic response function, for example, of the form

$$f(x) = (1 + e^{-x/T})^{-1}$$

which clearly satisfies the above two boundary conditions. Moreover, when the parameter T becomes very large the value of the neuron output will be the constant ½, independent of the input; this corresponds to a very "noisy" situation, when the neuron responds in a manner independent of the input: it has maximum noise in its response. On the other hand, when $T = 0$ the response function is identical to the step function

$$Y(x) = 1 \ \text{ for } \ x > 0; \qquad Y(x) = 0 \ \text{ for } \ x < 0$$

In this case the neuron is a pure decision response machine, only responding if its activity is greater than the net of the threshold and the external input.

We have only considered here formal neurons which have a graded or continuous response. The living neurons described briefly in the previous sub-section send out "spikes", single pulses of electrical activity, which lasts for about a millisecond or so. There has been considerable interest in modelling such neurons by artificial neurons, especially for problems in vision, where problems of binding of different features of an object have to be achieved across different modules. There has not yet been any extensive application of such model neurons to financial applications.

11.4 Neural Network Architectures

Neural networks could be connected together in any manner. However, the most effective architectures have been found from practice to be one of two types:

- Feedforward (FF)
- Recurrent (RNN)

11.4.1 Feedforward Networks

The FF network has inputs arriving from the left, as seen in Fig. 11.2, and outputs leaving after going through the network, on the right. This allows the output to be obtained by repeated application of the input → output functions at each neuron, as defined earlier. At each step in the calculation the input to a given layer is determined only from activities arriving from the left. Each of the layers except the last on the right is termed a hidden layer, since its outputs are not seen by any external observer. On the other hand, the last layer on the right is seen, and is termed the output layer. The overall map can be given as a sequence of mappings of repeated applications of the input–output formula given earlier.

A number of functions may be achieved by this FF architecture:

- **Auto-association**, where a given input is associated to itself. The value of this is to allow for noisy inputs leading to clean versions on output.
- **Hetero-association**, where a given input is sent into a different but specific output. This thereby allows for pattern mapping of a more flexible form, as well as helping clean degraded inputs.
- **Classification**, in which a given set of inputs gives as output one of a specified set of outputs specifying to which class the input belongs.

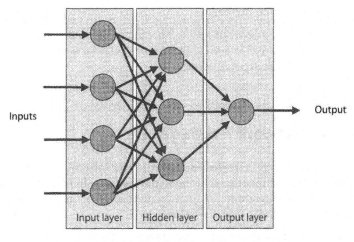

Fig. 11.2 Feedforward neural network.

It is these three functions which make neural networks so useful for applications across a wide field, since the training set, the set of specified input → output pairs, is well defined. It is then possible to develop training methods which allow the required function defining the input to output transform to be suitably approximated.

11.4.2 Recurrent Networks

Before doing that, we note the other extreme of architecture: the recurrent network (Fig. 11.3). This has feedback from outputs or hidden layers back into earlier layers through a buffer. In this way, the network, when processing input from time t, also has information fed back through the buffer from time $t - N$. This enables the

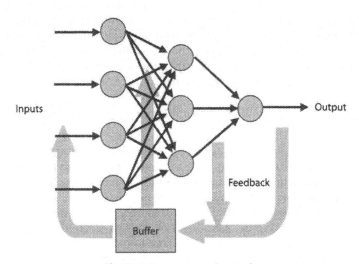

Fig. 11.3 Recurrent neural network.

network to take account of errors or predictions from the past, as represented by outputs or hidden unit activity, to give a more accurate prediction of the future. Such nets can also be trained by similar techniques as those we will now turn to, so we will not consider them explicitly further here.

11.5   Neural Network Training Rules

The simplest of these, the perceptron learning rule, was introduced over thirty years ago by Frank Rosenblatt for the single-layer net (with no hidden layer). The rule allowed a two-class classification task to be learnt in a finite number of steps, and is of the form (for outputs with only the value 0 or 1):

- If the output is correct, then there is no change in the weights.
- If the output is 0 and it should be 1, then increase each weight on each input by the corresponding input value on that input line.
- If the output is 1 and it should be 0, then decrease the weight on each input by the corresponding input value on that input line.

The overall effect is to change the weights on each input line by an amount equal to the error on the output multiplied by the input on the line:

$$\Delta w_i = \text{error} \times x_i$$

where the error is taken to be the difference (desired output – actual output), and x_i is the input on the ith input line.

This perceptron learning law could not be used to train networks with hidden layers, since the credit assignment problem was not soluble: how to assign praise or blame to each output of a hidden layer neuron. This problem was solved in 1986 by Paul Werbos, and since then has been shown to have great effectiveness, by using the method of back-error propagation (BEP). This uses the formula for differentiation of a function of a function to drag the change of a given weight for a hidden layer neuron, using a gradient descent method, to take account solely of expressions able to be calculated locally in the network associated with that node. It led to the result that the error could be propagated backwards from the output layer (where this was known) to earlier layers, using the associated connection weights, in the formula:

$$w_{ij} \leftarrow w_{ij} - \eta \frac{\partial E}{\partial w_{ij}}$$

As noted above, this learning law allows for gradient descent on the overall error surface of a task, defined from the training set. Such a process can be slow, as well as the net settling into a local but not a global minimum. However, there are several techniques to avoid this and related problems.

Other training methods for neural networks have been developed, both to exploit other methods of learning by the brain (which very likely does not use BEP, although the jury is still out on that), such as reinforcement training (see Chapter 12) or unsupervised learning. One very popular method is the Kohonen self-organising map, which is a cluster detection method, leading to a two-dimensional map of the set of input vectors representing a data set. However, whilst these methods have been used in some applications to financial prediction, they are not presently at the centre of attention. The most common and successful approach uses the feedforward network, along with some applications of recurrent nets.

11.6   Further Comments on Neural Networks

It is appropriate to underline that the above comments are only a very brief introduction to the large subject of neural networks. Thus we have not covered the important areas of applications of neural networks to computational neuroscience, nor of large efforts going into building hardware neural devices. One aspect to consider before closing these introductory remarks is the Universal Approximation Theorem, which gives some justification for the present ubiquity of neural systems. This states that a neural system can be constructed which approximates arbitrarily closely any given function

$$x \to F(x) \text{ from the space } \Re^m \to \Re^n$$

for any integers m, n. Only one hidden layer is needed for this to be true, although in order to approximate a probability distribution of a random variable it is necessary to have at least two hidden layers. An extension of this is that any dynamical system can be approximated by a suitable recurrent net. Thus neural systems are able to give universal underpinning of a broad class of functions met in the industrial environment by suitable neural networks. Moreover, these nets can be trained by BEP. We will develop these ideas on typical neural networks and their training more fully in Chapter 18, where application will be made to the USA bond market.

12. *Learning Trading Strategies for Imperfect Markets*

N. Towers and A. N. Burgess

12.1 Introduction

In the last decade much interest has been shown in the possibility of using sophisticated forecasting techniques as the basis of trading systems that will beat the market. Recent empirical evidence has indicated that financial markets can exhibit some degree of predictable behaviour (as described in Chapter 3). These results are justified on the basis that markets are only truly efficient, or unpredictable, with respect to information or modelling techniques that are commonly available to other market participants. Sophisticated modelling techniques in effect generate new information with respect to which markets are not necessarily efficient. In principle, this effect is encapsulated in the relative efficient market hypothesis (Lo and MacKinlay, 1999).

The degree of predictability which can be captured in a forecasting model, however, is typically small, and the ability to extract any meaningful economic advantage from this predictive information is critically dependent on the particular trading strategy which is used to exploit the forecasts. From this perspective, exploiting the flexibility of neural network techniques within a decision-making framework provides a powerful method for performing empirical optimisation of trading strategies. The performance of dynamic trading strategies is typically influenced by transactions costs which arise from market microstructure effects, which cause real markets to deviate from the idealised case of frictionless markets, in many cases severely limiting the usefulness of traditional portfolio theory (Markowitz, 1959). These effects give rise to non-linear conditional transactions costs which can significantly influence trading performance. This sensitivity is particularly exacerbated in the case of high-frequency trading, in which predictive models are employed to achieve excess profits at low levels of risk. There is good reason to believe that such profits can be achieved, but only at marginal levels which reflect the intellectual capital invested in developing new trading systems, as argued by Lo and MacKinlay (1999). In general, the trading of statistical arbitrage models is a sequential decision task which cannot be solved analytically. This motivates the development of a modelling framework that can account for the future consequences of trading decisions and so provides a means of optimising the trade-off between exploiting predictability and minimising the costs of trading.

Reinforcement learning algorithms offer such a mechanism as they are capable of learning approximate solutions to stochastic dynamic programming problems with incomplete knowledge of the underlying dynamics of the system (Bertsekas, 1995). In this chapter reinforcement learning is used to optimise trading strategies, based upon predictive signals, for imperfect markets. Specifically, a Q-learning algorithm is designed to take advantage of the independence between asset prices and trading decisions to learn over a range of possible states in each time period.

12.2 Trading Predictability

12.2.1 Introduction

In recent years, in apparent contradiction to the random walk hypothesis for asset returns, explicit empirical studies have produced significant evidence to conclude that financial markets are to some degree predictable and that predictive ability may be maximised using a forecasting model. Furthermore, trading strategies have been applied to these forecasts and shown to produce economically significant trading, further reducing the reliability of the efficient market hypothesis. These empirical discoveries raise the issue of whether predictable models can be systematically exploited in practical trading environments, through market timing or tactical asset allocation, and also how trading should be controlled in order to optimise an investment objective.

The high complexity and almost stochastic nature of financial markets have spurred the development of sophisticated forecasting techniques that attempt to capture different deterministic components of market dynamics. This has led to many methodological developments in modelling non-linear and time-varying modelling relationships in non-stationary stochastic environments. However, by concentrating on improving the accuracy of forecasting, financial modelling research has in some part neglected to consider that ultimately forecasting models are essentially just another input into the process of making investment decisions. In practice, the development of trading strategies for predictability involves combining not only forecast information, but also inventory, transactions costs and risk controls or constraints.

The natural difference between forecasting and decision making, and the complexity involved in developing reliable financial forecasting models has often led to a decoupling of the optimisation of forecasting models from the rest of the investment decision-making process. This strong emphasis on forecasting has often occurred at the expense of considering the development of decision modelling tools for trading applications. This is demonstrated by a plethora of over-simplified trading rules, whose purpose is to create "profitability" tests for predictability rather than focusing on whether genuine trading, which utilises predictive forecasts, is economically significant in practical trading environments. One common example is the application of classical mean–variance analysis which constructs a portfolio with maximum expected return for a given level of expected risk. This method does not take into account transactions costs and consequently only optimises decision-making over the current time period. The optimal portfolio is thus considered "myopic", as decisions only maximise risk-adjusted return on a period by period basis, and so ignore any interdependence between periods caused by transactions costs which may arise from taxes, market impact, trading restrictions etc. The performance of dynamic trading strategies in practical trading environments is often critically dependent on the extent of these frictional forces.

Typically, when these factors are considered the optimal dynamic portfolio is no longer myopic but may be improved by employing optimisation techniques that consider multiple time periods where the longer term effects of actions are also taken in account. Under imperfect trading conditions, the sequence of trading positions is *interdependent*, so a "best" decision cannot be estimated myopically (i.e. simply looking over the current period) but must be determined from a decision policy (i.e. looking longer term over a sequence of actions). In this case, modelling techniques for sequential decision making need to be incorporated with the predictive information from a forecasting model in order to approximate the optimal trading strategy.

12.2.2 Transactions cost Models

In investment finance, standard assumptions in modern portfolio theory assume away the effect of market imperfections such as transactions costs arising from market impact, taxes and trading restrictions. Under idealised conditions the optimal portfolio can be considered myopic and so does not depend on the longer-term consequences of trading. This aspect of the financial market's microstructure can usually be ignored when considering the "efficient markets" perspective, as these do not significantly effect long-term passive investment strategies. However, these trading costs often have a significant effect on the performance of short-term dynamic trading strategies. In practice, trading opportunities must include all costs associated with transacting a trade to determine whether the marginal cost of execution outweighs the potential profits.

Trading costs are driven by the market microstructure, which is due to the organisation and control of the trading process in financial markets and is associated with trading through both market makers and order-driven exchanges. In most well-established markets these structures are designed so that investors can buy or sell significant quantities of securities quickly, anonymously and with relatively small market impact. Usually this liquidity is maintained by investors incurring a trading cost, usually in the form of the stable bid/ask spread on the price of a security. However, in times of low trading volume or when trading relatively large quantities of assets, sufficient liquidity cannot be maintained cheaply by the market, so the trading of specific assets may have significant market impact. In these circumstances the factors that affect transactions costs fall into two categories:

- Trade information (e.g. percentage size of trade, market capitalisation of stocks)
- State of the market (e.g. volume, volatility)

Under these conditions, the minimisation of execution costs typically involves breaking down large trades into smaller blocks to spread trading over a number of time periods (Bertsimas and Lo, 1998). The optimal trading strategy is no longer myopic, but depends on optimising sequences of trades over a given time period.

Transactions cost models are typically developed by market participants who wish to rebalance portfolios of assets that experience wide variations in the cost of trading. Typically, trading methods are devised to ensure that all trades are completed at the same time for some pre-agreed spread away from the mid-prices. This cost covers the bid–offer spread, compensation that the broker receives for taking over the market impact risk, and also market- and stock-specific price risks. In the case of statistical arbitrage trading, market-specific risk is eliminated as the trade usually comprises roughly equivalent values of buy and sell orders from the same market. The transactions cost model tries to explain/forecast the spread away from the mid-price charged by the broker.

The main factors that explain variations in the cost of trading can be developed in a model which takes the general form:

$$T = C(\sigma, \nu, S, \kappa) \tag{12.1}$$

where C is some function of the market volatility, σ, market volume, ν, relative size of the trade, S, and capitalisation/liquidity of the assets in the trade, κ.

In general, we expect that trading costs will increase in times of increased market volatility, or reduced market volume, or for relatively large trades, or for trading small capitalisation stocks. The specific functional form of equation (12.1) is dependent on the privileges of the market participant, the traded instruments and the specific market. These transactions cost models are becoming increasingly important as practitioners address the significant costs that can be associated with trading portfolios of assets.

12.3 Modelling Trading Strategies

12.3.1 Introduction

In trading environments with stable transactions costs, decision models can be developed for trading predictability (e.g. a class of decision rules: Towers and Burgess, 1999; Towers, 2000). Other authors have developed model-based trading systems that optimise trades on the basis of macro economic variables rather than predictive signals, such as recurrent reinforcement learning (Moody *et al.*, 1998), Q-learning (Neuneier, 1996, 1998), and neural networks (Choey and Weigend, 1997). The sequential decision models that use reinforcement learning (RL) algorithms consider interdependence between time periods due to a path dependent performance criterion (Moody, 1997) or a combination of proportional and fixed transactions costs (Neuneier, 1996). In these papers, simulation and empirical results indicate that RL methods offer potential for optimising asset allocation tasks subject to some path-dependent factor.

In this chapter we consider trading environments that may include market impact effects, which cause "non-linear" conditional transactions costs. In these circumstances decision rules are too complex and restrictive, so we resort to developing empirical modelling techniques, based on reinforcement learning, for optimising the trading strategy.

Reinforcement learning is based on a control system adhering to the Markov property, which requires that all relevant information be retained in the state and that all states and actions can be specified. For a simplified trading system, the state only includes the predicted return, the existing trading position and the state of the market. In practice, this trading system could describe a statistical arbitrage trading system, as described in Chapter 22, where a portfolio of assets has fixed percentage asset weightings which can be represented by a single trading position.

The reward associated with each trading position represents the investment return received at the next observation of the system. In trading systems, rewards from trading decisions are not instantaneous, but are delayed until the asset prices are next observed. We therefore attribute a reward to a selected action, at time t, although the actual time the reward is received is $t + 1$. Specifically, the reward at time t is influenced by the trading position, a_t, the synthetic asset return, Δy_{t+1}, and the state of the market, X_t, which is expressed as

$$r_t = \Delta y_{t+1} * a_t - C(\Delta a_t, X_t) \tag{12.2}$$

where C is some function of the change in the trading position and the state of the market.

In equation (12.2), the first term equates to the profit or loss assuming no trading costs, and the second term approximates the transactions cost due to changing the trading position, as indicated in equation (12.1).

12.3.2 Reinforcement Learning

For RL systems the learning process typically takes place by updating the value function on the basis of the trading reward and an approximation of the investment value of following the best policy from the next time period. For one-step Q-learning (Watkins, 1989) this may be written as

$$Q(s_t, a_t) \leftarrow Q(s_t, a_t) + \alpha[r_t + \gamma \max_{a \in A} Q^*(s_{t+1}, a_{t+1}) - Q(s_t, a_t)] \tag{12.3}$$

where α is the learning rate and γ is the discount factor subject to $0 \leq \gamma \leq 1$.

The discount parameter, γ, specifies the present value of future rewards, so if $\gamma = 0$, then the policy is "myopic" and so only maximises immediate rewards. As γ moves away from zero, the objective takes more account of future rewards, and so the trading policy becomes more farsighted.

For trading systems, standard RL algorithms such as Q-learning, may have practical limitations that reduce their ability to exploit predictability. The main problem, which is common in many RL applications, is that the learning process requires large quantities of data in order to approximate the optimal policy. However, we have developed a method of addressing this drawback by exploiting the nature of the trading environment to boost the effectiveness of the learning stage by redesigning the algorithm to learn from actions that *could have been taken* as though they *had been taken*. This is a specific property of the financial domain which is not normally found in RL applications, in that we assume a partial separation between actions and subsequent states of the system.

This ability to learn from all possible actions is based on the assumption that the market is fully elastic, so that an individual trade cannot permanently affect the state of the market. Thus actual returns (and also predicted returns) are not adversely effected by previous trading decisions. This enables the learning process to consider other actions (trading positions), in addition to the selected action, without affecting the state in the next time period. Thus an entire region of the value function can be updated in each time period as opposed to only a single state corresponding to the selected action.

For trading systems, the learning stage in standard RL can be extended to cover a region within the state–action space. This enhancement to the learning stage of the standard RL algorithm can be implemented using additional loops to evaluate possible actions and states, as illustrated in Fig. 12.1.

The modified algorithm proceeds in the same manner as the classical algorithm by selecting the trading actions based on the current value function. At the next time step the state of the market is observed, including the actual return from the portfolio (or combination of assets). The trading reward is calculated and a forecast generated for the next time period. However, in the learning phase, a feature specific of financial markets is exploited on the basis of independence between asset returns and trading decisions. This separation enables the reward to be computed for different actions and states of the market and so allow the learning stage to explore a region of the state–action space in each time period. This differs from the typical sequential learning in which an outcome (i.e. the next state) is dependent on the action taken; hence the value function is only updated for the selected action. This

---

$s_t = \{s_t^i, \hat{y}_{t+1}\}$ where $\hat{y}_{t+1}$ = predicted return and s_t^i = state of the portfolio/market

Initialise value function $Q(s, a)$

Initialise state of portfolio/market s_0^i and generate first prediction $\hat{y}_1$

Repeat

    decision stage

    change trading position, a_t, using current policy derived from $Q(s, a)$

    when $t = t + 1$

    observe state of market, s_{t+1}^i and actual asset return, y_{t+1}

    calculate trading reward, $r_t(a_t, y_{t+1}, s_t^i)$

    generate new prediction, $\hat{y}_{t+2}$

    learning stage

    For (all possible states s_t^i)

        For (all possible actions, a_t)

            approximate "would have been" reward r_t

            compute temporal difference, $d_t = r_t + \gamma \max_{a(t+1)} Q(s_{t+1}, a_{t+1}) - Q(s_t, a_t)$

            update value function, $Q(s_t, a_t) = Q(s_t, a_t) + \alpha d_t$

        Next

    Next

Until t is terminal

Fig. 12.1 On-line Q-learning with additional loops in the learning phase.

creates a trade-off between exploration (trying all actions) and exploitation (choosing best option given current model). This modification allows the RL algorithm to avoid the normal trade-off between exploitation and exploration and so increase learning efficiency. The increased efficiency is dependent on the relative size of the region of the state–action space that can be explored in each time period. This modification can be applied to other reinforcement learning algorithms to enhanced learning.

12.4 Experimental Design and Simulation Experiments

12.4.1 Experimental Design

Trading systems are considered continuous state–action space problems with continuous variables describing predicted returns, trading positions and state information. In these types of problems function approximation techniques are typically the most efficient way of preserving the salient information extracted during the learning stage while also generalising to other states. In trading environments, rewards from trades are typically subject to considerable noise, so the learning process introduces the possibility of *overfitting* the training set. This occurs when the function approximator learns the noise component of the data, thus reducing its ability to generalise to unseen data (see Chapter 7). The choice of a suitable parameterisation requires some knowledge of the shape of the function to be approximated.

For the simplified trading example, we have indicated that a portfolio of assets can be traded on the basis of predicting some component of the asset price dynamics. For example, if we ignore transactions costs, then for a trading strategy to maximise profits the optimal trading policy and value function can be simply computed, as shown graphically in Fig. 12.2.

The left-hand graph shows that for constrained asset allocation the optimal trading policy is a step function of the sign of the predicted return. The optimal trading position (fractional allocation) switches between the two extreme positions $(-1, +1)$ depending on the sign of the predicted return, indicating a buy in the case of a positive forecast and a sell for a negative prediction. In a trading environment with no costs, the previous trading position is of no consequence and the optimal trading policy is relatively straightforward. The associated value function is, however, a complex non-linear function consisting of two quadratic functions. If we consider this to be representative of the functional form of possible value functions then a flexible non-linear function approximation technique is most appropriate. For this work, we use a neural network as a suitable function approximation technique given its ability to control overfitting and its wide use within other RL applications.

For these simulation experiments, we assume that transactions costs are influenced only by the state of the portfolio and not by market conditions. Under this assumption we ignore the effects of trading volume and volatility and so allow the state of the system to be described simply in terms of the predicted return and the

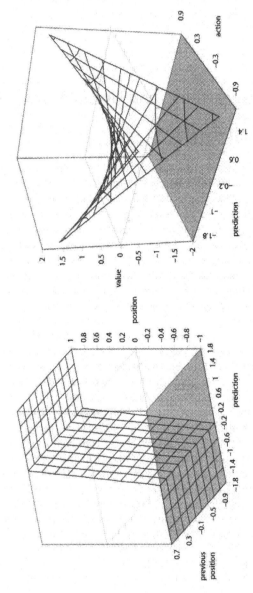

Fig. 12.2 The optimal myopic trading policy and the optimal myopic value function (expected return function) for maximising profitability with no transactions costs.

existing trading position. The transactions cost is then a function dependent on the change in the trading position.

Specifically, let the investment return r_t be determined by the trading position a_t and the asset return Δy_t and also some transactions cost function C which is due to some market impact effect defined as

$$r_t = a_t \Delta y_t - C(a_t, a_{t-1})$$

$$\text{where } C(a_t, a_{t-1}) = \begin{array}{ll} 0 & \text{if } |a_t - a_{t-1}| \le \lambda \\ c & \text{if } |a_t - a_{t-1}| > \lambda \end{array} \tag{12.4}$$

where λ is a tolerance parameter and c is some additional transactions cost.

For this simple transactions cost model, the cost of trading is significantly different from the proportional cost associated with stable bid–ask spreads and is motivated by the fact that, while small trades have negligible market impact, large trades cannot be executed without incurring extra additional costs. If we consider c to be large, we penalise moves more than λ sufficiently to consider it as a trading restriction around the movement of the existing trading position. In this case the percentage trading restriction is defined as

$$\%\text{Trading Restrictions} = 1 - \frac{\lambda}{\text{trading limit}} \tag{12.5}$$

where the trading limit equals 2 for fractional asset allocation $(-1, +1)$.

For this trading system, trading opportunities are limited depending on the existing trading position and the tolerance parameter, λ. Although this model is an oversimplification of a practical transactions cost model, its use for simulation purposes can be motivated by the fact that practical trading conditions often restrict trading on the basis of existing trading positions. An interesting effect of this trading restriction is that the trading environment is now path-dependent, so expected trading profits should benefit from considering both the immediate and longer term effects of trading. The optimal myopic trading policy is now no longer a simple step function which switches the trading position between the two states $(-1, +1)$ given the sign of predicted return, as illustrated in Fig. 12.2. The myopic policy is now dependent on the existing trading position, the tolerance parameter λ and the predicted return. However, we can still specify the optimal myopic policy assuming the trading position will increase (or decrease) as much as possible for a positive (or negative) forecast within the trading limits $(-1, +1)$, which is defined as

$$\begin{aligned} a_t &= \min(a_{t-1} + \lambda, 1) & \text{if } \hat{y}_{t+1} > 0 \\ &= \max(a_{t-1} - \lambda, -1) & \text{if } \hat{y}_{t+1} < 0 \end{aligned} \tag{12.6}$$

where $\hat{y}_{t+1}$ is the predicted asset return.

The optimal myopic policy exploits the information of the predicted return to the full, in order to maximise the immediate profits without considering the consequence to profits in subsequent time periods. For trading subject to some restriction, the path dependency in the trading sequence indicates that the optimal myopic policy should be sub-optimal and provides motivation for the development of a multi-period trading policy using RL.

For experimental purposes, we can simulate the predicted and actual using a data generating process to provide a method of controlling the characteristics of the forecasts.

Specifically, let some asset price y, be constructed using a data generating process with an explanatory variable, x, which represents the deterministic component and a noise variable, ε, which represents the stochastic component of y, and is defined as

$$\Delta y_t = \beta x_t + \sigma_t \varepsilon_t \quad \text{where} \quad \varepsilon_t \sim NID(0,1)$$
$$\text{and} \quad x_t = \phi x_{t-1} + \sigma_\eta \eta_t \quad \text{where} \quad \eta_t \sim NID(0,1) \tag{12.7}$$

thus the coefficient β, represents the information the explanatory variable contains regarding future returns and σ_ε the strength of the noise variable. The coefficient ϕ represents a stability factor in the explanatory variable and so with σ_η controls the level of autocorrelation in the asset return series. This characteristic is typical of trending or mean reverting behaviour found in statistical mispricings and common for predictive time series.

To set the noise level of the two processes, let the standardised variance of the explanatory variable equal the variance of the actual asset returns so that two of the coefficients are defined as

$$\sigma_\varepsilon^2 = 1 - \beta^2$$
$$\sigma_\eta^2 = 1 - \phi^2 \quad \text{where} \quad \phi < 1 \tag{12.8}$$

where ϕ now defines the degree of autocorrelation in the explanatory variable and β the correlation between the returns of the asset and the explanatory variable.

If we assume that the forecasting model is constructed to capture the deterministic component of the asset return series (i.e. maximally predictive), then the predicted returns series $\Delta \hat{y}$, is defined as

$$\Delta \hat{y}_t = \beta x_t \tag{12.9}$$

For this data generating process, the correlation coefficient between predicted and actual returns equals β, which is considered to be the measure of prediction accuracy.

We have now specified a trading environment with a transactions cost model using a trading restriction, an associated optimal myopic trading policy and a data-generating process for predicted and actual returns series. However, for this simulated trading system the optimal trading policy is unknown, so we use RL to approximate the optimal trading policy. In order to avoid imposing significant bias, which may degrade performance while learning the value function, we employ flexible estimation procedures provided by neural networks. A single neural network is required to store the value of all possible states and actions. The RL algorithm, defined in Fig. 12.1, is modified so that the learning stage updates the neural network weights, w, rather than a Q-function represented by a look-up table using the update rule:

$$w = w + \alpha d \nabla Q(s, a; w) \tag{12.10}$$

where d is the temporal difference error and the derivative of Q is computed in the usual way using error backpropagation techniques.

It is anticipated that connectionist RL will accurately approximate the optimal trading policy, which we can compare against the optimal myopic policy.

12.4.2 Simulation Experiments

Simulation experiments are developed for the trading system with predicted and actual returns generated using equations (12.7) and (12.8). The value function is stored in a neural network specified with one hidden layer and six hidden units. The neural network weights are initialised close to zero and the learning rate set to 0.1. A training set is generated consisting of 1000 observations of predicted and actual returns with a predictive correlation of 0.2. The discount parameter that represents the present value of future rewards is set to 0.9. The reward for each action-state is specified using equation (12.4).

Batch learning is used (i.e. weight changes are stored and weights updated when all training patterns have been presented to the network) so that the data set can be reused. Performance is measured by computing the average profit of the current optimal policy over the in-sample data set during training.

In the case where there is no trading restriction and so there is no advantage from a multi-period trading policy, we expect the optimal myopic policy to at least match the RL trading policy. For this example, we trained the network for 8000 epochs and recorded the average profit for the current trading policy during training, as shown by the training curve in Fig. 12.3 (top). At convergence we computed the approximation to the optimal value function, as shown by the lower graph in Fig. 12.3.

At convergence, the average profit of the RL trading policy is 0.162 compared to 0.161 for the optimal myopic trading policy derived from equation (12.6). The value function stored in the neural network also corresponds to the shape of the optimal myopic value function shown in Fig. 12.2. These indicate that, in the trivial case, the RL trading policy closely matches the optimal myopic policy. This provides evidence that the RL method can accurately approximate the optimal trading policy.

We completed further experiments to test the effect of a trading restriction on trading performance and compared the RL trading policy with the optimal myopic policy. To accurately test out-of-sample performance we generated additional 100 data sets of 1000 observations with the same predictive characteristics. We then computed the average profit of both the RL policy and the optimal myopic policies for a range of trading restrictions, which are summarised in Table 12.1.

The results show that for trading with no restriction ($\lambda = 2$) the difference between the average out-of-sample profits of the RL and optimal myopic policy is

Table 12.1 Average profits for different percentage trading restrictions

	Trading restriction				
	0% ($\lambda = 2$)	20% ($\lambda = 1.6$)	40% ($\lambda = 1.2$)	60% ($\lambda = 0.8$)	80% ($\lambda = 0.4$)
MA – RL	0.1642	0.1303	0.1201	0.0921	0.0579
Optimal myopic	0.1642	0.1295	0.1182	0.0892	0.0547
Difference	−0.0000	0.0008	0.0020	0.0029	0.0031
Percentage difference		0.63%	1.61%	3.12%	5.37%
Std error (difference)	0.00065	0.00061	0.00077	0.00066	0.00075

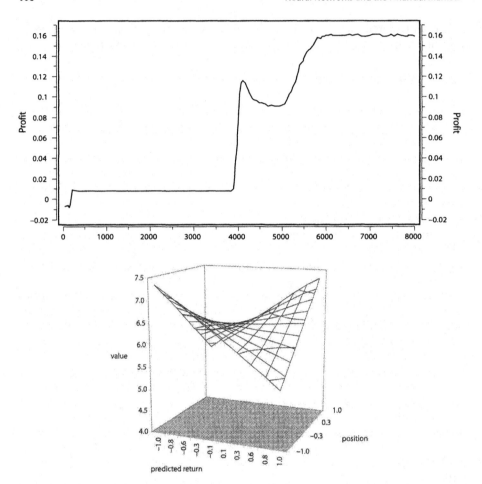

Fig. 12.3 The training curve for optimising trading with no trading cost restriction (top) and the value function approximated by a neural network (bottom).

statistically indistinguishable. For trading with a restriction, performance degrades considerably for both policies with the optimal myopic decreasing from an average profit of 0.164 to 0.058, a deterioration of 64%. However, in the presence of a trading restriction, the performance of the multi-period RL policy improves upon the optimal myopic policy. In addition, the larger the trading restriction, the greater the path dependency, and so, as expected, the more significant the impact of the multi-period policy. In terms of investment performance, the RL policy with a 60% trading restriction ($\lambda = 0.8$) results in a small increase in average profit of 3.12%. To highlight the difference between the myopic and RL trading policies we plot the two trading policies in terms of the change in the trading position against the predicted return, as shown in Fig. 12.4.

The graphs show the myopic and RL trading policies in terms of the relative change in the trading position against predicted return for a 60% trading

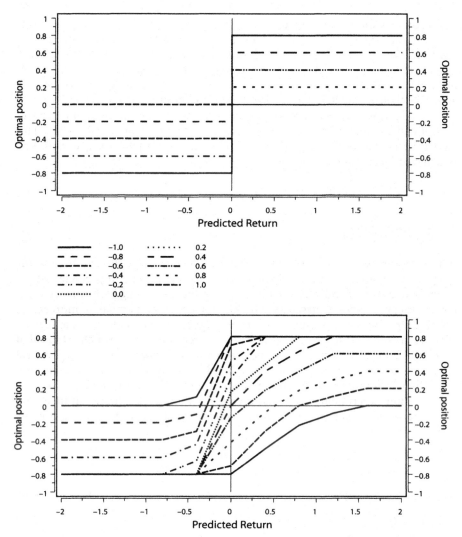

Fig. 12.4 The optimal myopic policy (top) and multi-period RL trading policy (bottom) for a 60% trading restriction.

restriction. For the optimal myopic policy, the trading position only changes if the sign of the predicted return changes. No account is taken of the future consequences of moving the trading position. For the multi-period RL strategy, however, the trading position changes with respect to the magnitude and sign of the predicted return. If the magnitude of the predicted return is small then the trading position does not necessarily change by the maximum allowable by the trading restriction. A smaller change may be recommended, as even though there is no direct transactions cost from a trading restriction, there is an associated opportunity cost which limits the future exploitation of predicted returns.

We can explain the difference in trading policy in terms of an analogy with the bias–variance trade-off. In this analogy, bias is due to the stability of the trading position through time and variance is due to the ability of the policy to adapt in order to exploit predictability. Trading strategies which exploit the predicted return but which do not take into account the current or future trading costs are considered models with small variance (maximally exploit predictability) and high bias (no consideration for the future cost of trading). The RL trading policy outperforms the optimal myopic policy by trading off some variance in order to reduce bias. This has the effect of moving along the bias–variance curve until the best generalisation is achieved (i.e. maximise expected performance).

12.5 Summary

In this chapter we have developed and tested a methodology for training trading systems in imperfect markets. We have discussed the trading of predictability in financial markets and how transactions costs influence trading performance when rebalancing portfolios of assets. The methodology uses a popular reinforcement learning algorithm, Q-learning, which is redesigned in order to learn from regions of states in each time period rather just the selected action state which is typical of standard RL implementations. The value function is parameterised using a neural network and market imperfections considered in the form of a trading restriction which limits trading opportunities on the basis of the existing trading position.

Simulation experiments show that even for a trading restriction that incurs no direct transactions cost the RL trading policy outperforms the optimal myopic policy.

13. Dynamical Systems Perspective and Embedding

Neep Hazarika

13.1 Introduction

The analysis of experimental time series for prediction based on a dynamical systems approach remains a challenging problem. A scalar time series $x(t) \in \Re$ can be considered to be a single component of a many-dimensional process of unknown dimension. In this chapter we adopt the working hypothesis that many classes of experimental time series may be analysed within the framework of a dynamical systems approach. We are assuming that the state of a system is given by a point s evolving in a multidimensional state space Γ. Then the motion of s in Γ characterises the dynamics of the system.

In the case of non-linear systems with many degrees of freedom it may not be possible to keep track of the motion in high-dimensional space. However, we are fortunate in that many systems with apparent high dimensionality are really characterised by a small number of *effective* degrees of freedom (due to nonlinearity, dissipation and symmetry, for example). The motion of the system in a high dimensional space Γ settles down, after some time has elapsed, to an attracting subspace, Γ_A. Thus the problem reduces to identifying the coordinates that characterise the much lower dimensional attractor Γ_A. In fact, it has been argued that an adequate choice of coordinates is a set of previously measured values of the quantity to be predicted (Packard *et al.*, 1980). Such a set could consist, for example, of a sequence of m such measurements of past values. This sequence should contain enough information to capture the dynamics of the attractor in order to predict the motion on it, provided that m is sufficiently larger than the attractor dimensionality d.

Even if the assumption of an underlying deterministic system is correct, we do not observe the state s_t of the system directly. Instead we rely upon sensors which provide (scalar) observations on the underlying system states through a measurement function, $X(t) = Xs_t$. Typically this measurement function is unknown. We cannot invert the measurement function, but we can use a delay reconstruction to construct a vector $X(t) = X(t-\tau), ..., X(t-(n-1)\tau) \in \Re^n$ (where τ is the lag, and n is the number of lags) with the same information content as the original system state (assuming that the measurement function has not introduced its own dynamics into the observations). Here n, the number of lags, is often called the "embedding dimension." The time $(n-1)\tau$ spanned by each embedding vector, is called the "window length" of the embedding. In the above discussion, τ is introduced to allow for the fact that, for time series encountered in the real world, the sampling interval is often set without accurate prior knowledge of the time-scales intrinsic to the system under study. Thus, determining the value of τ becomes an essential part of the analysis.

Takens' theorem (Takens, 1981) gives conditions for this to be an embedding; in fact, his formulation of the reconstruction theorem using delay coordinate maps enables the non-linear predictor of a dynamical system to be directly derived from a system's time series. The theory employs a *dynamical systems* approach to time series forecasting, where a state variable evolves within a system manifold M of dimension m via a *diffeomorphism* (a one-to-one differentiable function with a one-to-one differentiable inverse) of a lower-dimensional manifold D, and gives rise to the scalar observable time series. This is depicted in Fig. 13.1. Takens' theorem

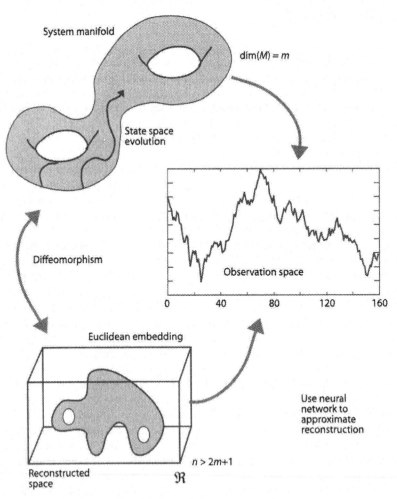

Fig. 13.1 Dynamical systems approach.

states that the embedding dimension n and the dimension m of the manifold satisfy the inequality ("Takens' criterion")

$$n \geq 2m + 1$$

The fundamental assumption is that the data $x(t)$, $t = 1, 2, \ldots, N$ are generated by a finite dimensional non-linear system of the form

$$x(t) = f(x(t-1), x(t-2), \ldots, x(t-m)) + \varepsilon_t$$

for a particular value of m, where $x(t) \in \Re$ and ε_t is iid with zero mean and unit variance.

The usual analysis strategy in such a case is to employ an embedding procedure involving the generation of a vector time series (Packard *et al.*, 1980). Since the underlying system is a finite-dimensional non-linear system, it is appropriate to consider using a neural network to approximate the underlying function. Normally this is done by training a neural network with the input sequence

$$[X(t), X(t-\tau), X(t-2\tau), \ldots, X(t-(n-1)\tau)]$$

with the known output $X(t + T)$ at time T as the target value, for previous values of t. What is essentially being performed is an approximation of the true mapping by a *non-linear* function which can, for example, be parameterised by the weights and thresholds of a neural network. It is therefore possible to predict a future point at time T using the trained network as a surrogate for the unknown non-linear function. This method has been used successfully for the prediction of non-linear systems and, in conjunction with artificial neural networks, has been shown to yield accurate results (Lowe and Webb, 1994; Weigend and Gershenfeld, 1993) in some problem domains.

Similar methods have been used in earlier work by Lapedes and Farber (1988).

The same principle has been used by Sauer (1993) to predict time series using delay co-ordinate embeddings. Studies indicate that, for a given time series, it is sufficient to prescribe only the window length $(n - 1)\tau$, and not necessarily the embedding dimension n or the lag τ separately (Broomhead and King, 1986; Mees *et al.*, 1987). It is this simpler approach that we have chosen to implement for the purposes of this chapter. In this case, the delay embeddings have the form

$$[x(i) = \{x(i), x(i+1), x(i+2), \ldots, x(i+n-1)\} \in \Re^n] \quad \text{for} \quad i = 1, 2, \ldots, N-n+1$$

Our results indicate that the predictive capability of a system model is a function of the embedding dimension, although other factors such as sampling rate may also have to be taken into account.

13.2 Practical Problems

There are a number of practical problems that need to be addressed with regard to the Takens' delay coordinate maps. The first is that the theory has been developed around deterministic smooth dynamical systems. However, most real-world time series have a high level of noise. Secondly, no *a priori* knowledge regarding the unseen dynamical system is available. As such, careful consideration must be given to the choice of parameters of the delay coordinate map.

In practice, theoretical considerations do not address the level of complexity of dynamical generators of real-world time series, such as electricity load demand or financial futures contracts.

The presence of noise obscures the true intrinsic dimensionality of the generator. In addition, the noise could have a random component as well as a dynamic component, and such non-stationary effects have to be taken into account. Further, it is also possible that the generator itself is non-stationary. It should be assumed that the generator of the time series is not static, but dynamic, and this is what gives rise to the resulting non-stationarity. Commonly, quasi-stationary time-scales are employed to seek evidence for non-stationarity in a time series. Thus, a study of the dynamics of the generator is equivalent to the study of the non-stationarity of a time series, and this can be performed either in the time domain itself, or via a suitable transformation in "phase space."

A key point we wish to make is that in order to reliably construct a model of the underlying generator of the observations, it is necessary to determine and characterise the *complexity* of the model in order to match the complexity of the unknown generator. In the context of system models, this implies both the embedding dimension (which dictates the appropriate number of delays), and the number of degrees of freedom of the model. If we have little or no prior knowledge, then the degrees of freedom of the model have to be derived from experimental data and, in general, the model should have fewer degrees of freedom than the information content supported by the data itself.

There are generally two ideas that one may use in constructing system models. The first is based on the assumption of deterministic dynamics. The second alternative is stochastic modelling. A typical approach is to combine the two approaches to include both a non-linear component describing the system's internal dynamics and a stochastic term that takes into account perturbations caused by random fluctuations in the system parameters. However, the addition of noise induces an apparent increase in the intrinsic dimensionality of the data. If the model architecture has not been accurately specified, then the long-term behaviour of the iterated dynamics of the model can be severely distorted.

Additional complications arise in time series that are oversampled, since in this case successive time series samples are highly correlated, and hence the number of delays needed to adequately capture the dynamics would be greater than if the time series samples were more sparsely sampled and less correlated. Hence we see again that what is important is the total information content contained in a length of time series, which is determined both by its sample rate and the number of delays. Typically, we have no control over the sample rate of real world data.

Despite the assumption of a stochastic component, well-founded methods exist to determine and characterise the complexity of the model and of the data. The methods developed in this paper essentially provide prescriptive information regarding how to specify the number of delay vectors for the appropriate long term dynamics.

13.3 Characterising and Measuring Complexity

In this section we demonstrate how characterising the *degrees of freedom* by the singular spectrum of the delay vectors allows us to estimate the intrinsic dimensionality of the data (which determines the number of delays needed to map the deterministic component of the data generator).

Previous work (Broomhead and King, 1986) has indicated that an embedding and a signal–noise subspace decomposition for dynamical systems is possible by using a singular value decomposition of the data matrix constructed from overlapping delay vectors of the time series of suitable size. We now extend this insight to determine the model complexity which can be matched to the data for "best" predictive performance.

Structure in the singular spectrum (which includes the sum of the eigenvalues and any fine detail discontinuities in the spectrum) provide information on the intrinsic dimensionality of the information content of the signal. In particular, if the delay window does not sufficiently capture the dynamics of the generator, we would not expect convergence of the singular spectrum. We expect a general stability of the spectrum as sufficient information content is captured with the window size. Hence *convergence* of the singular spectrum is the criterion for obtaining a sufficiently large delay window. However, because of serial correlations in data, the length of the delay vector is not equivalent to the intrinsic degrees of freedom of the data. Rather, the number of degrees of freedom is determined by the location of structural discontinuities or "kinks" in the converged spectrum (Fig. 13.2).

If the signal were free of noise, the spectra would be expected to show a smooth decline. The kinks observed may therefore be attributed to the various noise processes of the system.

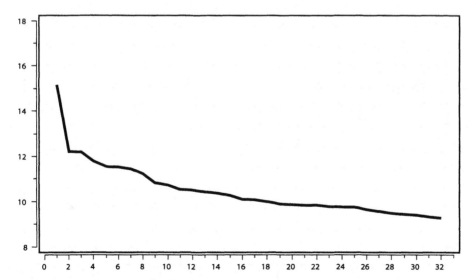

Fig. 13.2 A sample singular spectrum. There are two kinks in the spectrum, at $x = 2$ and $x = 3$, after which the spectrum is smooth. This indicates two degrees of freedom in the system.

13.4 SVD Smoothing

As described in the previous section, the embedding dimension of the reconstruction space $2m + 1$ is determined by systematically increasing n until a prior condition is reached. An example will illustrate this procedure. Figure 13.3 shows the eigenspectra for different numbers of delays for a synthetic signal generated from a mixture of sinusoids with added noise. From the figure, we note that there is a convergence of the spectra when the number of delays is of the order of 32. It could therefore be assumed that the manifold and its attractor are approximately 32-dimensional structures; however, $n = 32$ is only an upper bound on the dimension $2m + 1$ because the noise present on the attractor is amplified in reconstruction space. The true attractor is therefore contained within a subspace of these 32-dimensional structures. Considering the eigenspectra in Fig. 13.3, it is apparent that, although this indicates the embedding size required to capture the relevant dynamics, the actual complexity of the deterministic component in this signal is only of the order of two degrees of freedom, as indicated by the first major "kink" in the spectrum, i.e. the attractor is most likely a two-dimensional structure. As such, the remaining 30 components are assumed to be responsible for the noise in the time series. If the signal were free of noise, the spectra would be expected to show a smooth decline. The kinks observed may therefore be attributed to the various noise processes of the system. An assumption can therefore be made that, as these 30 spectral components represent the noise in the system, they may be discarded. The underlying "noise-free" signal can be extracted by reconstructing the signal from the first two dominant singular values, with the rest of the singular values from 3 to 32 being set to zero. This may be viewed as a smoothed approximation to the original time series, where the singular values are the fundamental tools used for smoothing. In a similar manner, the noise can be modelled by reconstructing the

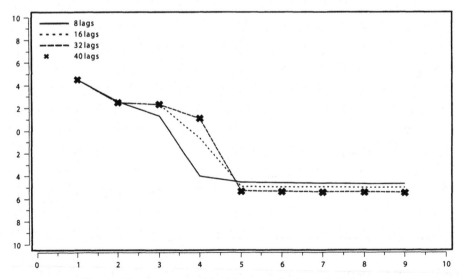

Fig. 13.3 The eigenspectra of the delay vectors for the synthetic data set.

signal corresponding to singular values 3 to 32, and extracting a second time series from this.

13.5 Summary

The dynamical systems view has been introduced in this chapter to allow the definition of the embedding dimension to be given. The method of calculation was shown in Section 13.3, after the notions of complexity and degrees of freedom were introduced. We will later show how these ideas can be used to help build prediction models by looking for evidence of the presence of a certain number of degrees of freedom in the time series; the remainder of the possible variables will then be treated as noise and so discarded.

14. Vector Machines

Neep Hazarika and John G. Taylor

14.1 Introduction

One of the basic problems of data analysis is that of classes of data points which are not linearly separable. The vector machine solves this by the expansion of the dimension of each data vector x into a new space by the mapping $x \to \phi(x)$ with values in a higher dimensional space. Any quadratic error expression will then contain inner products of two higher dimensional mapped vectors, say $\phi(x)$ with $\phi(y)$. Conditions are then imposed so that this inner product is reduced to the evaluation of a suitable kernel at the two original data values: $K(x, y)$. The non-linear mapping: $x \to \phi(x)$ leads to an extension of non-linear regression by this higher dimensional embedding method.

14.2 Support Vector Machines

The support vector machine has recently been introduced as a new technique for solving a variety of learning and function estimation problems. It is firmly grounded in the framework of statistical learning theory which has been developed over the last three decades (Vapnik, 1982, 1995). The theory characterises properties of learning machines which enable them to generalise well into unseen data. Thus, the support vector machine (SVM) program allows a user to carry out pattern recognition and regression estimation, using support vector techniques on some given data. In many cases, SVM generalisation performance (i.e. error rates on test sets) either matches or is significantly better than that of competing methods. For a more exhaustive description of support vector machines, the reader is referred to Vapnik (1995).

14.2.1 Basic Formulation

Given a training dataset $\{(x_1, t_1), (x_2, t_2), ..., (x_N, t_N)\} = (x, t)$, the aim is to determine, in the case of ε–SV regression, a function $f(x)$ that deviates from all the actual target

117

values (t_i, $1 \leq i \leq N$) by a value of at most ε. Further, we also want $f(x)$ to be as flat as possible. Thus, we are not concerned with errors that are smaller than ε, but the formulation does not accept errors of a larger magnitude.

In general, we can begin by describing the case where f is a linear function of the form $f(x) = \langle w, x \rangle + b$ where w are the weights, and $\langle .,. \rangle$ denotes the dot product. In this case, *flatness* implies small values of w. This may be achieved by a minimisation of the Euclidean norm $\|w\|^2$. The introduction of non-linearity into this formulation of the SVM enables the problem to be rewritten as a kernel regression problem, where we now use the kernel regressor

$$t = \Phi w \qquad (14.1)$$

where Φ is the "design" matrix whose elements are $\Phi(m,n) = K(x(m), x(n))$, where $K(.,.)$ is a *kernel* function that is chosen to satisfy Mercer's condition. For details, the reader is referred to the report by Smola and Schölkopf (1998).

14.3   Relevance Vector Machines

A recent improvement upon the support vector machine is the relevance vector machine (RVM) (Tipping, 2000). The SVM uses state-of-the-art methodology for regression and classification problems, which results in excellent generalisation properties using a sparse kernel representation. Nonetheless, the SVM does have a number of disadvantages, the most notable among them being the absence of probabilistic outputs. The RVM employs a probabilistic Bayesian approach and is therefore suitable for sparse data sets that are generally encountered in finance. Although the RVM is a generalised linear model of similar functional form to the SVM, it displays comparable generalisation performance with substantially fewer kernel functions.

The RVM was devised as an alternative to the SVM because the latter suffers from a number of disadvantages:

- The SVM predictions are point estimates, and are not probabilistic.
- The SVM requires too many support vectors, and the number increases rapidly with the size of the training set.
- One needs to employ an estimation procedure to evaluate the error/margin trade-off parameter C, as well as the insensitivity parameter ε;
- The kernel function $K(.,.)$ must be chosen to satisfy Mercer's condition.

The relevance vector machine is identical in functional form to the support vector machine, but uses a probabilistic model. It has none of the drawbacks of the support vector machine. An iterative procedure is employed to determine hyperparameters for the weights, and the kernel functions associated with large values of the weight decay parameters α are then pruned. One such decay parameter is associated with each weight. We will outline briefly the derivation of the RVM algorithm. For details, the reader is referred to the paper by Tipping (2000).

14.3.1 Basic Formulation

Given a dataset $\{x(n), y(n)\} = (x,t)$ (where $1 \leq n \leq N$), we use the kernel regressor

$$t = \Phi w$$

where Φ is the $N \times (N+1)$ "design" matrix with $\Phi(m,n) = K(x(m), x(n))$, $\Phi(n, N+1) = 1$ and $w = (w(1), w(2), ... , w(N), w(0))$ is the vector of weights. Then, following a Gaussian assumption for $p(t \mid x)$, the likelihood of the dataset can be written as

$$p(t|x,w,\sigma^2) = (2\pi\sigma)^{-N/2} \exp\left\{-\left(\frac{1}{2\sigma}\right)\|t - \Phi w\|^2\right\} \tag{14.2}$$

Combining a further Gaussian prior for the weights w, we get

$$p(w|\alpha) = \prod_{i=0}^{N} \exp\left\{-\frac{1}{2}w(i)^2 \alpha(i)\right\} \tag{14.3}$$

where α is a vector of $N+1$ hyperparameters. Bayes' rule is then invoked to obtain the posterior over the weights:

$$p(w|t,x,\alpha,\sigma^2) = p(t|x,w,\sigma^2)p(w|\alpha)p(\alpha) / p(t) \tag{14.4}$$

Then, combining equations (14.2), (14.3) and (14.4), we obtain

$$p(w|t,x,\alpha,\sigma^2) =$$
$$\frac{1}{M}(2\pi\sigma)^{-N/2} \exp\left\{-\frac{1}{2\sigma}\|t - \Phi w\|^2\right\} \prod_{i=0}^{N} \exp\left\{-\frac{1}{2}w(i)^2 \alpha(i)\right\} \tag{14.5}$$

An explicit expression for the normalising factor M in equation (14.5) can be obtained by recognising that the exponent is quadratic in w of the form

$$-\left(\frac{1}{2\sigma}\right)w^T \Phi^T \Phi w - \left(\frac{1}{2}\right)w^T A w + \left(\frac{1}{\sigma}\right)t^T \Phi w = -\left(\frac{1}{2}\right)w^T \Sigma^{-1}w + t^T B\Phi w$$

$$= -\left(\frac{1}{2}\right)(w - \mu)^T \Sigma(w - \mu)$$

where we have defined $A = \mathrm{diag}(\alpha_0, \alpha_1, ... \alpha_N)$ and $B = \sigma^{-2}I_N$, with

$$\Sigma = (\Phi^T B\Phi + A)^{-1}, \quad \mu = \sigma\Phi^T Bt$$

Upon Gaussian integration over w we obtain the normalisation factor $M = |\Sigma|^{1/2}$, and equation (14.5) can be written as

$$p(w|t,x,\alpha,\sigma^2) =$$
$$\left(\frac{1}{M}\right)(2\pi\sigma)^{-(N+1)/2} \exp\left\{-\left(\frac{1}{2\sigma}\right)(w - \mu)\Sigma^{-1}(w - \mu)\right\} \tag{14.6}$$

Upon further integration over the weights w, and using Bayes' formula,

$$p(t|\alpha,\sigma^2) = \int dw\ p(t|x,w,\sigma^2)p(w|\alpha) \tag{14.7}$$

the final expression for the *evidence* for the hyperparameters is obtained, after suitable manipulation of matrix inverses, as

$$p(t|\alpha,\sigma^2) =$$
$$(2\pi)^{-N/2}|B^{-1} + \Phi A^{-1}\Phi^T|^{1/2}\exp\left\{-\frac{1}{2}t^T(B^{-1} + \Phi A^{-1}\Phi^T)^{-1}t\right\} \tag{14.8}$$

If priors were defined for α and σ^2, it would have been possible to integrate over the hyperparameters. However, it is not possible to perform such a marginalisation in closed form, so we use an iterative procedure to compute the hyperparameters that optimise the evidence (14.8).

14.4 Optimising the Hyperparameters for Regression

In this case, the target t is assumed to be uniformly distributed, and is not considered relevant to the calculation of the optimal hyperparameters. We therefore replace possible hyperpriors over α and σ by an iterative approach, optimising on their values in $p(\alpha,\sigma|t) = p(t|\alpha,\sigma)$.

Upon differentiation, and setting derivatives of the probability (14.8) to zero, we obtain the following estimates:

$$\alpha(i)^{\text{new}} = \frac{\gamma(i)}{\mu(i)^2} \tag{14.9}$$

where $\gamma(i) = 1 - \alpha(i)\Sigma_{ii}$, and also

$$(\sigma^2)^{\text{new}} = \|t - \Phi\mu\|^2/(N - \gamma.1) \tag{14.10}$$

14.5 Optimising the Hyperparameters for Classification

In his paper, Tipping (2000) employs the logistic sigmoid function to obtain the class probability in the case of classification. This can be extended to the multi-class problem using SOFTMAX. The most probable weights are then calculated from $p(t|w)$, using the iteratively re-weighted least-squares algorithm described by Nabney (1999). The Hessian is then computed at the optimal weight value directly (Tipping, 2000), and used to update the hyperparameters α as described by equation (14.9) above (but without the σ^2 hyperparameter).

14.6 Summary

A brief survey of vector machines has been given in this chapter. The basic idea was introduced of expansion of the dimension of each data vector by the mapping

$x \rightarrow \phi(x)$, with values in a new higher dimensional space. In this way it is hoped that non-linear separation problems of data points can be made easier to handle. Any quadratic error expression will then contain inner products of two higher dimensional vectors $\phi(x)$ with $\phi(y)$. Conditions are imposed so that this inner product can be reduced to the evaluation of a suitable kernel at the two original data values: $K(x, y)$. The non-linear mapping: $x \rightarrow \phi(x)$ leads to the expression (14.1) as an extension of non-linear regression by this higher dimensional embedding method. The removal of many of the support vectors in the regression expression (14.1) was then described by the relevance vector approach, based on use of Bayesian methods to optimise the likelihood of the data set. Optimisation of the hyperparameters was then discussed for regression; classification was considered only briefly at the end of the chapter.

15. Bayesian Methods and Evidence

Sebastian Larsson

15.1 Bayesian Methods

The Bayesian interpretation of probabilities has a natural appeal in the context of pattern analysis and forecasting in the way that it provides an intuitive and flexible framework for dealing with many different possible hypotheses, even in situations when data is scarce. As a consequence, Bayesian methods have enjoyed a much wider following in this subject area than they perhaps have in the wider statistical community. Since Bayesian thinking is often implied in many of the methods described throughout this book, we feel that it is worthwhile outlining briefly what we mean by Bayesian methods and the type of statistical analysis to which it naturally lends itself.

In this section we introduce the Bayesian interpretation of probability theory and the type of analysis to which this viewpoint typically leads. The Bayesian treatment is compared with the more traditional "Frequentist" approach and the differences between the two approaches, in particular the use of prior probabilities and the use of probabilities in hypothesis testing, are highlighted. We conclude with an application of Bayesian analysis to the problem of assessing the performance of a time series predictor from data about its historical performance.

15.2 A Bayesian View of Probability

Any introduction to Bayesian methods must appear somewhat philosophical in nature, since at the heart of the Bayesian theory lies a fundamentally different interpretation of what a probability actually *is* as compared to the more traditional "Frequentist" view. Once these ontological issues have been dealt with, all the usual expressions we are familiar with from school day probability theory (including Bayes' theorem itself!) remain unchanged, and it is easy to be left wondering what practical purpose has been served by the whole exercise. However, as we shall see, the Bayesian interpretation of probability does have some profound implications, including the assignment of *a priori* probabilities and the use of probabilities in hypothesis testing.

What is not at issue in our discussion of probabilities is the general mathematical framework used to describe probability theory, as set out in any basic text (see e.g. Grimmett and Welsh (1986) or Williams (1991)). Rather, we wish to compare the traditional and Bayesian ways of assigning probabilities to real stochastic systems and how these quantities are to be interpreted.

In the Frequentist way of thinking, the probability of a certain event is a number associated with the underlying random system, the value of which can, in principle, be determined by repeatedly sampling the system and observing the frequency with which the said event occurs as a fraction of all possible outcomes. As the number of samples grows without bound, the frequency estimate of the probability becomes arbitrarily good, but note that the actual probability is just a number whose value we might not know but which is knowable by performing this frequency analysis. We note that probabilities defined in this way are objective, in the sense that they are properties of the system at hand, independent of the observer.

From the Bayesian point of view, on the other hand, the probability assigned to a particular outcome is largely arbitrary as long as it is consistent with all the information already known about the stochastic system. Bayesian probabilities are subjective and are interpreted as a way of assigning numerical values to the degree of ignorance of a given observer about the observed system. In contrast with the Frequentist, it is therefore possible for two Bayesian observers to assign different probabilities to the same event.

It is important to realise that, although this subjective view of probabilities has some very significant consequences, Bayesian probability assignment does not lead to the state of anarchy we might at first think. Firstly, many probabilistic systems we consider are made up of combinations of simpler stochastic processes, and the probabilities must then be assigned consistently with those calculated according to the rules of probability. So, once we have assigned the probability of obtaining "heads" in a simple coin toss, the probability of obtaining any sequence of heads or tails in a series of tosses is completely determined by the usual binomial probability model, irrespective of our interpretation of probabilities.

Eventually, however, we need to consider the assignment of probabilities to "primitive" systems, where we have no knowledge of any inner workings of the random process. At this stage it is common for both Frequentists and Bayesians to quote some form of the "Principle of Insufficient Reason" and assign *equal a priori probabilities* to all the possible states of the system. To the Frequentist this is justified since the probabilities are ultimately determined by performing an infinite frequency sampling, but if there really is nothing to distinguish the possible states of the system, symmetry would seem to dictate that the outcome must be equal probabilities. For the Bayesian there is more scope for individual expression, since any assignment of probabilities is valid; however, an unequal assignment of probabilities would not be consistent with the perceived symmetry.

Thus, in the more orthodox view there are probabilities associated with each possible outcome of the primitive system, but we might not know what they are without conducting an infinite sampling experiment. To Bayesians the whole notion of a probability that is unknown is something of a contradiction in terms, so they would simply assign a reasonable seeming set of probabilities and then make sure that these numbers were updated to keep them consistent with any new data.

15.3   Hypothesis Testing

We have seen that for simple probabilistic systems, such as dice rolls and coin tosses, the Frequentist and Bayesian viewpoints lead to identical probabilities, even if the interpretation of what the numbers mean is somewhat different. However, we now turn to the issue of statistical inference, and we shall see how the two interpretations can lead to quite different methodologies.

For definiteness, let us consider a random variable with a Gaussian probability distribution function specified by the two parameters (μ, σ) denoting the mean and standard deviation. We will refer to the parameter pair (μ, σ) as our model hypothesis[1]. It is frequently the case that we do not actually know what these parameters are, but would like to *infer* their values given some set of data, D say, obtained by actually sampling the random variable a finite number of times. What we need is a procedure for establishing which set of parameters are the best estimate of the real, unknown, model parameters, and thus deciding which model hypothesis is the best in light of the data.

The starting point in both the Frequentist and Bayesian methods is to consider the probability of obtaining the observed data on the *assumption* of a given model (μ, σ) which we might write as $p(D \,|\, \mu, \sigma)$ and which we will refer to as the *likelihood* (or *evidence*) of the hypothesis given the data. The notation we have chosen for the likelihood strongly suggests that it is the same thing as the probability distribution of the data conditional on the model parameters. However, we have to be careful here, because from the Frequentist point of view this conditional probability does not really exist, since (μ, σ) is *not* a set of random variables! In other words, (μ, σ) is a set of parameters whose values are not known, which automatically makes them random variables from the Bayesian standpoint, but to a Frequentist they are just two real numbers.

This distinction is the key to understanding the difference between hypothesis assessment as performed within the two probabilistic frameworks. We are going to risk clouding this issue slightly for the sake of notational simplicity by allowing ourselves to treat deterministic parameters as random variables with delta-function distribution functions, so that the conditional probability $p(D \,|\, \mu, \sigma)$ exists even in the Frequentist case.

Whatever our choice of notation, however, the likelihood function still takes the same form irrespective of interpretative framework and it tells us the probability of the sampled data taking on values in an infinitesimal neighbourhood around the actual observed value, given the assumed model parameters. Thus the likelihoods serve as an intuitive "plausibility" measure for comparing different hypotheses, since for a given data set, a large likelihood means a large probability for the observed data as we repeat the sampling experiment over and over. From the Frequentist point of view this is about as far as we can go using purely probabilistic

---

1   Note that some authors (e.g. MacKay, 1991) make a distinction between hypothesis testing and parameter fitting. From this point of view we might say that the assumption that our p.d.f. was Gaussian (as opposed to Poisson, say) constitutes our model hypothesis, whilst any numbers (μ, σ) are model parameters which we need to be fitted. Here we will treat any distinct p.d.f. as a separate hypothesis.

arguments, although it is common to integrate the likelihood function over regions of the data-space to obtain the usual one- or two-tailed tests, such as χ^2 and t tests.

For the Bayesian, however, the likelihood is only a start. Next we use Bayes' theorem to write

$$p(\mu, \sigma | D) = \frac{p(D | \mu, \sigma) p(\mu, \sigma)}{p(D)} \tag{15.1}$$

thus obtaining an expression for $p(\mu, \sigma | D)$, the probability density function for our model parameters, conditional on the observed data[2]. To the Bayesian way of thinking this is exactly the quantity we want to be considering, since this distribution summarises everything we know about μ and σ. In equation (15.1) we see how the likelihood of the data is used to update our prior (to the arrival of the data) distribution $p(\mu, \sigma)$ of the model parameters to give an *a posteriori* distribution (up to a normalisation constant). The use of a prior is clearly a feature which distinguishes Bayesian inference from its Frequentist counterpart, where we are effectively forced to perform our inference of model parameters as if this prior were just a constant, i.e. a uniform prior.

In practice, the use of non-uniform priors only affects our hypothesis testing if we do not have sufficient amounts of data. Any assumptions about the prior will sooner or later be dominated in equation (15.1) by the contribution from the likelihood as we gather sufficient quantities of data. A good choice of prior will help us obtain good estimates for our model parameters even with small amounts of data, whilst a bad choice will have the opposite effect. Essentially, the Bayesians permit themselves to encode more diffuse information into their hypothesis testing than can be encoded in the likelihood. So, for example, if the random variable we have considered is the distribution of the returns on a certain investment, we know that very extreme return–risk profiles would mean that it would either be untradable or so desirable that it would distort the entire market. Thus, with no direct pricing information, but with a general idea of the market conditions, the Bayesian could easily justify writing down a non-uniform prior incorporating this notion.

But perhaps the most important aspect of the Bayesian use of $p(\mu, \sigma | D)$ as a model plausibility criterion is that it is actually a probability density. This property not only agrees with many people's intuitive way of thinking about the inference of model parameters, but also means that it is straightforward to deal with cases when the data does not strongly favour a single hypothesis. For any property of our system, represented by the variable A say, that we might be interested in we can write

$$p(A | D) = \int p(A | \mu, \sigma) p(\mu, \sigma | D) d\mu \, d\sigma \tag{15.2}$$

so that our best description of A is a straightforward average over all the possible models with weights that are just the model probabilities as calculated form equation (15.1). When the likelihood function is sharply peaked at some one set of model

---

2 N.B. We could use Bayes' theorem in the Frequentist case as well, since it remains a valid identity. However, the quantity $p(\mu, \sigma)$ on the r.h.s. is a delta-function peak around the actual, unknown, values, which means that the l.h.s. is also a delta-function peak around these, still unknown, values. In other words, it is a true statement, but it tells us nothing we did not already know.

parameters this average will produce the same result as finding the most likely model (μ, σ) and then using the distribution $p(A \mid \mu, \sigma)$ for A. We would then obtain the same results (assuming a uniform prior) as in the Frequentist assessment. However, if $p(A \mid \mu, \sigma)$ varies significantly over the region where $p(\mu, \sigma \mid D)$ is significant we will generally obtain much more robust estimates of A by using the full expression (15.2) and combining the behaviours of several competing hypothesis with weights corresponding to their probability of being the "true" model, conditional on the observed data.

Thus we see that Bayesian techniques come into their own when we are dealing with systems where, as is often the case in practice, there is a scarcity of solid data. In such cases the ability to incorporate difficult-to-quantify prior information, and the possibility of working simultaneously with a number of possible models, become very important tools.

15.4   The Bayesian Evidence Ratio

An important problem to which Bayesian methods naturally lend themselves is in assessing the performance of various predictive techniques. We will use the ratio of evidence assessment described below in subsequent chapters to illustrate general performance levels, but in addition this section serves as a simple example of how Bayesian methods can be applied to testing various competing theoretical explanations of observed data.

We consider the problem of how, given a time series of target values and a series of predictions, we would find a robust way of determining how good the attempt at prediction has proven to be over some historical time period. In this section we will address the whole issue of prediction performance assessment from first principles by posing the question "What is the *probability* of this model being a correct description of the observed data?". Such lines of questioning quickly lead us into the realms of Bayesian evidence estimation.

If we are given a hypothesis H and some data D we write the probability of the hypothesis H being true given the data as $p(H \mid D)$, and then Bayes' theorem states that

$$p(H|D) = \frac{p(D|H)p(H)}{p(D)} \tag{15.3}$$

We also say that the *a posteriori probability* for the hypothesis H based on the data D is equal to the *evidence* times the *a priori probability* of the hypothesis, divided by a (hypothesis independent) normalisation factor.

The data we use to evaluate the performance of a given hypothesis will be taken to come in the form of a set $D = \{(y_i, t_i)\}_N$ of N prediction–target pairs. In order to make progress with our analysis we will now assume that the target series can be explained by the prediction plus some unknown noise component

$$t_i = y_i + \sigma \varepsilon_i \tag{15.4}$$

where the ε_i are iid Gaussian random variables with zero mean and unit standard deviation and the σ is a constant to set the expected level of residual noise. Because of the parameter σ we strictly speaking have a continuum of possible models, one for each non-negative value for the expected noise level. Since, we do not know what this value is we will integrate over all such possible values[3] (we will phrase this integral in terms of the equivalent parameter $\alpha \equiv 1/\sigma^2$)

$$p(H|D) = \int p(H,\alpha|D)\mathrm{d}\alpha$$
$$= p(D)^{-1} \int p(D|H,\alpha)p(H,\alpha)\mathrm{d}\alpha \tag{15.5}$$

Using our assumption about Gaussian distributed residuals we can write

$$p(D|H,\alpha) = \left(\frac{2\pi}{\alpha}\right)^{-N/2} \exp\left(-\frac{\alpha N}{2}.\mathrm{MSE}\right) \tag{15.6}$$

where the MSE is the mean square error calculated from the data sample. Assuming a uniform prior $p(H, \sigma) = p_0$ in terms of the standard deviation (i.e. some H and σ independent constant) we easily find the prior in terms of a by calculating the usual Jacobian factor

$$p(H|D) = \frac{1}{2}\alpha^{-3/2}p_0 \tag{15.7}$$

Substituting for this quantity in equation (15.5) and introducing the variable $b = 2/N$ MSE we obtain

$$p(H|D) = \frac{1}{2}\frac{p_0}{p(D)}\int_0^\infty \left(\frac{2\pi}{\alpha}\right)^{-N/2} e^{-\alpha/b}\alpha^{-3/2}\mathrm{d}\alpha$$
$$= \frac{1}{2}\frac{p_0}{p(D)}(2\pi)^{-N/2}b^{(N-1)/2}\Gamma\left(\frac{N-1}{2}\right) \tag{15.8}$$

in terms of the usual gamma function. The assumption of a uniform prior for σ might seem a bit over-liberal, but in practice our result is not overly sensitive to the exact choice of prior since the evidence $p(D|H,a)$ will in general be distinctly peaked for some finite value of a and our result should not be influenced significantly by including models with zero or very large levels of noise on an equal footing with more plausible values.

As it stands, this expression is not of much use, since we have no way of knowing $p(D)$, the full probability distribution of the observed data (such knowledge would be tantamount to knowing the correct hypothesis to explain the target data). However, since this factor is independent of our chosen hypothesis, it is possible to evaluate the ratio of the probabilities of the two competing hypotheses

---

3   **N.B.** The integration over σ is the only step in the calculations in this section which is inherently Bayesian.

$$\frac{p(H_1|D)}{p(H_2|D)} = \left(\frac{\text{MSE}_1}{\text{MSE}_2} \right)^{-(N-1)/2} \tag{15.9}$$

where we are assuming that both of our data sets contain the same number of points N as evidence for both hypotheses (in general these will be the same set of target points and the corresponding predictions). We will refer to this quantity as the *ratio of evidences* for the two hypotheses, since, with the choice of uniform priors, that is indeed what we have calculated. In addition, the name is aesthetically somewhat more pleasing than the (perhaps more accurate) ratio of posterior probabilities.

Of course, we still have to choose N, the amount of history we consider when assessing model performance. In this regard we will argue that we should use *all genuinely out-of-sample predictions* in calculating the evidence for a model. This stance might seem at odds with the use of a twelve month average relative variance (ARV_{12}) as introduced in Chapter 6, but is justifiable as it is used within the *NewQuant* prediction process; see Chapter 25. However, in judging the performance of a prediction model all genuine predictions should be used. Within our suggested assessment programme a model could only be excused for going through bad periods of prediction if it also predicted when those periods occur!

The evidence ratio, as described above, is used throughout this book to measure prediction performance; see for example Section 18.4. Although this performance statistic has been designed to have an intuitive interpretation in terms of the relative probability of two model descriptions given the available data, we will take a moment to discuss what constitutes a "good" evidence ratio. Firstly we must agree on a "benchmark" model against which we are going to measure all our prediction efforts. In *NewQuant* we have chosen a twelve month moving average prediction as our baseline for prediction performance: it is simple enough to be virtually insensitive to harmful over-training effects, whilst still being able to follow general trends in the data.

Any evidence ratio larger than one then indicates better prediction performance than this benchmark model. What constitutes a "good" evidence for a model depends partially on how good we expect this benchmark to be (in our case the moving average is considered a "soft" lower bound: we would not want to tolerate performance significantly less than this model provides), and partially how stable the evidence statistic is as a running assessment. By this last part we mean that our models are continually being assessed for performance and all our performance statistics show some level of monthly fluctuations, even though we expect both the evidence and ARV_{12} to converge for large enough data sets. For the time series and available history within the *NewQuant* process we see substantial fluctuations even in our largest assessment data sets, and as a consequence we take the conservative stance of only considering model performance as "good" if it is beating the benchmark by at least an order of magnitude. Thus, we would feel justified in referring to any evidence greater than or equal to ten as good.

There are a number of refinements we might choose to make to the assessment method using the ratio of evidence; for example, the use of a non-trivial prior for the noise level would be a relatively straightforward exercise. We have, however, chosen to use the evidence ratio as derived above because of its simple form and relatively transparent interpretation.

15.5 Conclusions

In this chapter we have provided a brief introduction to the Bayesian view of probabilities and how such concepts shape our approach to hypothesis testing. At each step we have tried to show, as far as possible, how the equivalent Frequentist method would apply. We hope that introducing Bayesian methods in this way will be more palatable to a reader used to the more traditional ways than a sudden barrage of prior probabilities and seemingly *ad hoc* uses of Bayes' Theorem.

We have also introduced, in a simple form, the use of ratios of evidence in assessing model performance. Since this technique has become commonplace within *NewQuant* we felt it was useful to describe this method in some detail and, in addition, it provides a very straightforward example of Bayesian type methods in action.

PART IV
Prediction Model Applications

In this part of the book application to explicit prediction of bond and equity series is made of the various modelling technologies described so far; the part concludes with predictions obtained by combining over all the predictions.

We start in Chapter 16 with a description of initial attempts to predict the shape of the bond yield curve. The nature of this shape is first described, and then possible parameterisations of the yield curve are discussed. Prediction of the parameter time series is then considered.

In Chapter 17 bond prediction is considered using the relevance vector machine introduced in Chapter 14. A linear regression method has been developed specifically to deal with both the problem of handling many inputs (so providing a Bayesian-optimal approach to input selection) as well as leading to a linear regression model for the selected inputs. The results of this approach are given for a benchmark series constructed so as test the efficacy of the variable selection approach in the presence of a fixed and known amount of noise. This is extended to the problem of predicting Australian bonds.

Application of neural networks are given in Chapter 18, where both feedforward and recurrent nets are developed after using input selection by the relevance vector-based method of the previous chapter. Specific examples of prediction of US Government bonds are described, with a more general discussion given of results across a range of other markets.

A specialised neural network approach, the adaptive lag method, is described in the following Chapter 19, with a training rule developed for the best lags. This allows the optimal lags to be learnt from a given set of input for a given target series. The results of this approach for prediction of German government bond returns are then described.

A further neural network approach is then considered, in Chapter 20, which uses random generation and subsequent selection of neural networks. Those nets are kept which are more effective than chance (by a small but specified amount) in prediction on a specific data set, the prediction being by majority vote. The resultant weak classifier is applied to US bond returns.

The method of co-integration is discussed in Chapter 21. This uses the detection of trend following to allow prediction by a co-integrated time series of the series of interest. This is applied to enable the construction of effective models of prediction of suitable combinations of FTSE 100 stocks.

Chapter 22 applies the reinforcement training method of Chapter 12 to a portfolio of assets. This combines the development of both a prediction and a trading scheme. The approach is extended to take account of trading costs, which leads to important modifications of the results obtained on their neglect.

Results obtained from various univariate models are then described in Chapter 23. The models considered are: Nearest Neighbours, Group Method of Data Handling (GMDH), Support Vector Machine and Relevance Vector Machine.

Predictions made by these approaches are given for various bond series (UK, European, German).

Chapter 24 develops the combining of predictions across a number of model technologies. Such a process is essential to enable the best of a set of predictions to be used, with poorer approaches being penalised before they are allowed to degrade prediction effectiveness. The temperature-dependent combiner is described in this chapter. This allows an adaptive approach to determining the optimal weights to assign to set of predictions and their associated technologies, as determined by a suitable assessor of the effectiveness of the particular prediction approach over the recent past. The combiner is shown to give as good predictions as those of the various models being combined.

16. *Yield Curve Modelling*

Sebastian Larsson

16.1 Yield Curve Modelling

The purpose of the investigations described below was to find techniques for predicting the maturity structure of various bond markets. In particular, we wanted to make monthly predictions of the yield curve, with a long-term view of using such information to formulate profitable trading strategies for a global bond portfolio. At present, our attempts at profitable maturity predictions are very much a work in progress. Nevertheless, some of the results we have obtained so far shed some interesting light on the problem, as well as highlighting some of the challenges which we still face.

We start our analysis by describing the data which we have had available and how we have used this data to evaluate various ways of describing the yield curve in various markets. This data is then fitted using various parametric models. The resulting time series of parameters can then be used as a basis for attempts to make predictions of the bond maturity structure. We show some preliminary results obtained using univariate prediction techniques, as outlined elsewhere in this book. Lastly, we sum up our results to date and indicate the most urgent directions for further research.

16.2 Yield Curve Data

The scarcity of good data available for our yield curve analysis has been a significant factor in shaping the directions in which this investigation has proceeded. We will therefore start by spelling out the nature of the data which has been available and what additional data we would expect to be of most value in extending this investigation.

For the present analysis of the maturity structure of global government bonds, we analyse data using 10 maturity buckets[1]. In each one of these buckets we have data for the average yield and average maturity. Thus, since there are only 10 distinct

---

1 At the date when the data was supplied these were: Total, 1–3 yrs, 3–5yrs, 3–7yrs, 5–7yrs, 7–10yrs, 1–5yrs, 5+yrs, 1–10yrs and 10+yrs.

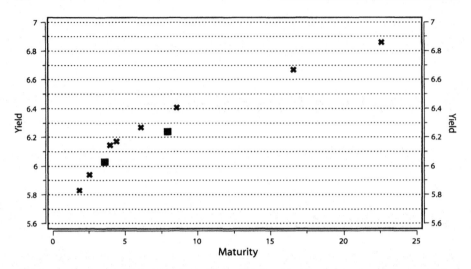

Fig. 16.1 Yield curve data for the USA. We see that the "Total" and "1–10 yrs" points (squares) seem to lie beneath the curve traced out by the other data points.

buckets to choose from, we have at most 10 data points for any yield curve. A typical yield curve taken from this data set is shown in Fig. 16.1.

After a preliminary inspection of the resulting yield curves we deleted the "Total" and "1–10 yrs" buckets from our data set, since these points frequently did not seem to lie on the curve traced out by the other data points in all of the markets considered. We do expect some distortion in the data brought on by the averaging performed over values in any one bucket, and it is reasonable to expect the most significant distortions to occur for the wider buckets, such as the "Total" and "1–10 yrs". However, there are other wide buckets, such as the "10 + yrs" bucket, which we retain since they do not seem to be affected to the same degree. Thus, we retain eight points per time slice for use in our maturity analysis, as described below.

Since any averaging over a maturity bucket will entail a loss of detail of the yield curve, it would be highly desirable to have yield and maturity data available in a large number of narrow and non-overlapping buckets (such as the data used in (Orr, 1997)). With such data we would be able to study, with some accuracy, the detailed dependence of yield on maturity in the various markets under consideration. However, as we shall see, the data that we do have still allows us to use simple parametric models to describe the overall yield curve shape.

We should also note that the yield data contains contributions due to coupons. In theoretical discussions of the yield curve, such as the one described in Chapter 4, it is more usual to consider the zero-coupon curve, since a knowledge of this curve allows us to calculate the price of any bond in a straightforward manner. Such a curve can be calculated by combining yield and coupon data for an array of individual bonds. However, such data was not available to us in a format which would allow the historical analysis we needed in order to provide a basis for a forecasting technology. Furthermore, it is not certain that the overall maturity structure which we need to know in order to make informed trading decisions cannot be obtained equally well from the raw yield curve, although it is not as straightforward to interpret.

16.3   Yield Curve Parameterisation

The first step we are going to take in trying to predict the future shape of the yield curve, is to choose a simple parametric function which fits to the overall shape of the curve at a given time slice. Given such a model, we can perform a least χ^2 fit for its parameters and thereby obtain a small number of monthly time series which encode the shape of the curve. The hope is that the model chosen incorporates some significant information about the overall yield curve structure and that the fitted parameters will therefore describe the yield curve more efficiently than the time series representing points on the yield curve itself.

In deciding which parametric model to use in describing our yield curve data we considered a number of possibilities. Some of these models, such as the Pareto and Willner models (Haugen, 1993) described below, are suggested by theoretical considerations (e.g. the Willner model can be justified starting from the Vasicek short rate model (de La Grandville, 2001) using a "no arbitrage" argument), whilst others, such as the simple Exponential model, also described below, are purely empirical models. However, all models we considered are capable of describing the overall shape of the yield curves described by our data.

The majority of the data shows the yield curve levelling off to a constant value for large maturities, although this behaviour is not always evident at our highest maturity point, usually at about 23 years. Such behaviour is to be expected since there is no reason for yields to depend on maturity once the maturity exceeds the investment horizon of all investors. The yield curves are also expected to intersect the zero maturity axis at some finite and positive value (the short rate) and with some finite slope. The most frequently seen shape is similar to that seen in Fig. 16.1, where the yield rises with increasing maturity, but occasionally we must also cater for inverted shapes and for more complicated intermediate cases.

A large number of possible yield curve parameterisations were tried, but most of these were found to be too complicated, i.e. contained too many free parameters, to provide robust fits to our eight data points. For large numbers of model parameters we can always obtain very good χ^2 error on our fits, but we are prone to overfitting, where the values of fitted parameters are sensitively dependent on the exact positions of individual data points. As well as being at odds with our attempt to find a parameterisation that encodes the overall yield curve structure, such overfitted parameter series are also found to fluctuate wildly from month to month, making them unlikely candidates for a successful attempt at prediction. All the models that we proceeded to consider in some detail had three or four parameters.

Having singled out our simplest models as favoured candidates for yield curve fitting, we proceeded to examine how well such models could be made to fit the curves for all the available historical data and for all available markets (USA, Japan, UK, Germany, France, Canada and Australia).

$$Y(x) = a_0 + a_1 e^{-x/a_{\exp}} \qquad\qquad \text{Exponential Model}$$

$$Y(x) = a_0 + (a_1 + x a_2) e^{-x/a_{\exp}} \qquad\qquad \text{Pareto Model}$$

$$Y(x) = a_0 + (a_1 + a_2)\frac{(1 - e^{-x/a_{\exp}})}{x/a_{\exp}} - a_2 e^{-x/a_{\exp}} \qquad\qquad \text{Willner Model}$$

The models considered were the Exponential, Pareto and Willner models described by the above equations, where x is the maturity value. As already mentioned, there are some theoretical reasons why the Pareto and Willner models might fit the yield data well in general, whilst the Exponential model is an empirically motivated simplification of the Pareto model.

If we do the χ^2 fit, using the Levenberg–Marquardt method (Press *et al.*, 1992), to obtain the parameter time series, we find that all three models can consistently produce parameterisations with low fitted errors over most of our historical data. However, although the parameter series will look quite reasonable (i.e. predictable) in most cases, we find that there are isolated regions of extreme values, or "spikes". Thus the time series obtained for the parameters looked to be difficult to predict and this expectation was borne out when predictions were attempted on these series using a univariate GMDH predictor (see Chapter 23).

On closer examination the spikes were found to occur when the yield curve data was well fitted by a straight line (of non-zero gradient). In other words, the gradual levelling out of the yield curve expected at large maturities was not found in the data. In such cases we intuitively feel that our data simply does not have enough points at large enough maturity to capture the asymptotic behaviour. In line with this intuitive idea, we would like to constrain the parameter associated with the scale of the exponential term, as set by a_{exp}, in such a way that the parameter never becomes smaller than 1 over the largest maturity in the data set. In order to effect this constraint we made the substitution $1/a_{exp} \rightarrow k_0 + a_e^2$ where k_0 is the minimum value desired for the exponent parameter, which we set to 1/25 throughout, and a_e was always taken to be positive. Effectively we are minimising the χ^2 error with the additional constraint that the scale parameter a_{exp} never becomes larger than 25.

With this modification, none of the fitted parameter series suffer from the erratic spiky behaviour described above and we were able to study the relative merits of our three parameterisation methods. Looking at the three plots in Figs. 16.2, 16.3 and 16.4 we see that we were able to obtain good fits to the overall yield curve structure

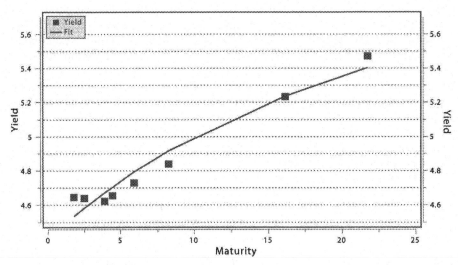

Fig. 16.2 USA February 1999 yield curve, simple exponential fit. $\chi^2 = 0.035$.

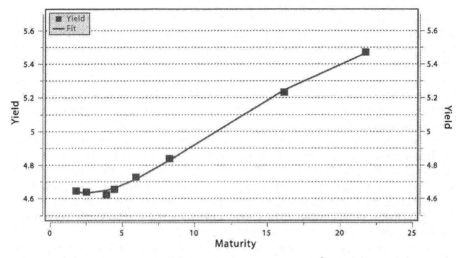

Fig. 16.3 USA February 1999 yield curve, Pareto fit. $\chi^2 = 0.001$.

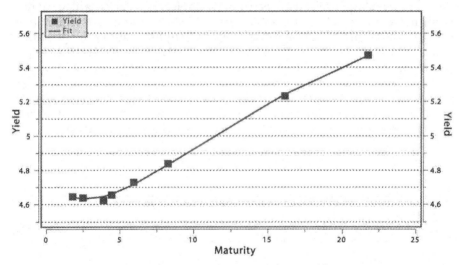

Fig. 16.4 USA February 1999 yield curve, Willner fit. $\chi^2 = 0.001$.

using either of the three methods, but that the simple exponential fit (Fig. 16.2) was slightly too simple to capture the more complicated structure at low maturities evident in the data (USA yield curve data for February 1999) and consequently it has a noticeably higher χ^2 error.

However, the very clear inverted structure of the yield curve at short maturities, as seen in this example, is the exception rather than the rule. In most cases the Exponential model performed at a comparable level to that of the other two models, being able to capture all the broader features: general level, whether the curve is rising or falling, and the overall convexity. On the other hand, the more flexible models sometimes generated parameter series which jump suddenly between two different minima of the χ^2 error surface, as the error surface changed from one month to the next. In some cases, such jumps can be the correct identification of a new feature developing in the yield curve during the month, but more often these jumps seem to be artificial features brought on by slight overfitting to a small number of points. In other words, given the amount of data available to us, the four parameter models seemed to generate series with occasional hard-to-predict jumps, thought to be mainly due to data artefacts.

In the light of this lack of robustness, we decided to leave the four parameter models in favour of the simpler Exponential model, which yielded less erratic parameter series. However, as we can clearly see from Fig. 16.2, there is some loss of information in performing an Exponential fit, since there are "real" features of the USA yield curve which cannot be represented by this simple parameterisation. (Note that in Orr (1997), where data is less scarce, the author still favours the simpler parameterisation, which in that case is the Pareto model.)

Looking over the historical period January 1997 to November 2000, the Exponential parameter series as calculated from the USA yield data can be seen in Figs. 16.5, 16.6 and 16.7. Both the a_0 and a_1 series are well behaved, with no huge spikes or obvious regime shifts, whilst the exponential scale factor still looks hard to handle, mainly because it spends a substantial part of 1998–99 saturating the minimum curvature constraint, i.e. the USA yield curve was nearly linear during this period.

Thus, we have decided on a favoured parameterisation technique, the simple Exponential fit, because of its relative robustness in producing well-behaved parameter series for all the data considered whilst still yielding reasonable overall χ^2 errors. Some yield curve features which are present in the data cannot be adequately modelled by a functional form of this simplicity, but the principal maturity structure of the yield can be represented by the Exponential parameterisation.

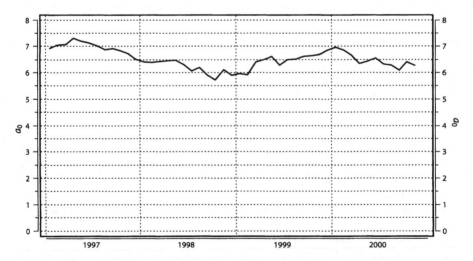

Fig. 16.5 USA January 1997–November 2000. Exponential fit: a_0 parameter series.

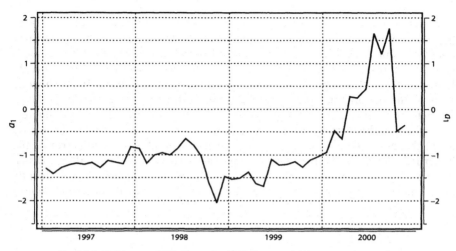

Fig. 16.6 USA January 1997–November 2000. Exponential fit: a_1 parameter series.

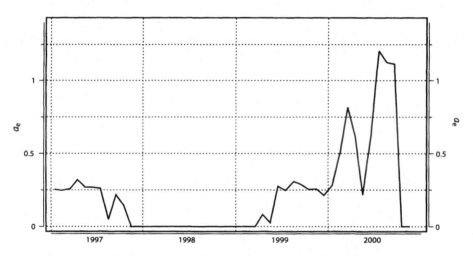

Fig. 16.7 USA January 1997–November 2000. Exponential fit: a_e parameter series.

16.4 Predicting the Yield Curve

Once we have decided on the use of the Exponential parameterisation of the yield curve, we must turn to the problem of performing actual predictions. First we produce time series representing the three Exponential model parameters for each of the markets under investigation (so far we have focused mainly on the USA, Japan and Germany) over the historical period covered by our data. Then we apply any appropriate prediction technique in order to produce a series of predictions for each of our parameters.

To date, in our investigations of yield curve forecasting, we have only investigated the use of univariate predictions, and in what follows we will be showing results obtained using the GMDH method, as described in Chapter 23, which turns out to give the best results in most of the markets. The results for Germany, for the period January 1997 to November 2000, can be seen in Figs. 16.8, 16.9 and 16.10, showing each of the exponential parameters, together with the corresponding GMDH prediction, in turn. The ARV_{12} figures are quite low for all the parameters throughout the historical period, but as we can see from the graphs, these figures are not all that descriptive because of the relative sizes of month-on-month errors to the larger long-term trends. It is also the case (as is fairly convincing after a casual inspection of the graphs) that the GMDH predictions do not perform significantly better than the fairly trivial lag-by-one-month prediction and, in short, that none of

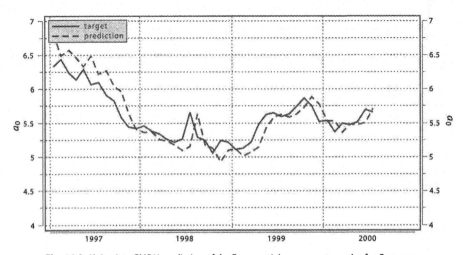

Fig. 16.8 Univariate GMDH prediction of the Exponential a_0 parameter series for Germany.

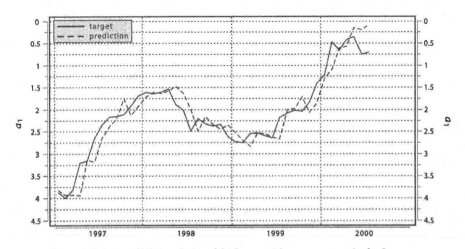

Fig. 16.9 Univariate GMDH prediction of the Exponential a_1 parameter series for Germany.

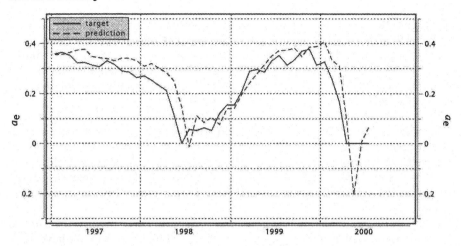

Fig. 16.10 Univariate GMDH prediction of the Exponential a_e parameter series for Germany.

the univariate prediction techniques were able to extract much in the way of patterns within these parameter series.

However, it is by no means obvious that prediction performance at this level is not enough to enable us to predict the overall yield curve shape with a reasonable degree of accuracy. To investigate this possibility we reconstruct the predicted yield curve form the GMDH predicted parameters and compare the resulting curve to the actual yield curve data at the relevant date.

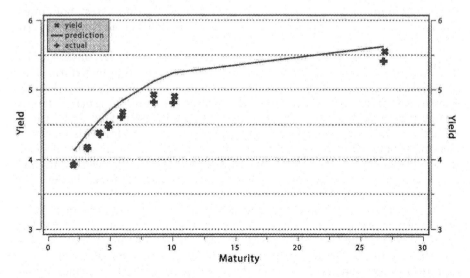

Fig. 16.11 Yield curve prediction for Germany, March 1998, using an Exponential parameterisation with GMDH predictions. We see that the overall level of the actual curve dropped over the course of the month (the + shapes show the actual yield curve for February), whilst the predicted curve shows the right shape but the level has risen. Prediction $\chi^2 = 0.533$.

In Figure 16.11 we show a typical result for a German yield curve prediction. It is clear that there is a lot of room for improvement, since the level shift of the curve has been in the opposite direction to that predicted. However, the general shape of the curve is not too far off the mark, giving us some hope that we might obtain some useful results with this type of method, given a better attempt at predicting the various parameter series.

The average χ^2 error of Exponential model fits over the historical period January 1997 to November 2000 is 0.023, which is the prediction performance obtained for perfect predictions of the yield curve parameters. Using the GMDH the χ^2 error achieved over this same period is 0.627, indicating that the average yield curve prediction is much worse than the best possible Exponential result, giving a general performance level fairly close to (if slightly worse than) than that shown in Figure 16.11.

At this point, we conclude that obtaining good yield curve predictions using a parameterisation, such as the Exponential model, is a tough problem. We have tried to obtain credible forecasts using various univariate techniques in various markets, but with no really remarkable success. However, our results are not completely off the mark, and we retain some hope that we will be able to obtain interesting performance in the near future using a complete multivariate prediction effort.

16.5 Conclusion

In this chapter we have considered the problem of using *NewQuant* prediction techniques to obtain a prediction for the bond yield curve in any of our target markets. The ability to forecast the bond maturity structure is of great interest, both in its own right and as a possible way of increasing the profitability of our core bond portfolio product.

At the present stage of this analysis, we find that we are somewhat constrained by the available data. However, the size of our data set still permits us to perform plausible yield curve parameterisations, provided we only use models with relatively small (three or four) numbers of parameters. Looking at the resulting parameter fits we find that, with the scarcity of data, we need to put in by hand our expectations about the overall scale of the parameter fit in order to obtain stable results. Our analysis singles out the Exponential model as our favoured parameterisation, since its simplicity ensures that the resulting parameter series are well behaved, whilst still containing enough structure to describe most of the features found in the yield curve data.

Although there is still much work left to be done in order to obtain credible prediction performance for the yield curve parameters, the results obtained so far, using only univariate techniques, are not completely discouraging. The predicted yield curves obtained to date still have fairly large χ^2 errors, but we seem able to capture in a very rough way the general shape and trends of the shape of the curve in a consistent way across markets.

We can see several ways in which the research described in this chapter can be extended. Considering first the issue of the underlying data, we note again that we are somewhat starved of points on our yield curves and we could clearly benefit from being able to resolve the yield curve structure in greater detail. It would also be of great interest if we were able to obtain zero-coupon yield curve data directly, since the techniques explored here could be applied directly to this data in order to obtain a spot rate prediction. Such a predictive technique would allow us to perform predictions of bond prices in a very flexible manner.

As we have seen, in order to make competitive maturity predictions the yield curve parameterisation holds some promise, but it needs to be backed up with genuine multivariate predictions. In practice, it should not be very difficult to construct such multivariate prediction models for our yield curve parameters, and in fact this extension of our investigation is already under way.

Finally, it is worth remarking, that the ultimate performance assessment of our attempts at maturity forecasting is whether they enable us to construct a more profitable bond portfolio, but we clearly have some work left to do before we reach such a stage.

17. Predicting Bonds Using the Linear Relevance Vector Machine

Neep Hazarika and John G. Taylor

17.1 Introduction

As described earlier in this book, a large part of the problem in modelling financial markets is to select the relevant inputs. Even if we restrict ourselves to only 40 input time series, and allowing for a choice of lags of up to 24, this still leads to a selection process involving up to 960 variables. This is difficult to achieve automatically in a single step, so various methods have been developed in an attempt to solve this combinatorial explosion.

- Random variable search methods (as described, for example, in Chapter 10).
- Pruning and ridge regression (also known as *shrinkage methods*), in which predictive models are built using automatic reduction of input weights for irrelevant inputs (see Chapter 7 on regularisation and Section 9.6 on ridge regression) (Banfield and Raftery, 1993; Eriksen, 1987; Flury, 1986; Flury *et al.*, 1994; Frank and Friedman, 1993; Hastie and Mallows, 1993; Hastie *et al.*, 1995; Hoerl and Kennard, 1970a, 1970b; Manly and Rayner, 1987; Owen, 1984; Sen and Srivastava, 1990).
- Stochastic search variable selection (SSVS), based on Bayesian methods and Gibbs sampling techniques to obtain *a posteriori* probability distributions on the importance of the inputs. This approach uses an iterative search through the regression coefficients to optimally determine the parameters assumed *a priori* in parameter and hyperparameter distributions for a given set of inputs (Carlin and Chib, 1995; George and McCulloch, 1993, 1996; George *et al.*, 1995; Raftery *et al.*, 1994).
- Special methods are developed that attempt to handle large numbers of inputs, such as network integration (see Chapter 20) and the random vector functional link (RVFL) method. This approach uses random assignment of weights in a multilayered perceptron (MLP), with training to select the hidden-to-output weights, and subsequent sub-selection of those models that gives better prediction accuracy with respect to a pre-set standard (see Chapter 20).

In this chapter we describe an approach which, in principle, would be able to handle up to about a thousand putative inputs, and builds predictive models which allow a ranking of the importance of these inputs. Models can then be constructed using subsets of these variables. Alternatively, models using all the inputs can be developed which contain an explicit ranking of the importance of these inputs, and hence are more transparent than the other approaches.

17.2   The RVM as a Predictor

The version of the RVM described in Chapter 14 was constructed only to act as a pattern recogniser. We will describe its extension for use in both univariate and multivariate prediction.

17.2.1 Linear Univariate Prediction

For the linear univariate case, we describe the dataset as $\{x(d, t), x(t+1)\}$, where $x(d, t)$ is the d-dimensional embedded vector formed by $x(d, t) = \{x(t), x(t-1), ..., x(t-d+1)\}$, normalised to zero mean and unit variance. Then the RVM may be extended as

$$x(t+1) = \sum_{k=1}^{N-d+1} w(d,k)K[x(d,t), x(d,t-k)] + w_0 \qquad (17.1)$$

where $w(d, k)$ is the weight attached to the lag k, $K[.,.]$ is the kernel function associated with the lags, and the overlap of the lagged and unlagged embedded vectors is used to give a prediction at the next time step. Note that if the kernel is taken linear in the lagged variables, this case essentially reduces to fitting an *autoregressive* model to the data.

The RVM described in equation (17.1) may now be applied as a predictor as follows:

1. Iterations are performed on a training set to recalculate values of the hyperparameters $\alpha(d, k)$ and $\sigma^2(d)$ associated with the weights $w(d, k)$ in a manner similar to the methodology discussed in Section 14.4. These are computed for all values of d and values of $\alpha(d, k)$ above a certain critical level (set by some performance criteria) are rejected. This implies that the associated weights $w(d, k)$ are set to zero.

2. The prediction mean squared error (MSE) is then calculated by applying equation (17.1), in a one-step-ahead predictive mode, to an out-of-sample test set.

3. Steps 1 and 2 are repeated for a set of values of the embedding dimension d, and the value of d which achieves a minimum prediction MSE is then selected.

17.2.2 Multivariate Prediction

This may be achieved by including further series $y(t, l)$ (where l is a label for the particular indicator series). The appropriate input data set for the case of a set of indicator variables is then given by the set of corresponding embedding variables $y(d(l), t, l)$, where $d(l)$ is the dimension of the embedding vector associated with the lth indicator variable, and t is the time step. The extension of (17.1) is then given by:

$$x(t+1) = \sum_{n,l} w(d,n,l) K[x(d(l),t), y(d(l),t-n,l)] + w_0 \qquad (17.2)$$

where the summation in equation (17.2) is over the lags n as well as over the further indicator series represented by the indicator labels l, including the original target series, if necessary. There may be different choices of the embedding dimension $d(l)$ for the different indicator series, so $d(l)$, in general, will not be the same for different indicators l.

Equation (17.2) can now directly be used with a set of indicators. The determination of the relevant vectors is performed by evaluation of the non-zero weights, as in the previous linear univariate case. The formulae in Section 14.4 can be applied directly, although labelling of the rows of the Φ matrix will now have to be performed by taking into account the extended vector representation of the weights w; these are now of total dimension LM, where L is the number of indicators, and M is the number of lags. Thus, if the training set consists of N data points, then the dimension of Φ will be $N \times LM$.

17.2.3 Linear Regression Prediction

The above approach to solve the large input variable selection problem is still problematic, because of the very large dimensions of the design matrix Φ constructed from general non-linear kernels $K[.,.]$ in the embedding space.

Instead of a general kernel, a one-dimensional embedding may be constructed, and the kernel can be taken to be linear in the lagged variable. In equation (17.2), this reduces to $K[x(d(l),t), y(d(l),t-n,l)] = y(l)$ with $d(l) = 1, \forall l$. Then equation (17.2) reduces to the standard regression formula, with a corresponding reduction of Φ in equation (14.1). If we denote

$$Y(t) = (y(t,1), y(t-1,1), ..., y(t-L_1,1), y(t,2), y(t-1,2), ...,$$
$$y(t-L_2,2), ..., y(t,M), y(t-1,M), ..., y(t-L_M,M))$$

(where L_i is the maximum lag of the ith input $y(.,i)$, with $1 \le i \le M$), then Φ of equation (14.1) becomes, for the linear regression version of RVM:

$$\Phi = \begin{pmatrix} Y(0) & 1 \\ Y(1) & 1 \\ Y(2) & 1 \\ \vdots & \vdots \\ Y(N-1) & 1 \end{pmatrix} \qquad (17.3)$$

It is this $N \times (\sum_{i=1}^{M}(L_i+1)+1)$ matrix which we have used in our detailed analysis, with $L_i = 23$ and M up to 40.

17.3 Input Variable Selection

Input variable selection can now be performed by using the iterative process described in Section 14.4 and subsequent determination of the associated distribution of the weights (given by equation (14.6)). After convergence of the iterations, input selection can be done by selecting those embedded inputs whose associated α hyperparameters are below a certain pre-specified threshold. It will then be possible to restart the input variable selection process by omitting these inputs, and restarting the process with a smaller data set. The process itself can be iterated a number of times. Note that this approach should not suffer the problems associated with the removal of unimportant data points, since, at least initially, there will be a plethora of points, and so $LM >> N$.

17.3.1 Method to Obtain Variable Ranking

In order to test and benchmark the RVM, a testbed of targets was constructed. The target was composed of a linear sum of previous lags of each input series, with the weights chosen randomly in the interval $(-1, 1)$ $1/2^j, j = 1, 2, ..., 8$. This ensures that we have a range of input strengths, and will allow the determination of the sensitivity level at which a given input can be selected from an overall input appearance. Assessment of the goodness of fit of an RVM model to the test data was performed using the following technique:

1. For the single input case, an analysis of the accuracy of the weight extraction under addition of noise level to the target series is performed. In order to determine this noise scaling effect, we calculate the Euclidean distance between the input weights (used in constructing the target series), and the weights calculated by the RVM model (the trained weight vector): $\| W_{\text{input}} - W_{\text{RVM}} \|$. This metric, denoted by $d(W_i, W_{\text{RVM}})$, is computed for added increasing noise variances to the target. The "distance function" is expected to increase as noise is added to the test data set, and indicates the sensitivity of the RVM model to the correct calculation of the weights. This procedure is repeated for several separate input series from which a target series is constructed.

2. The variance estimated by the RVM model (σ^2_{RVM}) is compared to the variance of noise actually added to the target (σ_i^2). This gives an assessment of the accuracy of the model under varying added noise.

3. Items (1) and (2) are repeated for increasing numbers of inputs, using the normalised metric $d(W_i, W_{\text{RVM}})/\| W_{\text{input}} \|$.

4. The next step is to assess the related dependence of the accuracy of the weight estimation by the RVM model upon expansion of the target construction to more than one combined input series, and for a similar variation of noise levels. This will allow an estimate of the scaling of the computational time with respect to the number of inputs and noise levels.

5. The final step is the determination of the level of removal of irrelevant inputs by adding one or more further time series to the input set which do not contribute to the construction of the target series (hence having zero weights). The

effectiveness of the possible irrelevance detection may be assessed by determining the rescaled Euclidean length of the weight vector components of the linear RVM model along the irrelevant time series components $E_{\text{irrel}} = \| W_{\text{irrel}} \|/ \| W_{\text{input}} \|$, as well as determination of the rescaled weight reconstruction error ($E_W = \| W_{(\text{RVM,relevant})} - W_{\text{input}} \|/\| W_{\text{input}} \|$), where $W_{(\text{RVM, relevant})}$ denotes the non-zero weight values as determined by the model, and W_{input} denotes the input weights actually associated with the target. These quantities will also depend on the noise present in the target construction, so this reconstruction error E_W needs to be investigated for several values of the noise level.

17.3.2 Results for Benchmark Series

Results using the benchmark testbed, constructed as described in the previous section, are described below.

Figure 17.1 shows how the distance function $d(W_i, W_{\text{RVM}})/\| W_{\text{input}} \|$ varies with the noise variance σ_i^2 for the single input series case, two input series, four input series and eight input series respectively. A comparison of the noise standard deviation estimated by the RVM model (σ_{RVM}) with that actually added to the target input series (σ_i) for the corresponding cases is shown in Fig. 17.2. These results show a gradual increase of $d(W_i, W_{\text{RVM}})/\| W_{\text{input}} \|$ with σ_i^2, and also that the noise level in the target is captured accurately by the RVM model, as shown by the linear relationship in the figures, with very little degradation of the model for up to four input series.

We have considered three cases in order to determine the level of removal of irrelevant inputs, as described in Section 17.3.1. We have computed the quantities E_W and E_{irrel} for the following cases:

(a) Two inputs, with one input series irrelevant, i.e. the irrelevant series does not contribute to the construction of the target.

(b) Four inputs, with two irrelevant series.

(c) Eight inputs, with four irrelevant series.

The results are shown in Fig. 17.3. The efficacy of the RVM model for irrelevant input removal is quite robust for added input noise variances of up to 10^2, as can be seen from the relatively low values of E_{irrel}.

17.3.3 Results for Australian Bond Returns

In this section, we describe the results of applying the linear extension of the RVM to the Australian 7–10 year bond returns. We also demonstrate the input selection method using 25 indicator input series with a maximum lag of 24 for each series. This implies an input dimension of 600. Upon ranking the inputs and corresponding lags by the converged weights assigned by the RVM, we try to assess the target series prediction using all weights, only the first 50, and the first 100 of the total of 601 weights. A plot of the weights is shown in Fig. 17.4, and the corresponding histogram is shown in Fig. 17.5. Note that most of the weights have a very small magnitude, as shown by the clustering near $\mu = 0$.

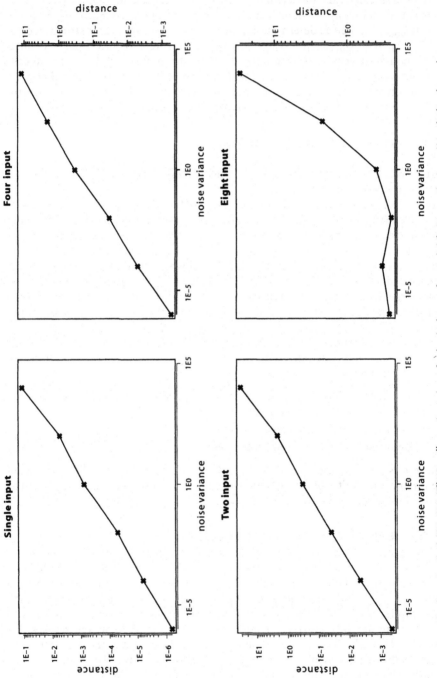

Fig. 17.1 Graph of $d(W_i, W_{RVM})/\| W_{input} \|$ vs. noise variance for the single, two, four and eight input series cases. Note the log–log scale.

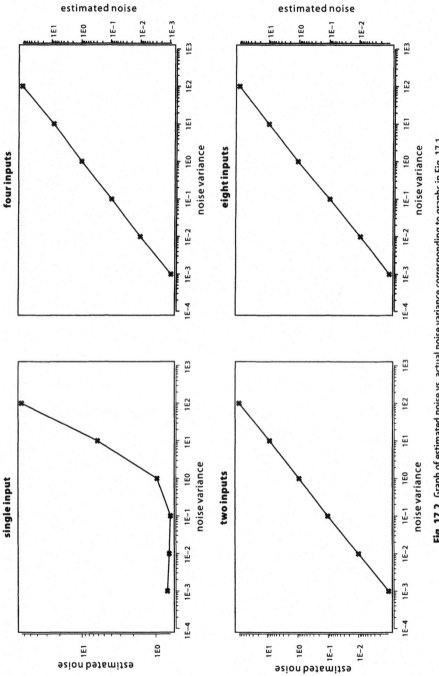

Fig. 17.2 Graph of estimated noise vs. actual noise variance corresponding to graphs in Fig. 17.1.

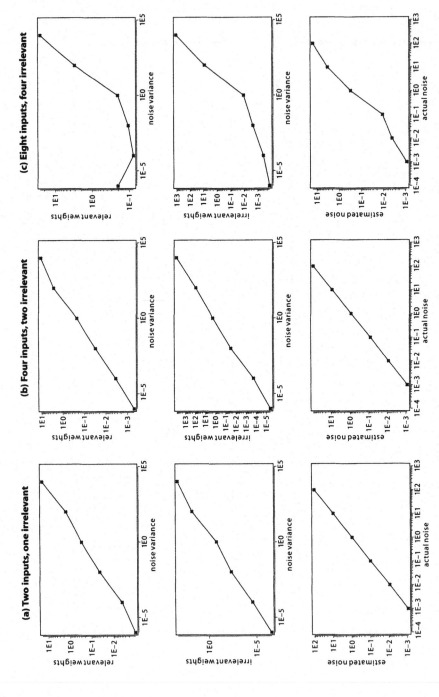

Fig. 17.3 Graph of E_W, E_{irrel} and estimated noise vs. noise variance for (a) two inputs, one irrelevant; (b) four inputs, two irrelevant; and (c) eight inputs, four irrelevant. Note the log–log scale.

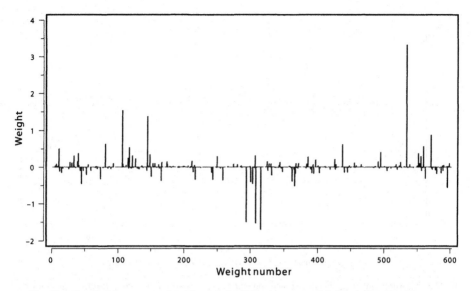

Fig. 17.4 Graph of the converged weights (μ), for 600 inputs to a model of Australian Bond Returns.

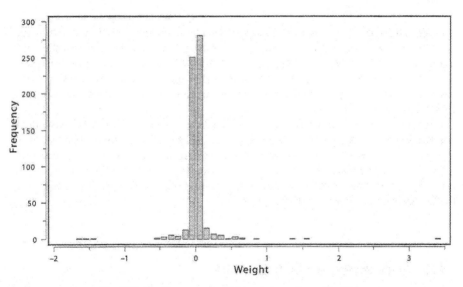

Fig. 17.5 The histogram of weights corresponding to Fig. 17.4.

The metric we use to measure the accuracy of the prediction is the *average relative variance* (ARV), which is defined as

$$\text{ARV} = \frac{1}{\sigma^2 N} \sum_{i=1}^{N} (t_i - \hat{t}_i)^2$$

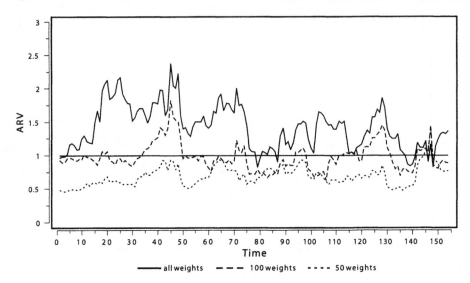

Fig. 17.6 Measurement of prediction accuracy, showing how the running ARV varies across the prediction interval.

where t_i is the true value of target sequence at time i, $\hat{t}_i$ is the prediction, and σ^2 is the variance of the true sequence over the prediction interval. In other words, the ARV is a measure of the ratio of mean squared errors of the prediction method in question, and the method which predicts the mean at every step. A value of ARV = 1 thus corresponds to simply predicting the average, or unconditional mean (see Chapter 15 for details).

In order to evaluate the accuracy of the prediction, the running ARV was calculated, using a moving window of 12 (Fig. 17.6). It is noted that when the number of weights is 100, the ARV has a value below unity throughout most of the prediction interval, implying that for this particular case, the resulting RVM model is not random, but that the model has been able to extract relevant information regarding the target from the input indicator series.

17.4   Summary and Conclusions

The problem of selecting relevant variables from a large potential set of them can be attacked in a number of different ways. The potentially most appealing method for statisticians is to use the full power of Bayesian technology. This leads, first of all, to the development of a Bayesian approach to linear regression, and secondly to the use of such models to rank the importance of variables by the relevant statistical parameter, in this case the weight parameter when it is significant. We developed the linear relevance vector machine based on the relevance vector machine described in Chapter 14. This is based on Bayesian methods for selecting the most appropriate values of the linear regression coefficients in a linear model. It is that model we use to extract a ranking of the input importance in a large set of potential candidates. This was shown in this chapter to be an effective approach to variable selection, firstly on a toy model and then on the non-trivial case of Australian bond series. The approach is thus initially justified. However, it still needs careful control and continued monitoring in its application to the live bond prediction process.

18. Artificial Neural Networks

David Attew

18.1 Introduction

The human brain is essentially a non-linear parallel computer, highly complex and responsible for all of the information-processing abilities that we possess. Its most basic component is the neuron, a specific type of cell used to store data enabling us to think, remember, and apply previously gained knowledge to current situations.

The enormous capabilities of the human brain are due to a massive number of these neurons and their interconnections. It is estimated that ten billion neurons function in the human cortex with many trillions of links or synapses existing between them. The synapses are capable of producing varying degrees of excitation or inhibition on receptive neurons. The output of the brain is determined by the neuron responses and hence the structure and relative strengths of these interconnections. These are developed and adapted throughout life as neurons die and new synaptic links grow – a procedure which provides us with what is commonly known as "experience".

In this chapter we develop the approach of artificial neural networks in greater depth, following from the introductory Chapter 11.

18.2 Artificial Neural Networks

Neural networks are based on the workings of the brain. They are parallel distributed processors that consist of artificial neurons referred to as nodes (shown diagrammatically in Fig. 18.1). These are much simpler in design when compared to a biological neuron (shown in Fig. 11.1). Inputs leading into the node are weighted and summed, and then passed through an activation function before output.

The activation function, $f(x)$, determines the amplitude of the node output and typically defines the limits between ± 1. Commonly used activation functions include the logistic sigmoid and tanh (see Fig. 18.2).

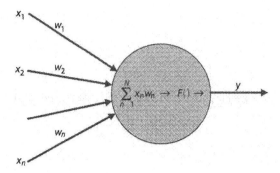

Fig. 18.1 Node diagram. Inputs multiplied by respective weight are summed then passed to the activation function before node output.

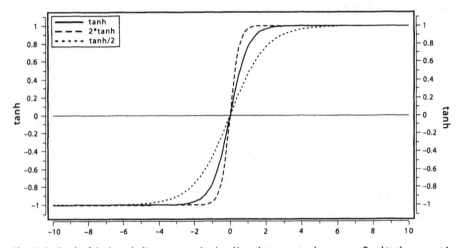

Fig. 18.2 Graph of the hyperbolic tangent activation. Note that output values are confined to the range ±1.

$$f(x) = \frac{1}{1+e^{-x}} \qquad f(x) = \tanh(x)$$

A linear activation function leaves input unaltered. It should be noted that the activation function for each of the hidden nodes is identical, as are the activation functions for each of the output nodes. However output and hidden activations do not have to be, and are usually not, the same.

Nodes are basically non-linear, ensuring that non-linearity is spread throughout the network – important for recognising patterns from an input signal whose underlying mechanism is itself inherently nonlinear.

A layered mapping of these nodes with adaptable links or weights between them comprises the network, which stores knowledge by modification of its own topology through a given learning process. Neural networks are of benefit due to their ability to learn and therefore generalise. Hence if the learning process is applied correctly, the output from the network should be reasonably accurate when used with

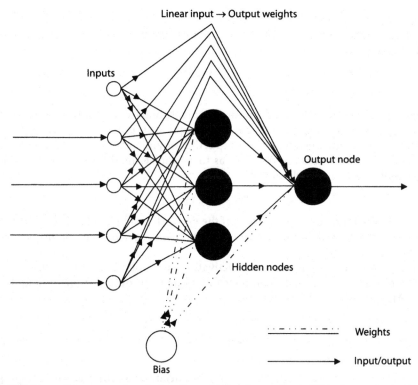

Fig. 18.3 The multi-layer perceptron displayed here with three layers – inputs, hidden layer and output layer. Bias node also included, which can be thought of as an additional input $x_0 = 1$.

previously unseen input data. This makes them a valuable tool for pattern recognition tasks and the modelling of financial time series.

The multi-layer perceptron is a common form of neural network containing several layers of nodes and adaptive weights, as in Fig. 18.3. Inputs are connected to all nodes in the hidden layer and these are linked to all nodes in the output layer. The hidden layer is so called as it constitutes the black box workings of the network, and is therefore hidden from the general user. The example topology in Fig. 18.3 contains only a single output. Nodes and weights from the input, hidden and output layers are designated by i, j, and k suffixes respectively. Let d, h, and a denote the numbers of nodes in each of these respective layers. Bias is also included here as a special case of input where $x_0 = 1$, and linked to hidden and output nodes. Notice in Fig. 18.3 that links exist from the inputs directly to the outputs. These are trainable linear links that add regressor functionality.

Network weights can be described with the following notation. A weight outputted from node i and inputted to node j is symbolised by w_{ij}. The output from any hidden node can now be represented as:

$$y_j = f\left(\sum_{i=0}^{d} w_{ij} x_i\right)$$

where output from node j is given as y_j, the hidden layer activation $f()$ of the sum of d weighted inputs to the node. The basic summed input to any node, e.g. k, shall be written as a_k.

$$a_k = \sum_j w_{jk} y_j$$

Note that in the case for the hidden nodes, y_i corresponds to just the input value x_i.

The weights between nodes are adapted by applying sets of training examples, i.e. an input pattern with a given desired output that we aim to obtain from the network. The network parameters are tuned so as to minimise the difference between the actual and desired network output:

$$\delta_k = y_k - t_k$$

where t_k is the target or desired value. If the network is subjected to enough examples then the parameters should eventually fit the most general case of the problem to which it is exposed.

Let $\bar{f}$ represent the output layer activation function. Then for a three-layer perceptron, as in Fig. 18.3, the complete function for the output from any k node is given by:

$$y_k = \bar{f}\left(\sum_{j=0}^{h} w_{jk} f\left(\sum_{i=0}^{d} w_{ij} x_i \right) \right)$$

The definition of a suitable error function is important for correct network training. This is to be minimised with respect to the network weights. For simple regression problems the least squares error function is satisfactory. Activation functions for the output units are differentiable in terms of input variables and weights, and the least squares error function is differentiable in terms of the network outputs and hence the network weights. These derivatives can then be used to find weight values which minimise the error function using a technique such as gradient descent. A computationally efficient method known as backpropagation (mentioned in Chapter 11) is used to evaluate the derivatives of the error function, as represented by the following equation.

$$\delta_j = f'\left(y_j \sum_k w_{jk} \delta_k \right)$$

where δ_j is the error at node j and

$$\delta_k = f'(y_k) \frac{\partial E^n}{\partial a_k}$$

$$\frac{\partial E^n}{\partial w_{ij}} = \delta_j a_i$$

An input vector x^n is forward propagated through the network and the activations of all hidden and output nodes calculated. δ_k is then calculated using the above equation and this error is propagated backwards through the network to obtain the hidden node errors, δ_j. The required derivatives are then calculated, weights are adjusted, and the cycle begins again with a new input vector.

Initially the network weights are randomly initialised within some reasonable range. These need to be relatively small to avoid activation function saturation leading to tiny function derivatives and therefore a flat error surface that is difficult to minimise. Likewise weight values that are too small lead to slow, inefficient network training. During training there is a significant risk of finding and getting stuck in local minima whilst reducing the error function; therefore careful selection of these initial weights is of importance. Indeed, the quality of network results is very sensitive to initial conditions. An initial value of unity plus some small zero mean Gaussian contribution can be used to generate initial weights. To remove initial condition effects many networks can be trained using different initialisations and then the results averaged. This is known as a "committee" of networks.

As stated above, gradient descent is a simple and effective network training algorithm. The initial weights, which can be represented by the vector w_0, are adapted iteratively along a negative gradient to achieve the greatest decrease in overall error.

$$\Delta w^{(\tau)} = -\eta \nabla E_{w^{(\tau)}}$$

τ represents the current process step and η represents the learning rate, usually a small value, which controls the rate of descent (Bishop, 1995). Too large a value for η leads to wild swings in the error movement and will render the algorithm useless. The reverse and the descent will progress unbearably slowly.

18.2.1 Momentum

A problem with this method is the lack of speedy convergence to the minimum. The gradient vector $-\nabla E$ does not point to the minimum of the error function, but instead staggers towards it in a series of oscillations. A momentum term can be added to the formula to effectively introduce a level of inertia to the descent movement, smoothing these oscillations. The revised gradient descent formula can now be stated as:

$$\Delta w^{(\tau)} = -\eta \nabla E_{w^{(\tau)}} + \mu \Delta w^{(\tau-1)}$$

where μ is the momentum operator.

18.2.2 Stopping

Another factor crucial to training success is the stopping criterion. An effective method is to test network performance on previously unseen data during training and halt the procedure when the out-of-sample error no longer falls but begins to increase. The generalisation capabilities of the network are of paramount importance and overtraining on a particular training set will yield a very low training error, but give rise to extremely poor out-of-sample performance. This is known as overfitting, i.e. when the network parameters have been adjusted to fit the training examples too specifically.

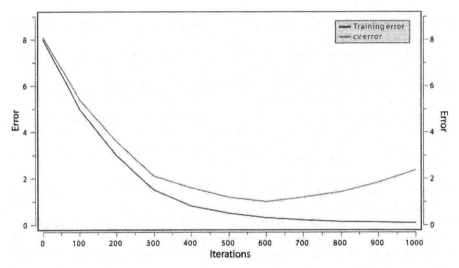

Fig. 18.4 Plot of training error versus number of backpropagated error minimisation loops. The error on the validation set is lowest after around 600, whereas the test error continues to reduce.

To achieve good performance on data previously unseen by the network it is necessary to divide the data into three distinct segments. The error function is minimised on the first segment, the *training set*, and generalisation performance is obtained from the *validation set*. However, constant appraisal of generalisation performance on the validation data can lead to overfitting on this also, so it is necessary to keep a segment of data that is completely unseen by the network in order to test true out-of-sample generalisation abilities. This is the *test set*.

The graph in Fig. 18.4 shows a plot of training epochs against error for a time series example. Also plotted is the network error on the validation set, highlighting their relationship. It can be seen that the lowest validation error occurs after approximately 600 training loops, long before the training set error begins to flatten out after around 900.

18.2.3 Cross-validation

A problem with training, validation and test set division is that usually monthly financial series suffer from a lack of available data. Here it becomes useful to utilise a technique known as cross-validation.

The data is divided into N separate divisions. The network is trained on $N - 1$ of these segments and its out-of-sample performance is evaluated using the one remaining. This is repeated for all possible combinations N; for example, if we divide the data into $N = 10$ sections the network will be trained 10 times. The results are then averaged over these 10 results. This ensures that all of the data is used in validation assessment whilst a high proportion at each stage has been utilised for training.

Another possible method is the bootstrap. This involves taking many random samples composed of individual points from the available data in order to provide a greatly increased number of network training examples. It is the hope that these will enable the network to approximate the underlying function that is generating the data.

Another important consideration with financial prediction is that the data is usually non-stationary with the fundamental dynamics changing over time. The network can adapt if the learning process (training) is ongoing, responding to any underlying changes in the input signal. It therefore can become an extremely useful tool for adaptive pattern classification, either in real time or over any chosen time frame window. The time frame for network retraining should be long enough to ensure that the system is largely unaffected by short-term changes in the input patterns which may be fallacious when considering the underlying general function to be mapped, but also short enough to adapt to any changes that are of significance.

18.2.4 Recurrent Neural Networks

Alternative topologies to be considered are neural networks with recurrence. These incorporate a feedback loop within the architecture to effectively provide the network with a one step memory of previous runs (Haykin, 1999). This can enable the network to model data series trends that were previously unrecognisable without this additional historical time delay feed. A great number of possible topologies can be constructed to this end, but in this example a layer containing *context* nodes is added to store information fed from the hidden layer for a single time cycle. The weights feeding from the hidden to the context nodes are fixed (untrainable) with a weight equal to unity. During a forward feed the context layer then introduces stored information back into the network through trainable weights linked to hidden and output nodes with a conventional mapping, i.e. each context node linked to each hidden and output. Note that the direct input to output links still exist affording a linear aspect to the network.

18.3 Models

To describe predictive neural network performance using financial time series, feedforward network architectures consisting of 20 inputs, bias, two hidden nodes and a single output were trained on the 13 major bond and equity series. Network design was equivalent to that shown in Fig. 18.3, with all nodes in adjacent layers connected and linear links existing between the input–output nodes. Cross-validation with 10 divisions yielded better results than the bootstrap and was therefore chosen as the preferred data sampling method. Bias, $x_0 = 1$, was applied to both the hidden and output nodes.

A recurrent neural network of the type displayed in Fig. 18.5 was also utilised. Fixed weights $=1$ linked the hidden to context nodes in a one-to-one mapping and trainable weights linked each context back to the hidden and output nodes.

In each of these architectures, important restrictions arise as a consequence of the size of the data set. With no more than 200 data points severe limitations emerge

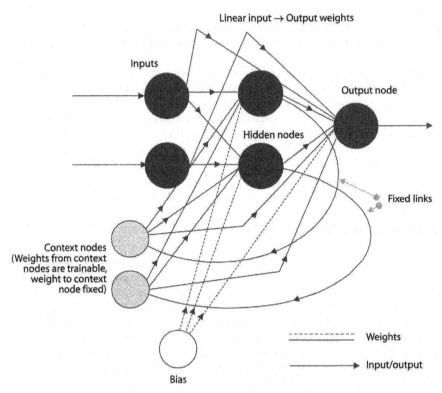

Linear input → Output weights

Inputs

Output node

Hidden nodes

Fixed links

Context nodes
(Weights from context
nodes are trainable,
weight to context
node fixed)

—————————— Weights

————————▶ Input/output

Bias

Fig. 18.5 The recurrent neural network. Linear links from the inputs through to outputs are included. Fixed weights from each hidden node to a context node carry information to be stored for a single time cycle, after which trainable weights feed this history back into hidden and output nodes.

due to the property (Amari *et al.*, 1995) that the generalisation error is proportional to the number of free parameters over the data set size. Keeping this to a minimum requires as few parameters as possible, restricting the number of inputs and hidden nodes dramatically. Thus for a feedforward network (N inputs and two hidden nodes) each new input gives a further two free parameters and each additional hidden node increases this number by ($N + 2$). With linear links from 20 inputs to a single output and two hidden nodes, the feedforward neural network yields 65 free parameters – which is already on the edge of good generalisation.

To consider practical examples, USA bonds returns with data dating back to 1985 are discussed. Bond series target and predictions (out-of-sample) for the period from January 1998 to December 2001 are shown (Figs. 18.6 and 18.7) for the feedforward and recurrent networks.

The USA bonds were the best market and the results are particularly favourable, with evidence for the neural network > 10 and for the recurrent network > 100. In all but three of the 13 major bond and equity markets the recurrent networks performed better than their normal feedforward counterparts, suggesting that the feedback memory was indeed adding value. However, this improvement was in some cases only marginal.

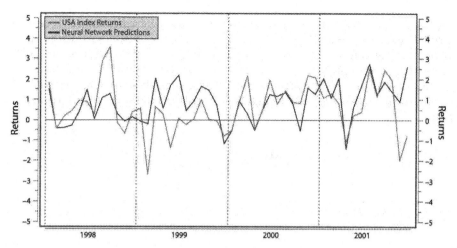

Fig. 18.6 Neural network predictions for USA bond returns.

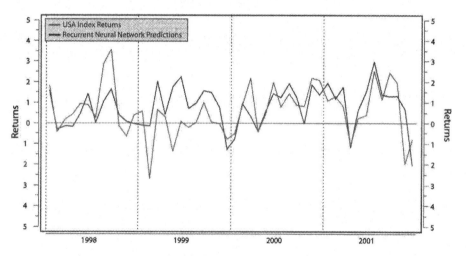

Fig. 18.7 Recurrent neural network predictions for USA bond returns.

18.4 Summary

Overall, although only a couple of examples have been touched upon here, a vast variation in neural network architectures can be designed and implemented, making the possibilities for experimentation numerous. Thus, for example, an increased number of hidden layers could be considered to achieve greater functionality. However, this is not possible with limited data sets, so we are restricted here to the single-layer network application with only two hidden nodes.

Artificial neural networks provide a flexible and robust non-linear modelling technique capable of adapting to market changes, which makes them powerful tools for financial prediction. With associated expertise and applications that stretch beyond identification and classification tasks, the many possibilities surrounding error functions, alternative parameter optimisation algorithms, data pre- and post-processing, the introduction of radial basis function networks, and Bayesian methods, there is clearly much more that can be written about what has become the wide-ranging subject area of neural computation than the space restrictions here permit.

19. Adaptive Lag Networks

Jimmy Shadbolt

19.1 The Problem

Standard distributed lag models have a number of built-in assumptions that are made to simplify the problem, but are difficult to justify in real-life applications.

They postulate that relationships between model inputs and the target data series have a fixed number of integer lags. There is no reason to believe that the influence of an explanatory variable should take exactly a whole number of months to impact on the target series. In fact, it would be very unlikely. The assumption is made purely because of the frequency at which the data is available.

If the lag on a relationship was a non-integer value of, say, 6.5 months, then examining the relationships using a monthly sampling frequency would show the lag to be switching over time between the integer values of 6 and 7 months. It is highly likely that the relationship would never be found.

Furthermore, there is no reason to believe that a lag is actually fixed at all. At different phases of the business cycle we would expect the influences to propagate at different rates. The lag may be 8 months in a slow growth period, but 6 months in high-growth periods. Given this, a search for a lagged relationship may fail even when a very strong relationship is present.

We must also confront the problem that we are doing some sort of linear filtering to select a small number of potentially important inputs from a large universe; then, if there is a non-linear relationship between a variable and our target, a search in a linear framework may find it (in the case of mildly non-linear functions), but most probably it will not.

19.2 Adaptive Lag Networks

To address these deficiencies we have developed a unique neural network model, using adaptive lags (Fig. 19.1). The network uses an adaptive filter (described by a kernel function) on each input. This applies a lag selector and a smoother to the input data, with both the lag selector and the degree of smoothing being

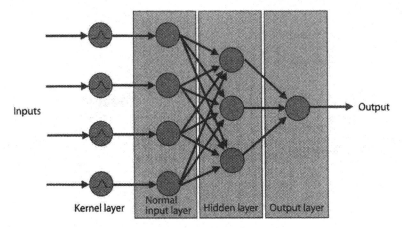

Fig. 19.1 The adaptive lag network.

adapted during network training. The lag (centre of the kernel) takes on real values, and the width of the kernel allows the influences from a number of adjacent integer lags to come through. The kernel is adapted by the network at the same time as the network weights, so that the lag is being selected on the basis of a non-linear relationship.

The filter is defined by a kernel function:

$$K = \frac{1}{(1+\eta_1)} \frac{1}{(1+\eta_2)} (1 - e^{-\beta}) \qquad (19.1)$$

where

$$\eta_1 = e^{-\beta(t-d+1/2)}$$
$$\eta_2 = e^{-\beta(d-t+1/2)}$$

The parameter d determines the centre of the lags selected by the kernel, whilst β fixes the width of the lag selection window.

Figure 19.2 shows the kernel for a lag of 6.5 months at various values of β.

The centre of the kernel is a real-valued lag, with an adaptive width which allows the function to estimate a distributed lag model. In the example shown, a lag of 6.5 and a β of 2 would imply a weighted smoothing using data between lags of 3 and 10 (the weights being the kernel values). The spread of the lags would allow the network to pick out an input with a lag that varied in this range.

The kernel is used to transform an input data series such that the input data value I at time t is given by:

$$I(t) = \sum_{i=-w}^{i=w} K(i)x(t-d+i) \qquad (19.2)$$

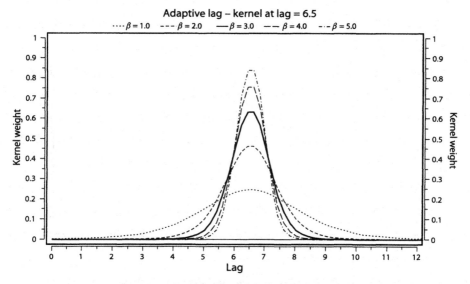

Fig. 19.2 The kernel used in adaptive lag networks.

19.3 Training the Adaptive Lag Network

The weights in the neural network can be trained in the normal manner by backpropagation.

The kernel training requires the derivatives of the error with respect to the lag d:

$$\frac{\partial E}{\partial d} = \frac{\partial E}{\partial y}\frac{\partial y}{\partial d}$$

y is the transformed input (the convolution of the kernel function with the actual input series). See Fig. 19.3.

$$\frac{\partial y}{\partial d} = \frac{\partial K(d,\beta)}{\partial d}x(t) = \beta K(d,\beta)\left(\frac{1}{\eta_3(1+\eta_1)} - \frac{1}{\eta_4(1+\eta_2)}\right)x(t) \tag{19.3}$$

where η_1 and η_2 are as above, and

$$\eta_3 = e^{\beta(t-d+1/2)}$$

$$\eta_4 = e^{\beta(d-t+1/2)}$$

We can train the width β using:

$$\frac{\partial K}{\partial \beta} = \frac{e^{-\beta}}{(1+\eta_1)(1+\eta_2)} + K\left(\frac{\eta_1(t-d+1/2)}{(1+\eta_1)} + \frac{\eta_2(d-t+1/2)}{(1+\eta_2)}\right) \tag{19.4}$$

See Fig. 19.4.

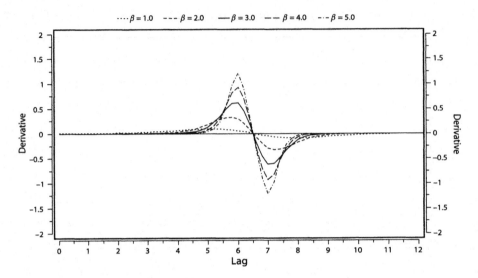

Fig. 19.3 The derivative of the kernel with respect to the lag.

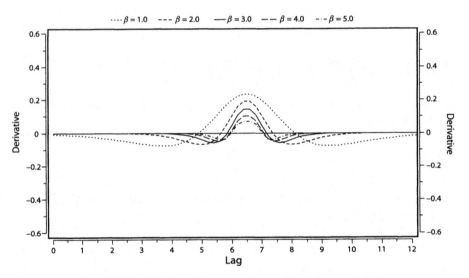

Fig. 19.4 The derivative of the kernel with respect to β, the kernel width.

19.4 Test Results

The network was tested on simple data where the target series is random data ($N(0,1)$) and the input is created by lagging the target by 4.0 and adding noise. The average results over 20 runs show that the lag can be picked up very well with a very high β (a narrow kernel) (Table 19.1).

Table 19.1 Test results for adaptive lag network on noise data

Noise level	Lag	σ_{lag}	β	σ_β
0.0	4.000	0.000	8.11	0.16
0.2	4.002	0.009	8.04	0.23
0.4	3.996	0.025	8.07	0.19
0.6	3.990	0.033	8.06	0.35
0.8	3.996	0.021	8.31	0.35
1.0	3.986	0.061	7.66	0.44

Table 19.2 Test results for adaptive lag network on data with varying lag

Noise level ε	Lag	σ_{lag}	β	σ_β
1.2	4.045	0.194	1.99	0.41
1.4	3.940	0.298	1.66	0.58
1.6	3.765	0.237	1.73	0.59
1.8	3.889	0.355	1.31	0.30
2.0	4.051	0.299	1.15	0.22

If we also add noise to the lag (such that lag $= 4.0 \pm \varepsilon$) we get the results shown in Table 19.2.

We see that if the lag drifts around about a centre at 4.0 the network will find a lag of 4.0, but with a wide kernel. From Fig. 19.2 we can see that a β of 2 corresponds to a kernel width of ~2, while a β of 1 corresponds to a width of ~6. This is in agreement with the widths expected from the noise levels.

19.5 Modelling

We use the adaptive lag networks for two purposes: scanning large datasets in a univariate (single input series) mode to establish which data inputs may be useful, and combining the best potential inputs to make multivariate models.

The univariate phase uses a bootstrap procedure to create a probability distribution function (PDF) along the temporal (lag) axis for each input, along with in-sample and cross-validation (CV) ARV statistics. The PDF enables lags to be chosen on the basis of maximum likelihood. The ARV statistics enable lags chosen on the basis of outliers to be excluded and so ensure good generalisation.

This information is used to choose the most likely lagged inputs for use in creating multivariate models.

Figure 19.5 shows an example plot of the statistics for the influence of the industrial sector on USA bonds. It shows that there are no particularly preferable lags, and that the out-of-sample ARV plot moves as a mirror image of the in-sample ARV. This is the behaviour of a model input that has no influence on the target series. Low in-sample ARVs lead to high out-of-sample ARVs, a typical demonstration of over-training and fitting into the noise.

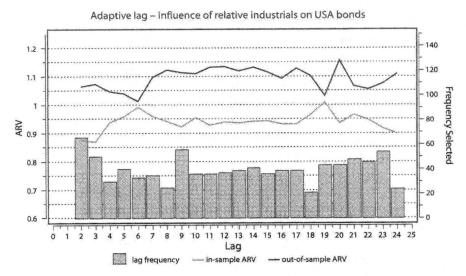

Fig. 19.5 Bootstrap results for the relative strength of the industrial sector as an influence on USA bonds.

Figure 19.6 shows a similar plot, this time for the influence of the relative service sector on Japanese bonds. It shows a clear preference for lags 5 and 21. At both of these lags the out-of-sample ARVs decrease with decreasing in-sample ARVs, indicating a clear influence of the service sector on the bonds.

Multivariate models use the lagged inputs chosen in the above manner. The lags will be initialised to their optimal value (found on a univariate basis), but during

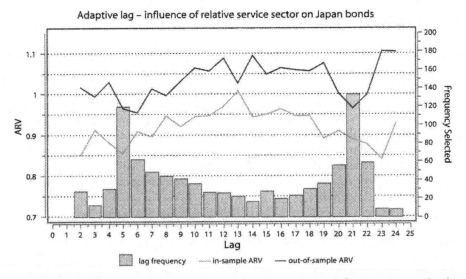

Fig. 19.6 Bootstrap results for the relative strength of the service sector as an influence on Japanese bonds.

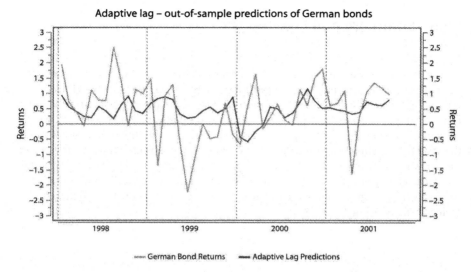

Fig. 19.7 Out-of-sample prediction of a model of German bond returns.

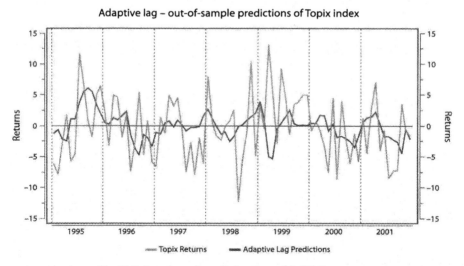

Fig. 19.8 Out-of-sample prediction of a model of Topix returns.

training the model is allowed to adjust the lags. This is done mainly to help avoid training getting trapped in local minima.

Figure 19.7 shows out-of-sample predictions for a model of average maturity German bond returns for a period of 45 months. Over the full period the evidence for the model (as defined in Chapter 15) is approximately 13. Figure 19.8 shows predictions for the Topix index. The evidence is approximately 32.

19.6 Summary and Conclusions

The chapter has described a highly adaptive approach to lag selection in the context of non-linear neural network models. A method for adaptively determining the optimal lags to be selected for a range of inputs, by using neural network training, was given. The training rule is that of gradient descent on the mean square error cost function, regarded as a function of the width and position of the lag kernel, which thereby allows choice of the appropriate lagged variables giving information about the target. This approach was applied in detail, first to a model in which the target was constructed as a linear combination of random series, and then to a particular bond model, showing the service sector effect on Japanese bonds. This approach has to be carefully monitored during live use in bond portfolio construction to ensure added value is being achieved.

20. Network Integration

Sebastian Larsson

In this chapter we will consider the network integration prediction technique. We will start by describing the general theoretical basis for making predictions using ensembles of neural networks. We will then proceed to describe the specific features of the implementation and then conclude by presenting some results for the USA bond market.

20.1 Making Predictions with Network Ensembles

In general, if we are trying to predict some quantity y_{t+1}, we need to consider the conditional probability distribution $p(y_{t+1}|D_t^+)$ where D_t^+ is all the data available at times up to and including the time t when the prediction is made. All statistical information about y_{t+1} which can be deduced at time t is contained in this probability distribution and in particular: the mean of the distribution

$$\hat{y}_{t+1} \equiv \int y_{t+1} p(y_{t+1}|D_t^+) dy_{t+1} \tag{20.1}$$

is the best prediction for y_{t+1} in the mean square sense.

Although it is this mean value which we are ultimately interested in, for the moment we will return to the full probability distribution $p(y_{t+1}|D_t^+)$. In order to make any progress in estimating this distribution, we are going to restrict our attention to some definite parametric family of probability distribution functions. Our analysis then reduces to the more manageable problem of estimating the distributions of out chosen parameters on the basis of the observed data. Thus, without explicitly stating what our set of parameterised distributions is, we introduce a family w of parameters, giving us

$$\begin{aligned} p(y_{t+1}|D_t^+) &= \int p(y_{t+1}, w|D_t^+) dw \\ &= \int p(y_{t+1}|w, D_t^+) p(w|D_t^+) dw \end{aligned} \tag{20.2}$$

which expresses the distribution for y_{t+1} in terms of the distributions conditional on the w taking on a specific set of values and the distribution of these w parameters.

Next, we split the past data into two parts: the information relevant to determining how the parameters w are distributed, which we will call D_t, and x_t on which the y_{t+1} distribution is directly dependent. Rewriting equation (20.2) with this new notation we obtain

$$p(y_{t+1}|D_t^+) = \int p(y_{t+1}|w, x_t, D_t) p(w|x_t, D_t) dw$$
$$= \int p(y_{t+1}|w, x_t) p(w|D_t) dw$$

(20.3)

and we can now evaluate the desired prediction by taking the mean of both sides to yield

$$\hat{y}_{t+1}(x_t) = \int \hat{y}_{t+1}(x_t; w) p(w|D_t) dw$$

(20.4)

where the x are some set of appropriate parametric functions.

Thus, the key to making a prediction, once we have chosen a specific method of parameterisation, is to estimate the probability distribution of the parameters which can be inferred from past data and to perform the above integral. Because of the well-known universal approximation theorem of artificial neural networks, such networks provide a natural candidate for the family of parametric functions in equation (20.4), where the parameters w are now simply the network weights.

Within this framework, the use of one single neural network for predictions is equivalent to assuming that the weight distribution $p(w|D)$ is a delta-function peak at some particular weight value, w_0 say. The usual neural network training is then tantamount to choosing that single optimal weight, in order to provide a good approximation to the integral in equation (20.4). In general, any reasonable estimate of what the weight-space distribution function actually looks like will be much broader than what is implied by the use of a single neural network, since a narrow distribution would require a plentiful supply of training data. The use of single networks in such situations frequently lead to poor, overtrained, predictions where too much credence is given to patterns observed in the limited data which is available.

If we were to become more ambitious in our attempts to approximate to the integral over weight-space in equation (20.4) by averaging the outputs produced by a large number of neural networks with weights drawn from the distribution $p(w|D)$, we would expect to see much better prediction performance. In practice, however, it can be difficult to estimate the form of the weight-space distribution from the available data (although we can make good progress here using Bayes' theorem and some reasonable assumptions about the data) and then to generate weights with the given distribution in a numerically tractable way. Thus the theoretical basis for *network integration* prediction techniques, i.e. using averages over large ensembles of neural networks, is relatively straightforward, although the exact method in which the appropriate sets of network weights are chosen can pose many practical difficulties.

20.2 The Network Integrator

We have experimented with a substantial number of methods for performing predictions using a network integration approach. To date, the most favourable results have been obtained when operating in the so-called "weak classifier" mode (Demiral *et al.*, 1995) and we shall proceed by describing briefly what this procedure entails.

The most important feature of the chosen operating mode is that we construct the network ensemble to give optimal predictions of the *sign* of target fluctuations, rather than directly predicting the amplitude of the target series. Once the target series is normalised to zero mean and unit variance, the performance of a given network predictor in the ensemble is assessed only on the basis of the number of times it predicts the correct sign for the data in the training set. This method is in effect making the simplifying assumption that the weight distribution is a decreasing function of the number of correct sign predictions only.

For every prediction target series an ensemble of 2000 sets of weights (each corresponding to a simple feedforward neural network) are generated. However, rather than trying to draw these weights directly from some appropriate estimate of the distribution function $p(w \mid D)$, we instead draw weights randomly from a Gaussian distribution (zero mean and fixed variance) and then try to capture the general shape of a more realistic weight distribution by rejecting networks with over 40% misclassified signs. In addition, we also assign a weight to each weight set in our ensemble so as to favour networks with high degrees of accuracy in predicting signs for the test set, thus allowing us to approximate to $p(w \mid D)$ even when the shape of this distribution is significantly different from the fixed Gaussian distribution.

The resulting sign-predicting network ensemble is finally re-scaled to the target mean and standard deviation in order to obtain a direct prediction for the chosen target. This use of sign rather than amplitude accuracy in accumulating the network ensemble allows us to obtain reasonable models of the weight space probability distribution using rejection sampling within manageable computing time, whilst still producing a respectable prediction performance for the overall target series.

As an example, we consider the use of the network integration method to predict USA bond returns over the 46 month period from January 1998 to October 2001. In Fig. 20.1 we see the target series as well as the predictions over the same period provided by the network integration technique and a prediction benchmark (here the average over the previous twelve months).

We see that both prediction series seem to capture the general trend of the target data whilst they differ substantially in their actual monthly values. The ratio of evidences (the use of evidence assessment is discussed in Chapter 15) over the entire assessment period is just over 13, indicating that the network integrator is providing a significantly better level of prediction performance than our simple benchmark.

In conclusion, we remark that, as well as being a natural extension to standard neural network techniques, the network integration scheme also adds value to our efforts of prediction by allowing large numbers of inputs to be used for each target series. Other neural network techniques, which are more susceptible to

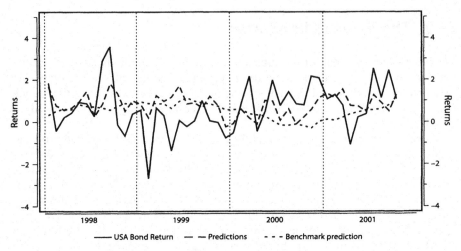

Fig. 20.1 The prediction performance of the network integration and the 12 month moving average benchmark for USA bond returns.

overtraining problems, can often only handle a limited number of inputs at a time. The extensive input selection process required for such models can potentially result in significant loss of information, which can be more easily captured by a network integration prediction. Further, by accumulating statistics of the weight space distribution during the rejection sampling part of the prediction process, it also possible to get some idea of the form of $p(w \mid D)$ and thus to perform an analysis of the relative significance of various input signals.

20.3   The Random Vector Functional Link (RVFL)

Although we do not use it, a brief mention of the RVFL is in order.

The RVFL method combines elements of network integration techniques with more traditional neural network training. The idea is simply to reduce the number of weights that we need to integrate over by performing a one-shot training step on the output weights. For linear output nodes the error function can be minimised exactly with respect to the output weights by a simple matrix inversion (using normal gradient descent training should also be very fast), since the error surface is quadratic in these terms. This training step effectively reduces the dimensionality of the parameter space for which we then perform a network integration whilst at the same time substantially reducing the in-sample error of any one network in our network integration ensemble. The expectation is that RVFL would be an attractive hybrid method which can efficiently train neural networks to obtain low in-sample errors whilst still maintaining the protection form over training that we expect from a network integration method.

20.4 Summary

The method of randomly throwing weight sets for neural networks, with subsequent averaging over suitably good randomly generated nets, has been developed over the past decade to obviate the problem of long training times for networks with a large number of variables (of the order of 50 or above). We have used that approach here, suitably developed, in order to speed up the creation of non-linear predictive models for bond and equity time series. The method we developed was shown to lead to efficient predictors of the actual values of the time series in the case of the USA bond series. It can be used effectively for up to about 100 inputs, although there is loss of effectiveness with many more inputs. Thus the approach is used in cooperation with an input selection method such as the RVM approach of Chapter 17, which would be used to reduce from 1000 or so inputs to lower than 100.

21. Cointegration

A. Neil Burgess

21.1 Introduction

A common theme in Computational Finance is that the predictability of financial time series is to some extent a function of the data-representation adopted (see Burgess (1999) for a review). In particular a number of authors use multivariate techniques to create *combinations* of time-series, generally as a preliminary step to performing predictive modelling itself. Such methods include factor models (Jacobs and Levy, 1988), canonical correlation (Lo and MacKinley, 1995), relative prices (Bentz *et al.*, 1996), principal component analysis (Burgess, 1996), cointegration (Burgess and Refenes, 1995, 1996; Steurer and Hann, 1996) and independent component analysis (Back and Weigend, 1998).

Such methods can be motivated from two perspectives: on a purely practical basis the combinations thus created represent time series which are not directly tradable in the market-place, and hence are less likely to have had any predictable component "arbitraged away"; a second motivation is that the combinations can be seen as a means of improving the signal-to-noise ratio of the data, and thus enhancing the predictable component in the data. This second view can be seen as a consequence of modern asset pricing models such as the capital asset pricing model (CAPM) of Sharpe (1964) and the "arbitrage pricing theory" (APT) of Ross (1976). Essentially these pricing models take the form:

$$\Delta y_{i,t} = \alpha_i + \beta_{i,M} \Delta Mkt_t + \beta_{i,1}\Delta f_{1,t} + \ldots + \beta_{i,n}\Delta f_{n,t} + \varepsilon_{i,t} \qquad (21.1)$$

In the CAPM model, $n = 0$ and the systematic component of asset price dynamics Δy_t is solely attributed to the link with market movements ΔMkt_t. In the APT model, and so-called "multi-factor" versions of CAPM, there may be a number of additional market-wide risk factors $\Delta f_{j,t}$. The essence of modern portfolio theory is that in well-diversified portfolios, the net effect of the asset-specific risks $\varepsilon_{i,t}$ is small and thus the major drivers of portfolio performance are the underlying risk factors, ΔMkt_t and $\Delta f_{j,t}$.

This distinction between the dynamics due to market-wide risk factors and the asset-specific component of price dynamics provides a strong motivation for believing that the returns of appropriate combinations of asset prices may be potentially more predictable than the raw (individual) returns. Consider a portfolio consisting of a long (bought) position in an asset y_1 and a short (sold) position in an asset y_2. If the asset price dynamics in each case follow a data-generating process of the form shown in equation (21.1), then the *combined* returns $\Delta y_{1,t} - \Delta y_{2,t}$ are given by:

$$\Delta y_{1,t} - \Delta y_{2,t} = (\alpha_1 - \alpha_2)$$
$$+ (\beta_{1,Mkt} - \beta_{2,Mkt})\Delta Mkt_t + (\beta_{1,1} - \beta_{2,1})\Delta f_{1,t} + \ldots \qquad (21.2)$$
$$+ (\beta_{1,n} - \beta_{2,n})\Delta f_{n,t} + (\varepsilon_{1,t} - \varepsilon_{2,t})$$

If the factor exposures are similar, i.e. $\beta_{1,j} \approx \beta_{2,j}$, then the proportion of variance which is caused by market-wide factors will be correspondingly reduced and the potential predictability correspondingly increased. This effect is illustrated in Fig. 21.1.

Thus the motivation for a relative value approach is that asset prices viewed in relative (i.e. combined) rather than absolute (i.e. individual) terms are both more amenable to statistical arbitrage and potentially more predictable. The analysis above demonstrates that, in principle, appropriately constructed combinations of prices can be largely immunised against market-wide sources of risk and will instead highlight the asset-specific aspects of the price dynamics. Such combinations of assets are amenable to statistical arbitrage because they represent opportunities to exploit predictable components in asset-specific price dynamics in a manner which is (statistically) independent of changes in the level of the market as a whole, or other market-wide sources of uncertainty. Furthermore, as the asset-specific component of the dynamics is not directly observable by market participants it is plausible that regularities in the dynamics may exist from this perspective which have not yet been "arbitraged away" by market participants.

This analysis helps to explain the popularity of relative value strategies amongst hedge funds, proprietary trading desks and other "risk arbitrageurs". In its simplest

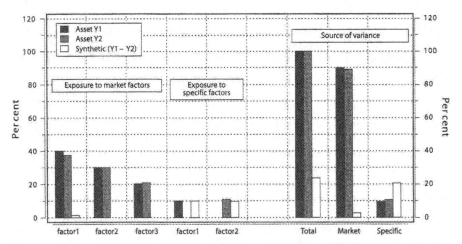

Fig. 21.1 Illustration of advantages of modelling within a combined price framework: whilst the individual assets Y1 and Y2 are primarily influenced by changes in market-wide risk factors, the price changes of the "synthetic asset" Y1 − Y2 are largely immunised from such effects and magnify the effect of stock-specific factors, which are more likely to contain systematic (and hence potentially predictable) components.

form this approach is called "pairs trading" and consists of trend and reversion analysis of a graph of relative prices, with the assets X and Y being selected on the basis of intuition, economic fundamentals, long-term correlations or simply past experience. Opportunities for pairs trading in this simple form, however, are reliant upon the existence of naturally similar pairs of assets, and thus are very limited. We describe below the details of our methodology in which cointegration techniques are used to create a wider range of opportunities, by constructing synthetic "pairs" in the form of appropriate combinations of two or more assets.

21.2 Construction of Statistical Mispricings

In an analogy to the no-arbitrage relationships upon which riskless arbitrage strategies are based, the objective of our methodology is to identify combinations of assets which represent statistical "fair price" relationships upon which to base "statistical arbitrage" strategies.

More specifically, given an asset universe U_A and a particular "target asset", $T \in A$, our objective is to create a "synthetic asset" $SA(T)$ such that the value of the synthetic asset can be considered a statistical "fair price" for the target asset:

$$E[T] = SA(T)_t \tag{21.3}$$

Furthermore, the fair price relationship in equation (21.3) should be such that deviations from the relationship can be considered as "statistical mispricings":

$$M_t = T_t - SA(T)_t \tag{21.4}$$

where the dynamics of the mispricing time series M_t contain a predictable component which can be exploited as the basis of a statistical arbitrage trading strategy.

Our methodology for constructing statistical mispricings is based upon the use of cointegration techniques to estimate the fair price relationships. A "cointegrating regression" (Granger, 1983) is used to estimate a linear combination of assets which exhibits the maximum possible long-term correlation with the target asset T. The coefficients of the linear combination are estimated by regressing the historical price of T on the historical prices of a set of "constituent" assets $C \subset U_A - T$:

$$SA(T)_t = \sum_{C_i \in C} \beta_i C_{i,t}$$

$$\text{s.t.} \quad \beta_i = \arg\min \sum_{t=1}^{n} \left(T_t - \sum_{C_i \in C} \beta_i C_{i,t} \right)^2 \tag{21.5}$$

and the "cointegrating vector" $\beta = [\beta_1 ... \beta_{nc}]^T$ of constituent weights is given by:

$$\beta_{OLS} = (C^T C)^{-1} Ct \tag{21.6}$$

where C is the $n_c = |C|$ by n matrix of historical prices of the constituents and $t = [T_1 ... T_n]^T$ is the vector of historical prices of the target asset.

The synthetic asset can be considered an optimal statistical hedge, conditioned upon the set of constituent assets C, in that the standard properties of the OLS procedure used in regression ensure both that the synthetic asset will be an unbiased estimator for the target asset, i.e. $E[T_t] = SA(T)_t$, and also that the deviation between the two price series will be minimal in a mean-squared-error sense.

We formally define a "synthetic asset model" as a triple:

$$SA = \{T \in U_A; \; C \subset U_A - \{T\}; \; \beta \in \Re^{|C|}\} \tag{21.7}$$

where U_A is the asset universe, $T \in U_A$ is the "target asset", $C \subset U_A - \{T\}$ is the set of "constituent assets" and $\beta \in \Re^{|C|}$ is the vector of constituent weights. Given such a model, we can derive the time series which represents the associated statistical mispricing:

$$M_t = T_t - \sum_{C_i \in C} \beta_i C_{i,t} \tag{21.8}$$

The statistical mispricing M_t can be considered as a composite portfolio consisting of the assets $\{T_t, C_1, C_2, \ldots, C_{nc}\}$ with weightings $\{1, -\beta_1, -\beta_2, \ldots, -\beta_{nc}\}$ respectively. The price of this portfolio represents the excess value of the target asset T, relative to the linear combination of assets $SA(T)_t = \Sigma_i \beta_i C_{i,t}$ and can be thought of as a "stochastically detrended" version of the original asset price T_t (i.e. detrended with respect to observed time series which are generated by (at least partially) stochastic processes rather than with respect to a deterministic function of time).

In this context the set of constituent assets C can be considered as acting as proxies for the unobserved risk factors which act as common stochastic trends in market prices. In maximising the correlation between the target asset and the synthetic asset the construction procedure cannot (by definition) account for the "asset-specific" components of price dynamics, but must instead indirectly maximise the sensitivities to common sources of economic risk. In the context of equation (21.2) the effect of the construction procedure is to artificially create a pair of assets (the target asset T and the synthetic asset $SA(T)_t$) which have similar exposures to the underlying (but not necessarily directly observable) risk factors which drive the asset price dynamics.

21.3 Conditional Statistical Arbitrage Strategies

Our conditional statistical arbitrage strategies are a mechanism for exploiting the predictive information which is contained in forecasting models of asset price dynamics. Rather than being concerned with changes in individual asset prices, as would be the case in a standard error correcting model, our models are concerned with changes in the prices of the *combinations* of assets which define statistical mispricings. The general form of our "mispricing correction models" or MCMs is:

$$\Delta\left(T_t - \sum_{C_i \in C} \beta_{i,t} C_{i,t}\right) = \Delta M_t = f(M_t, \Delta M_{t-\tau}, Z_t) + \varepsilon_t \tag{21.9}$$

where M_t is the deviation from the statistical fair price relationship, or "statistical mispricing", $\Delta M_{t-\tau}$ represents a set of lagged changes in the mispricing, and Z_t represents a selected set of exogenous variables which either directly influence the mispricing dynamics or serve to modulate the mispricing correction effect.

The "conditional statistical arbitrage" (CSA) trading rules which we use to exploit the predictions of the MCMs take the form:

$$\text{posn}(E[\Delta M_t],k,h) = \frac{\Sigma_{j=1}^{h}\text{sign}(E[\Delta M_{t-j}])|E[\Delta M_{t-j}]|^k}{h} \tag{21.10}$$

where h and k represent smoothing and sensitivity parameters respectively. The CSA rules can be considered as lying within a broader taxonomy of statistical arbitrage strategies based upon different functional forms of mispricing correction model, and thus the types of behaviour that they are designed to accommodate. Such a taxonomy is described in Burgess (1999).

21.4 Application of Cointegration-Based Methodology to FTSE 100 Stocks

In this section, we describe an application of the cointegration approach to exploiting statistical mispricings between the constituent stocks of the FTSE 100 index. The data consists of daily closing prices between 13 June 1996 and 5 October 1998. The 600 observations are divided into a 400 day "in-sample" period which is used to estimate the statistical mispricing models, and a subsequent 200 day "out-of-sample" period which is used to present an unbiased estimate of the generalisation performance of the models. After removing the assets for which continuous data samples were not available, the number of assets in the sample was 89 constituents plus the index itself.

In the remainder of this chapter we evaluate the performance of "Conditional Statistical Arbitrage" strategies on the set of 90 mispricings which result from each asset in the universe being compared to an associated synthetic asset consisting of three constituent assets.

21.5 Empirical Results of Conditional Statistical Arbitrage Models

In this section we describe the results of applying three neural estimation algorithms to each of the 90 statistical mispricings, a total of 270 models in all.

The three algorithms provide alternative methods for optimising the bias–variance trade-off in neural estimation. Although equally applicable to cases where the deterministic component dominates the noise term, the algorithms are specifically designed for the context where spurious variables may be present and the magnitude of the predictable component in the data is relatively low (accounting for between 0 and 25% of the variance of the target variable).

The three algorithms share a basic testing methodology in which the statistical significance of model components is calculated by comparing the degrees of freedom which they absorb with the additional explanatory power which they provide. The basic selection criterion which we use is a partial F-test of the form:

$$F_i = \frac{(\Sigma(y - \hat{y}_b)^2 - \Sigma(y - \hat{y}_a)^2) / (\Sigma df_A - \Sigma df_B)}{\Sigma(y - \hat{y}_b)^2 / ((n-1) - \Sigma df_B)}$$

$$= \frac{\Delta RSS / \Delta df}{RSS / n - df}$$

(21.11)

where $\hat{y}_A$ is the estimator which consists of the set of components A and $\hat{y}_B$ is the estimator which consists of the set of components B. The test compares the ratio of the *variance per degree of freedom* which is explained by the set of components f_i to the average residual variance (adjusted for both variance and degrees of freedom which are absorbed by the model). Under the null hypothesis that component f_i is irrelevant then the statistic F_i follows an F-distribution with df_i degrees of freedom on the numerator and $n - \Sigma_k df_k$ degrees of freedom on the denominator.

This F-testing approach is the basis of common statistical tools such as "stepwise regression" (e.g. Weisberg, 1985). It has a similar motivation to the econometric tests for neglected non-linearity used by Lee *et al.* (1993) for selecting the number of hidden units in a neural network. The partial F-testing approach was first applied to neural network variable selection by (Burgess, 1995) where a heuristic method was used to estimate the number of degrees of freedom associated with each input variable. In the algorithms described below the degrees of freedom for a neural network model are calculated from the smoother matrix according to the methods described in Chapter 8 of Burgess (1999).

The partial F-testing methodology can be used to optimise the bias–variance trade-off by approaching the optimal level of complexity either from below or from above. Methods which approach the optimal complexity from *below* are referred to in the neural network literature as "constructive" approaches in that they can be viewed as gradually building up or "constructing" a model. By analogy, we choose to refer to the alternative approach, of searching for the optimal complexity from *above*, as the "deconstructive" approach. The constructive and deconstructive approaches to the optimisation of model complexity are illustrated in Fig. 21.2.

The first of our three algorithms is based upon the use of a regularisation term to control global model complexity. The algorithm can be used in a "pseudo-constructive" manner by using a high initial level of regularisation which is then relaxed in order to add model complexity. The "pseudo-deconstructive" version of the algorithm uses an initially low degree of regularisation which is increased in order to remove complexity from the model. We refer to the algorithm as *pseudo-*(de)constructive because although the model complexity will vary in terms of the degrees of freedom in the model, the actual parameterisation of the model remains constant throughout.

The other two algorithms combine the use of regularisation with the explicit addition and subtraction of model components. In particular, these algorithms

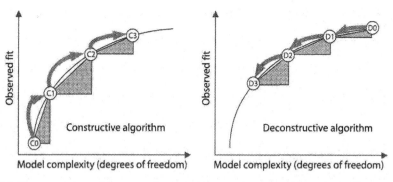

Fig. 21.2 The constructive and deconstructive approaches to optimising model complexity. The constructive approach starts with a null model which is successively enhanced whilst the additional components are found to be statistically significant. The deconstructive approach starts with an over-complex model which is successively refined by removing components which are found to be statistically insignificant.

combine the tasks of complexity optimisation and variable selection. The first is a constructive algorithm which operates by *adding* model components, whilst the second is a deconstructive algorithm which operates by *removing* model components. In all cases the model estimation procedure is guided by the use of statistical significance tests based upon the partial-F test of equation (21.11).

Having provided a brief overview of the algorithms by which the forecasting models were estimated, we now move on to examine the results achieved by the models, further description of the methodology can be found in Burgess (1999).

Before moving on to consider the collective performance of the forecasting models in a portfolio content, it is interesting to consider particular examples of models whose performance in some way typifies certain properties of the set of models as a whole. In particular we present below examples of models with *consistently positive* performance, with *non-stationary* performance, with performance which is *robust to non-stationarity* in the target mean, and with performance which is *highly sensitive to the level of transactions costs*.

21.5.1 Consistently Profitable Model

Figure 21.3 illustrates the out-of-sample equity curve of a consistently profitable model, created using the *deconstructive* version of the neural estimation procedure, and based on the mispricing of Smiths Industries against Rolls Royce, Rank Group and BSKyB. The characteristics of the model are reported in Table 21.1 (model ref = 228). The exogenous variables selected for the model were daily changes and 20-day volatility of the FTSE index.

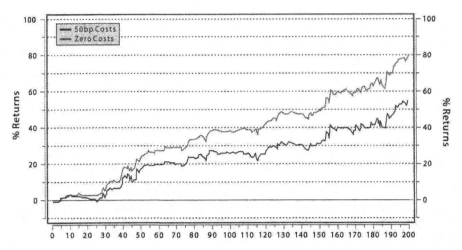

Fig. 21.3 Example of a consistently profitable model, created using the deconstructive neural estimation algorithm and based upon the mispricing between Smiths Industries, and a combination of Rolls Royce, Rank Group and BSkyB.

21.5.2 Model with Non-stationary Performance

Figure 21.4 presents the out-of-sample equity curve of Model 127 (see Table 21.1) whose performance undergoes a breakdown due to non-stationarity in the underlying relationships. The model was created using the *constructive* algorithm and based on the statistical mispricing between Lloyds TSB Group and a combination of the FTSE index, Allied Domecq and Rentokil. No exogenous variables were selected

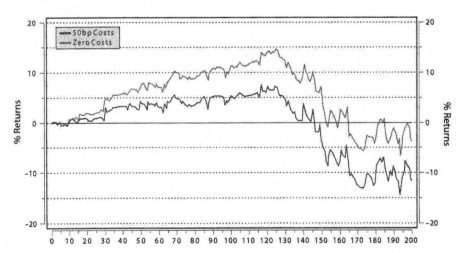

Fig. 21.4 Example of a model which exhibits performance breakdown, created using the constructive neural estimation algorithm and based upon the mispricing of Lloyds TSB against the FTSE index, Allied Domecq and Rentokil.

for this particular forecasting model, which was thus solely based upon the mispricing dynamics.

21.5.3 Model Which Is Profitable in Spite of a Negative R^2

Figure 21.5 shows the out-of-sample equity curve for Model 83, which is consistently profitable in spite of a negative R^2 during the out-of-sample period. The model was created using the *regularised* version of the neural estimation methodology and is based upon the mispricing of Diageo against Next, Granada Group and Safeway. The exogenous variables selected for inclusion in the forecasting model were 5-day changes in the FTSE index plus 5-day volatilities in both the DEM exchange rate and the S&P 500 index.

21.5.4 Model Which Is Highly Sensitive to Transactions costs

The final example, Model 235, which is highly sensitive to the assumed level of transactions costs, is illustrated in Fig. 21.6, and is based on the mispricing of Severn and Trent Water against the National Grid, Orange and P&O, with the forecasting model created using the *constructive* algorithm. Exogenous factors selected for inclusion in the model were 5-day changes in the FTSE and Dax indices, and 1-day changes in the S&P and Dax indices.

The performance statistics and other characteristics of the four models are described in Table 21.1.

The first set of table entries describe the forecasting model and are "Model": model reference number; "Algorithm": D=deconstructive, C=constructive, R=regularised; "Mispricing": reference to model used to generate the mispricings; degrees of freedom (MDOF) and F-ratio (F); the second set of figures present the

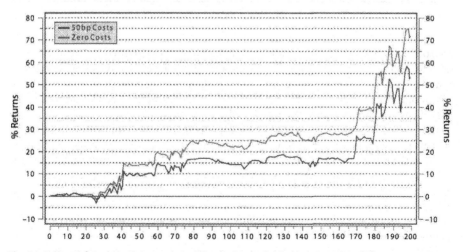

Fig. 21.5 The performance of the regularised forecasting model for the mispricing of Diageo against Next, Granada and Safeway. The model is consistently profitable in spite of a negative R^2 of –69% during the out-of-sample period. The correlation between the forecasts and the actual relative returns, however, is 0.15 – demonstrating that profitability is determined by correlation rather than R^2.

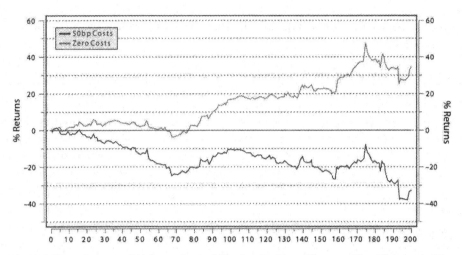

Fig. 21.6 The performance of the forecasting model for the mispricing of Severn and Trent Water against the National Grid Group, Orange and P&O. The model is profitable on a zero cost basis but consistently loses money when the transactions cost spread of 50 basis points (0.5%) is accounted for. This suggests that the magnitude of the mispricings with respect to this particular fair price relationship is too low to exploit profitably – at least using a trading rule of this type.

Table 21.1 Summary of cointegration model characteristics

Model	Algorithm	Mispricing	MDOF	F	H1/0bp	H2/0bp	H1/50bp	H2/50bp	Direction	Correl	R^2
228	D	76	12.04	5.31	4.38	3.39	2.96	2.31	53.8%	0.236	3.5%
127	C	43	2.55	9.82	2.78	−1.64	1.22	−1.84	45.4%	0.030	−7.8%
83	R	28	18.84	4.83	2.64	2.92	1.66	2.31	50.8%	0.153	−68.8%
235	C	79	2.09	6.63	2.61	1.35	−1.71	−1.63	58.3%	0.112	1.2%

Sharpe Ratio of the out-of-sample trading performance, divided between H1 and H2 and with costs at 0 and 50 basis points; and the final set of values are the out-of-sample statistical performance metrics: "Direction" = proportion of periods in which sign(forecast) = sign(actual); "Correl" = correlation between actual and forecasted change in mispricing; "R^2" = 1 – MSE/VAR(actual).

When considering a set of models, the appropriate method for evaluating a set of models is to evaluate the combined performance of the entire set, thus taking into account the extent to which the strengths and weaknesses of the individual models will compensate for each other. In this section we employ a very simple approach to model combination, in which the notional capital is simply divided equally amongst the set of models. More sophisticated approaches to model combination, and the various issues involved in jointly optimising a set of models, are discussed in Part III of Burgess (1999).

Table 21.2 presents the collective performance statistics of the sets of 90 models generated by each of the three neural estimation algorithms; the performance of a set of *linear* forecasting models is provided as a benchmark.

Table 21.2 Collective performance statistics

Algorithm	Sharpe Ratio	H1	H2	Profitable	H1	H2	Return	H1	H2	StDev	H1	H2
Linear	3.26	3.79	3.53	58%	60%	56%	28.2%	8.0%	20.2%	8.7%	2.1%	5.7%
Constructive	4.63	4.32	5.03	60%	60%	61%	19.4%	6.8%	12.6%	4.2%	1.6%	2.5%
Regularised	4.68	5.21	4.72	63%	67%	58%	19.9%	7.4%	12.5%	4.3%	1.4%	2.6%
Deconstructive	5.14	5.52	5.24	63%	65%	61%	22.5%	8.4%	14.1%	4.4%	1.5%	2.7%

The performance statistics reported are annualised "Sharpe ratio"; the proportion of trading periods which generated positive return across the portfolio as a whole; and first and second moments of the portfolio returns. Figures are presented across the out-of-sample period as a whole, and also broken down into two equal halves H1 and H2.

On the whole the results are broadly comparable across the different algorithms, with the deconstructive algorithm slightly outperforming in risk-adjusted terms. The linear models achieve the highest total return, but this is mainly due to the second period only and at a high cost in terms of increased risk. On a risk-adjusted basis the low-bias models outperform the linear models by a ratio of approximately 1.5, a result which is consistent across both sub-periods.

21.6 Summary

In this chapter we have described an empirical evaluation of a cointegration-based approach to exploiting predictability in appropriately constructed combinations of FTSE 100 stocks. The predictable component of the dynamics is captured by means of a low-bias methodology (Burgess, 1999) which incorporates model-free variable selection and neural model estimation and is exploited by means of a set of "conditional statistical arbitrage" (CSA) strategies.

Out-of-sample results suggest a potential annualised return of approximately 20% before trading costs are included.

22. Joint Optimisation in Statistical Arbitrage Trading

Neville Towers

22.1 Introduction

In Chapter 12 we discussed reinforcement learning, in which we optimise a function that is state-dependent. In this chapter we look at a portfolio of assets which is modified at each time step. If transactions costs are applied to all asset changes (as is the case in all real situations), then we have a state-dependent system and the principles of Chapter 12 apply. We will, however, extend those methods to allow us to jointly optimise two processes in a manner that allows maximum profit to be made from a trading system.

The process will be applied to the development of statistical arbitrage trading strategies for predictive models. The joint optimisation is of a prediction model, and a trading strategy based on the predictions made.

We build upon the methodology developed by Burgess (1999) and described in Chapter 21 for modelling the dynamics of statistical arbitrage which identifies and predicts statistical mispricings from amongst groups of assets.

A two-stage trading system for forecasting and trading a statistical mispricing is developed and applied to a set of 50 statistical mispricings, which were identified within the UK equity market (FTSE 100).

The trading systems are optimised for different levels of transactions costs, and the results demonstrate that the joint optimisation procedure can significantly improve trading performance over that of a system that makes optimal trades based on the independently optimal prediction model.

When trading costs are taken into consideration we find that a model that gives optimal prediction performance does not always give the highest profits. This is due to the predictions giving a number of buy/sell signals that lead to profits less than the cost of executing the trade. A model that has lower prediction accuracy but smoother predictions (which avoid the loss-making trades), can give higher profits. This leads to a trade-off between prediction correlation with the target and prediction autocorrelation.

22.2   Statistical Mispricing

Methods for constructing statistical mispricings between assets and testing for some predictable component have been investigated by Burgess (1999) and are described in Chapter 21.

The identification of statistical arbitrage relationships requires the construction of a time series of some linear combination of assets, which contains some deterministic component of the asset price dynamics.

We use a cointegration modelling framework to attempt to construct a mean reverting time series from a group of assets. In this process, some of the assumptions of the traditional cointegration technique can be relaxed in order to test for predictable behaviour rather than a stationary error-correction effect. Thus the stationarity tests of cointegration analysis, for example, the Dickey–Fuller test and the Cointegrating Regression Durbin–Watson test, can be replaced by tests for potential predictability, as discussed in Chapter 3.

For example, given a target asset T, a statistical mispricing M_t can be considered as a portfolio of assets $\{T, Y_1, Y_2, ..., Y_n\}$ with respective weightings $\{1, -\beta_1, -\beta_2, ..., -\beta_n\}$ where β is the cointegrating vector. The statistical mispricing can be considered as the value of the target asset T relative to the linear combination of constituent assets. This method of constructing a statistical mispricing using cointegration analysis has been extended to adaptive cointegrating vectors (using smoothing techniques or adaptive regression techniques). In the case of high-dimensional problems, with many potential combinations of assets, techniques may be required to search through potential permutations. For example, in the case of the FTSE 100, there are a vast number of potential combinations of assets, with almost one million possible combinations involving a target and a replicating portfolio containing just two assets. Obviously an exhaustive search across all combinations is computationally impractical, so a guided search mechanism is required to identify combinations which exhibit significant mean-reverting behaviour. One practical method of tackling this issue is by applying a stepwise linear regression approach to estimate the mispricing relationships, as suggested by Burgess (1999).

22.2.1   Testing for Return Predictability

A number of statistical tests have been developed for identifying non-random walk behaviour in a time series (for more details see Chapter 3). The power of these tests has been compared for bias corrected mean-reversion, as described by Burgess (1999). Results show that the VR statistic (equation (3.2), repeated here in equation (22.1)) is the most powerful test for the identification of potential predictability in relative asset prices.

$$VR(\tau) = \frac{Var(r_t(\tau))}{\tau Var(r_t(1))} \qquad (22.1)$$

22.2.2 Application to FTSE 100

The above procedure was applied to the 100 stocks in the UK equity market (the FTSE 100). The data set consists of 1100 observations of hourly prices collected from a live Reuters data feed from 9 a.m. to 4 p.m. daily during the period from the 15 May 1998 to 4 December 1998. The first 400 data points were used for constructing and testing the statistical mispricings and the remainder of the data for optimising model parameters and out-of-sample evaluation. To achieve this the second period was split into two datasets: an in-sample period of 500 observations to optimise the forecasting model and the trading rule parameters and the final 200 observations as the out-of-sample period.

A cointegration-based framework was used to construct statistical mispricings. It incorporated stepwise linear regression to direct the search for suitable combinations across the potential space of possible combinations, as discussed in Chapter 21. Furthermore, due to stability issues the number of constituent assets in the cointegrating vector was limited to 4. Using this method, 50 statistical mispricings were selected on the basis of the degree of mean reverting behaviour, which was tested against the random walk hypothesis using the Variance Ratio statistic (Burgess, 1999).

22.3 Controlling the Properties of the Forecasting Model

In this example we use a simple exponential smoothing model to predict the equity mispricing. It takes the form:

$$\overline{M}_t = \alpha M_t + (1-\alpha)\overline{M}_{t-1}$$

where α is the smoothing parameter. The predicted change in the mispricing (the return) is then simply computed as the difference between the current mispricing and the predicted mispricing.

$$\hat{y} = \text{expected } \Delta M = -k[\alpha M + (1-\alpha)\overline{M}] \qquad (22.2)$$

More advanced univariate models could be used, for example ARMA or ARIMA models (as described in Chapter 9), or we could use any of the other techniques described in this book, but as the purpose is to show the benefits of the joint optimisation approach we will keep things simple.

The construction of forecasting models for a statistical mispricing may also have a number of additional design factors that require specification. It is considered that these design factors influence the economic value of the forecasting model with respect to some trading strategy. In the case of statistical arbitrage trading systems, these factors may include the optimisation criterion, the forecast horizon and the forecast object. These factors may be particularly important as they influence the characteristics of the predicted returns. For example, the optimisation criterion may consist of two statistical characteristics, namely prediction autocorrelation and predictive correlation, which may both influence the economic value of the model. It is considered that statistical arbitrage trading, which involves exploiting predictability to overcome trading costs, may be particularly sensitive to the characteristics of the predicted returns. Joint optimisation allows us to control such characteristics by use of meta-parameters within an iterative optimisation procedure.

In the current example the trade-off between predictive correlation and prediction autocorrelation are controlled by the smoothing parameter (the more smoothing the higher the autocorrelation).

22.4 Modelling the Trading Strategy

For these experiments we compare three path-dependent trading strategies. The strategies all use a single parameter to control a trading position dependent on both the position we would take if we followed our prediction and the position we currently hold. The purpose of the path-dependent trading rules is to smooth the trading position through time. The trading parameter is to be optimised at the same time as the modelling parameter in order to maximise profits.

The first path-dependent trading rule (P1) is based on simple exponential smoothing of the trading position, a_t:

$$a_t^* = (1-\theta)a_t + \theta a_{t-1}^* \tag{22.3}$$

where θ is a decay rate parameter with constraint $0 \le \theta \le 1$. For example, if θ equals zero, no smoothing is applied to the trading position, but if θ equals 1, the trading position remains constant at the initial starting position.

The second rule (P2) is based on a simple moving average of the trading position, a_t, and is defined as

$$a_t^* = \frac{1}{h}\sum_{j=0}^{h-1} a_{t-j} \tag{22.4}$$

where h is the rolling window parameter controlling the number of past observations with constraint h [eq] 1. For example, if $h = 1$, no smoothing is applied to the trading position and increasing h produces a higher degree of smoothing.

The third rule (P3) is a "noise-tolerant" approach which attempts to decrease overall trading costs by reducing the number of relatively "small" changes in the trading position, and operates by only trading if the proposed change is significantly large. This rule is defined as

$$a_t^* = a_t \quad \text{if } |a_t - a_{t-1}^*| > \lambda \tag{22.5}$$
$$= a_{t-1}^* \text{ otherwise}$$

where λ is the tolerance parameter with constraint $\lambda \ge 0$. For example, if $\lambda = 0$, no smoothing is applied to the trading position, and increasing λ increases smoothness.

The path-dependent rules will be compared to two heuristic rules to assess the benefits of the joint optimisation. The first heuristic rule (H1) simply buys or sells a fixed amount depending on whether we expect returns to be positive or negative:

$$a_{t+1} = \delta \quad \text{if} \quad \hat{y}_{t+1} > 0$$
$$= -\delta \quad \text{if} \quad \hat{y}_{t+1} < 0 \tag{22.6}$$

The second heuristic rule (H2) buys or sells an amount proportional to the predicted returns:

$$a_{t+1} = \delta \hat{y}_{t+1} \tag{22.7}$$

22.5 Joint Optimisation

We can observe that in optimising the system we wish to make a trade-off between prediction accuracy and prediction autocorrelation, with the autocorrelation preventing trades with small potential gain but high cost. To implement the trade-off we introduce a meta-parameter κ that controls the balance between accuracy and autocorrelation in a cost function:

$$\text{Cost} = \kappa \, \text{accuracy} + (1 - \kappa) \, \text{autocorrelation}$$

The optimisation procedure is iterative, with the predictor optimising α for a specified meta-parameter value κ, passing the predictions to the trading system which optimises the trading rule. The trading system then passes back information which is used to modify κ the predictions are re-optimised with a new α, and so on.

It may be possible to develop a mathematical derivative of the change in trading profits with κ, but the simplest method is to estimate the derivative by perturbing the κ and recalculating the optimum predictions and hence trading strategy. In this way we can modify κ by:

$$\kappa \leftarrow \kappa + \eta \frac{\partial P}{\partial \kappa} \tag{22.8}$$

with η controlling the step size.

22.6 Empirical Experiments

Using the returns model (equation 22.2) and the five trading rules (equations 22.3–22.7), we used both single and joint optimisation procedures to optimise the Sharpe Ratio of a portfolio, as detailed below.

Single optimisation involves simply optimising the forecasting model to maximise predictive correlation and then optimising the parameterised trading rule given the set of predictions thus made. In the case of joint optimisation, we iteratively optimise both the prediction model and trading rule in order to trade off the two statistical characteristics of predictive correlation and prediction autocorrelation. The trade-off is achieved partly by the smoothing parameter in the predictor, and partly by the smoother in the trading rule.

For each experiment, transactions costs are kept constant. The trading performance is measured in terms of cumulative profit and annualised Sharpe Ratio. For these empirical evaluations we specified the optimisation criterion as the Sharpe Ratio, which we considered to be representative of the goals of risk adverse trading strategies.

22.6.1 Results for a Single Mispricing

An example of one of the 50 identified statistical mispricings is defined as follows:

$$M_t = NAM - 6.3334 - 0.182GLXO + 0.206HFX - 0.238UU \tag{22.9}$$

where *NAM*, *GLXO* and *HFX* and *UU* represent the price of stock in Nycomed Amersham, Glaxo plc, Halifax Group and United Utilities respectively.

The cumulative profit for trading this mispricing using the three parameterised rules and the two heuristics rules, using a single optimisation, are shown in Fig. 22.1 for the in-sample period and Fig. 22.2 for the out-of-sample period.

As expected, the three optimised trading rules (P1, P2 and P3) outperform the two heuristic trading rules (H1 and H2), with P1 producing the highest performance with 35.07%.

The in-sample performance ranking (Fig 22.1) is (from highest to lowest) P1, P3, P2, H2 and H1. The graph shows that performance is consistent over the trading period, with few sharp spikes to distort results. Figure 22.2 depicts the out-of-sample cumulative profit. This shows some variation in performance rankings compared to the in-sample period. The out-of-sample performance ranking (highest to lowest) is Rule P3, H2, P1, P2, H1. This highlights the need for further testing which can be achieved over longer data sets or across other mispricings.

Fig. 22.1 In-sample performance for the five trading rules. This is measured by cumulative profit for the 500 hour period.

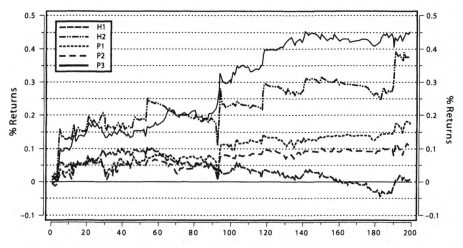

Fig. 22.2 Cumulative profit of the five trading rules for the 200 hour out-of-sample period.

Table 22.1 summarises the performance of trading systems for different trading rules using both single and joint optimisation methods. They are applied to the statistical mispricing described in equation (22.9), with transactions costs of 0.2%.

The results show that over the in-sample period the two heuristic trading rules give poor in-sample performance, in terms of Sharpe Ratio, of −1.460 and 0.425. As expected, optimising the three path-dependent trading rules using the single optimisation method gives better in-sample performance than the heuristic rules, with Sharpe Ratios of 2.519, 1.324 and 2.930 respectively.

The joint optimisation method applied to the parameterised rules, allowing trade-off between prediction accuracy and smoothness, gives improved performance. For the three parameterised trading rules this resulted in increased prediction smoothing, with α dropping to 0.05, 0.05 and 0.55 respectively, and reduced trading rule smoothing, with the smoothing parameters dropping by a factor of ~10. So it is better to smooth the predictions, thus sacrificing prediction accuracy, than to smooth the trading rule.

Table 22.1 Performance for a single mispricing

Rule	Method	Model parameters		Performance			
				In-sample		Out-of-sample	
		Forecast	Trading	Profit (%)	SR	Profit (%)	SR
H1	single	0.610		−13.17	−1.460	1.51	0.431
H2	single	0.610		8.51	0.425	39.07	4.123
P1	single	0.610	0.950	35.07	2.519	16.68	3.534
	joint	0.050	0.100	39.45	2.747	22.61	4.180
P2	single	0.610	10	18.18	1.324	10.38	2.693
	joint	0.050	1	39.62	2.717	23.96	4.252
P3	single	0.610	0.009	28.62	2.930	43.71	8.064
	joint	0.550	0.008	54.31	4.018	42.89	6.930

The out-of-sample performance is less conclusive with a wide variation in performance. On average, heuristic rules give a Sharpe Ratio of 2.28 compared to single optimisation of parameterised rules of 4.76 and jointly optimised rules of 5.12. For this example, the parameterisation of the trading rule increases performance by 88% and joint optimisation by an additional 8%. These results demonstrate the potential value of using parameterised trading rules and the joint optimisation method over a single mispricing.

22.6.2 Results for 50 Mispricings

We completed a more extensive study by generating trading systems for a series of 50 statistical mispricings. The results of this study are summarised in Table 22.2.

The table shows the average in-sample and out-of-sample performance, in terms of both cumulative profit and annualised Sharpe Ratio, across all trading systems for 50 statistical mispricings, with transactions costs of 0.2%. The three parameterised trading rules produce positive performance both in-sample and out-of-sample compared to negative returns from the two heuristic rules. In each case there is a slight deterioration in performance between in-sample and out-of-sample performance. In addition, the joint optimisation of both forecasting and trading outperforms the single optimisation approach. Overall, joint optimisation improves average performance, across all three rules, by 106%. These results show, using real data, the advantage of our parameterised trading rules and also of our joint optimisation methodology.

Table 22.2 Aggregate performance of 50 mispricings

Trading rule	Single optimisation				Joint optimisation			
	In-sample		Out-of-sample		In-sample		Out-of-sample	
	Profit (%)	SR	Profit (%)	SR	Profit (%)	SR	Profit (%)	SR
H1	−33.3	−4.58	−13.7	−5.24				
H2	−20.3	−1.67	−17.3	−3.63				
P1	22.8	1.17	0.03	0.89	32.7	1.87	0.06	1.54
P2	12.7	0.49	0.01	0.18	30.3	1.71	0.04	1.21
P3	36.5	2.15	0.07	0.69	51.9	3.57	0.03	0.88

22.6.3 Results for Different Trading Costs

Further experiments were conducted to analyse the influence of the level of transactions costs, as given in Table 22.3.

Table 22.3 shows the average Sharpe Ratios out-of-sample for all 50 trading models across trading rules for both single and joint optimisation methods, with transactions costs up to 70 basis points.

For no trading costs, the parameterised trading rules do not provide any significant improvement over the heuristic rules. Similarly, joint optimisation provides no benefit over the single optimisation approach, as expected.

Table 22.3 Performance (Sharpe Ratio) vs. Transactions costs

Costs bps	Single optimisation				Joint optimisation			
	H1	H2	P1	P2	P3	P1	P2	P3
0	3.11	4.09	3.86	3.83	3.71	3.44	3.25	2.82
10	−1.18	0.21	1.60	1.11	1.34	1.85	1.54	1.01
20	−5.23	−3.63	0.89	0.18	0.69	1.54	1.21	0.88
30	−8.81	−7.30	−0.26	−1.60	0.05	1.00	0.52	0.21
40	−11.84	−10.69	−1.23	−3.09	−0.52	1.00	0.80	−0.01
50	−14.32	−13.74	−2.23	−4.61	−1.12	0.99	0.72	−0.37
60	−16.33	−16.46	−3.24	−6.01	−1.49	0.80	0.57	−0.48
70	−17.95	−18.85	−4.31	−7.30	−1.98	0.72	0.53	−0.58

As transactions costs increase, however, trading performance deteriorates across all trading strategies with the parameterised trading rules significantly outperforming heuristic trading rules for costs as low as 10 basis points. At the 10 basis point level, average performance of the heuristic rules is −0.97 compared to 1.35 for parameterised trading rules using single optimisation. In addition, joint optimisation enhances performance with average Sharpe Ratio increasing from 1.35 to 1.47, which is an 8.9% increase. These results illustrate that joint optimisation can significantly improve performance for non-zero transactions costs.

22.7 Summary

Overall, the results show that trading strategies can be developed for statistical mispricings that lead to promising trading performance. As expected, profitability is influenced by transactions costs, with an increased level of costs leading to deterioration in trading performance. However, the three path dependent trading rules consistently outperform the two heuristic trading rules with additional performance improvements gained from the joint optimisation methodology. For transactions costs of 10 basis points, the average Sharpe Ratio is increased from −0.97 to 1.35 by using parameterised trading rules. Furthermore, joint optimisation increases performance from 1.35 to 1.47, an increase of 8.9%. We believe that these results on real data convincingly demonstrate the advantages of this approach.

23. Univariate Modelling

Neep Hazarika

23.1 Introduction

One of the methods of tackling the problem of predicting the future of financial time series is to look for patterns in the past; these are then used to complete patterns formed by the most recent data, and thus predict future values. For example, the "head and shoulders" pattern is a popular proposed clue from the past. Here we consider more general approaches. We gather together several univariate modelling techniques and show how they lead to models for various assets. We start with the nearest neighbour and GMDH (not described earlier in the book) and then move on to support vector machine and relevance vector machines (described in Chapter 14). We give examples of how these methods can predict various bond markets.

23.2 Nearest Neighbours

The nearest neighbour approach attempts to determine similar patterns, existing at earlier times, to a partial pattern developing presently. It searches for patterns in the past by using a distance matching technique based on the Euclidean distance between the patterns. The approach is similar to technical trading in that it is assumed that certain patterns are followed by certain market movements.

23.2.1 Method

The nearest-neighbour technique as a prediction method is based on the premise that the value of a time series x_t at time t can be represented as

$$x_{t+1} = f(x_t, x_{t-1}, x_{t-2}, \ldots, x_{t-N+1})$$

where $f(\cdot)$ is a non-linear function which can be applied to a (possibly smoothed) time series, and N is the dimension of the delay vector.

The nearest neighbour technique is one of the various implementations of a non-parametric method. The first step in the method is to look for similar situations in

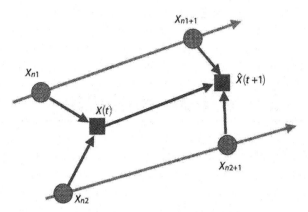

Fig. 23.1 Illustration of weighted average of two nearest neighbours.

the past and to select those points which have the nearest distance to the actual situation. This comprises examining the time series history for, say, k nearest neighbours, and using this information to predict that the system will exhibit a similar behaviour in the future. In this respect, this technique is essentially deterministic. Thus, x_{t+1} is approximated by $x_{t'+1}$, where $x_{t'+1}$ is the nearest neighbour of x_t; i.e. to predict tomorrow's value, the pattern most similar to that of today is sought. The forecast is that tomorrow's value will be the same as the weighted average of the neighbouring patterns one day later. This is illustrated in Fig. 23.1.

In the figure, if X_{n1} and X_{n2} are the nearest neighbours of of $X(t)$ at time t, then the predicted value $X(t + 1)$ at time $t + 1$ is given by the weighted average of X_{n1+1} and X_{n2+1}, which are the values that X_{n1} and X_{n2} evolve to at time $t + 1$.

Two parameters have, therefore, to be determined: one is the dimension N of the delay vectors, and the other is k: the number of nearest neighbours. The dimension N of the delay vectors can be taken to be the minimum size that causes a kink to occur in the singular spectrum, as described in Section 13.4: SVD Smoothing. Since the position of the kink n determines the number of "degrees of freedom" of the signal, we set $k = n - 1$, since constructing the return series from the smoothed index series has the effect of reducing the number of degrees of freedom by one. Further, a *distance function* $\lambda(\bar{x}_i, \bar{x}_j)$ has to be calculated. This is normally the Euclidean distance between the actual N-dimensional vector $\bar{x}_i$ and a historical N-dimensional vector $\bar{x}_j$. In particular, a *linear* combination of k nearest neighbours, using inverse distance weighting, gives a simple form of weighting function.

$$\hat{X}(t + T) = \frac{\sum_{i=1}^{N}(1/[X_{n_i} - X(t)])X_{n_i+T}}{\sum_{i=1}^{N}1/[X_{n_i} - X(t)]} \tag{23.1}$$

Note that there is a singularity when $X(t) = X_{n_i}$. In this case, we set

$$\hat{X}(t + T) = X_{n_i+T}$$

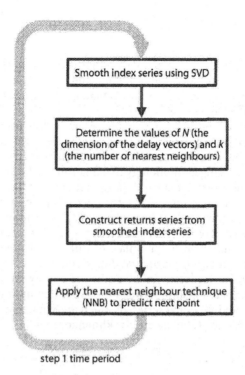

step 1 time period

Fig. 23.2 Flow chart depicting the nearest neighbour prediction technique.

Close sets of points are determined using a group of k nearest neighbours. These k nearest-neighbour vectors are then employed to construct a forecast of the next value by taking a weighted sum of the local forecasts one step later of the k nearest neighbours. Each point in the forecast is weighted in inverse proportion to its distance from the actual vector $\bar{x}_t$. A flow chart of the methodology is shown in Fig. 23.2.

23.3 The Group Method of Data Handling (GMDH)

In financial forecasting, problems often arise because of the large number of variables involved, coupled with the relatively small amount of available observations and the unknown dynamical relationship between the variables. Such problems occur due to the complex, often *ill-defined*, nature of the system, characterised by, for example, inadequate *a priori* information, a large number of parameters and short and noisy data samples.

One of the main problems encountered in the prediction of financial markets is the lack of sufficient data. This leads to problems with overfitting data, and therefore poor generalisation on relatively small data sets. This is true especially in the development of non-linear models which have large numbers of parameters.

23.3.1 GMDH

The group method of data handling (GMDH) algorithms provide a means to obtain accurate identification and forecasts for short and noisy input sample data. One major point of difference with neural nets is that, in the case of GMDH, the results are explicit mathematical models.

Forecasting involves the task of knowledge extraction from a mathematical description of the observed data. The *group method of data handling* is able to extract knowledge about the system under observation directly from data sampling. It employs a self-organising methodology that determines the optimal model based on a sorting procedure for model candidates that are evaluated according to the minimum that is obtained on an external accuracy condition (Madala and Ivakhnenko, 1994; Müller and Ivakhnenko, 1984). The basis for GMDH is to construct a polynomial fit of a given degree, using pruning of coefficients to prevent overfitting. Models built with polynomials of different degrees are assessed by overall mean squared error on a cross-validation set.

The model sorting methodology involves the use of polynomial reference functions. In general, the relationship between the input and output variables can be expressed as a Volterra functional series, of which the Kolmogorov–Gabor polynomial is a discrete analogue (Madala and Ivakhnenko, 1994):

$$y = w_0 + \sum_{i=1}^{N} w_i x_i + \sum_{i=1}^{N}\sum_{j=1}^{N} w_{ij} x_i x_j + \sum_{i=1}^{N}\sum_{j=1}^{N}\sum_{k=1}^{N} w_{ijk} x_i x_j x_k \qquad (23.2)$$

where $X = (x_1, x_2, ..., x_N)$ is the vector of input variables and $W = (w_0, w_1, ..., w_N)$ is the vector of coefficients or weights. The components of the input vector X may be lagged values of the series.

There are a number of GMDH algorithms that exist. We will describe only two such algorithms below:

23.3.2 The Combinatorial GMDH Algorithm

In the combinatorial GMDH algorithm, we develop a sequence of progressively complex models according to an external criterion, e.g. minimisation of the normalised RMS prediction error. The technique has a multilayered iterative structure. A particular difference between this algorithm and other iterative procedures is that, in the case of the combinatorial GMDH algorithm, the iteration rule does not remain constant but expands as each new series is generated. At the initial stage, all models are described by a simple structure in the form

$$y = w_0 + w_1 x_i \qquad i = 1, 2, ..., N \qquad (23.3)$$

Each of these models is then tested for accuracy according to the criterion mentioned above, and the best M models are selected, where $M \le N$. The next step is to increase the complexity by constructing models for the observed variable y in terms of the best models of the previous series, i.e.

$$y = w_0 + w_1 x_i + w_2 x_j \qquad i = 1, 2, .., M; \quad j = 1, 2, ..., N; \quad M \le N \qquad (23.4)$$

The next stage in the model sorting process involves even more complex polynomials of the form

$$y = w_0 + w_1 x_i + w_2 x_j + w_3 x_k$$

$$\text{where } i = 1, 2, ..., M; \quad j = 1, 2, ..., M; \quad k = 1, 2, ..., N; \quad M \leq N$$

(23.5)

This process is continued until the external minimisation criterion is met. Thus a
sorting of the polynomial models in order of accuracy is accomplished.

23.3.3 The Iterative Multilayered GMDH Algorithm

In this case, unlike the combinatorial case described above, the iteration rule
remains constant for all series. As an example, for the development of the first
series, we consider a particular model description of the form

$$u = c_0 + c_1 x_i + c_2 x_j + c_3 x_i x_j$$

(23.6)

The second series is then an iterated function of the best models obtained at the
previous step, and can be described as follows:

$$v = d_0 + d_1 u_i + d_2 u_j + d_3 u_i u_j$$

(23.7)

In a similar manner, the third series can be described by

$$w = e_0 + e_1 v_i + e_2 v_j + e_3 v_i v_j$$

(23.8)

In other words, the output values from a previous series are then input as arguments
for the development of the next series.

The GMDH technique thus automatically generates models of a given class by
sequential selection of the best models based on an external accuracy criterion
determined by cross-validation. It may be noted that this self-organising modelling
technique is based on statistical learning networks. These are networks of mathematical functions that are capable of capturing complex, non-linear relationships in
a compact and rapidly executable form. This method of model selection has its place
alongside such modern approaches based on model entropy maximisation (Akaike
approach) and average risk minimisation (Vapnik approach).

23.3.4 Example Model

Figure 23.3 shows the out-of-sample predictions of a model of UK bonds. The
evidence for this model (as defined in Chapter 15) is approximately 20.

23.4 The Support Vector Machine (SVM) Predictor Model

We will describe here the method for carrying out model selection using the SVM.

As in the case of the ARMA and nearest neighbour predictive models, the first step
(Fig. 23.4) is to smooth the raw index series using SVD. The return series is then
constructed from this smoothed series. For the SVM, we use *radial basis functions* for
the kernel. Radial basis functions are of the form $e^{-\gamma |x-y|^2}$ where γ is user-defined.

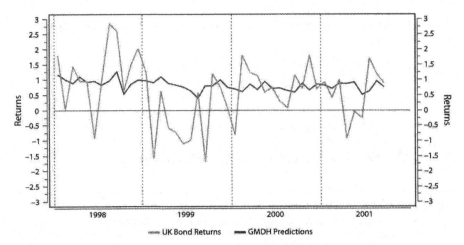

Fig. 23.3 Predictions from GMDH model of UK bond returns.

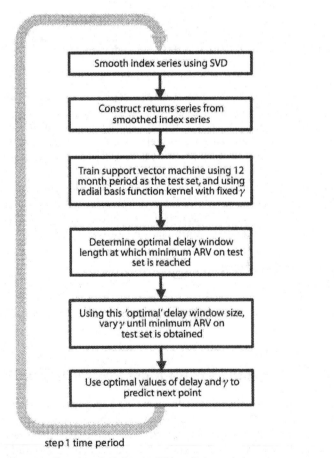

Fig. 23.4 Flow chart depicting the SVM prediction technique.

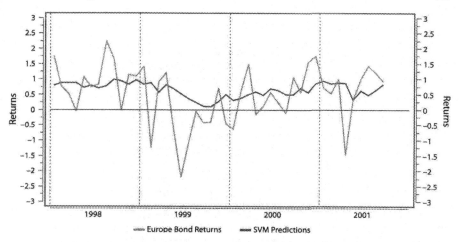

Fig. 23.5 Predictions from SVM model of European bond returns.

Next, training and test sets are created using variable delay windows, and the SVM is trained on these sets for fixed γ. The test set consists of the input window and the target over the last twelve-month period. The optimal delay window size is then fixed at that which gives the minimum ARV on the test set. Using this optimal delay window, the value of γ is varied, and the SVM again trained on the training and test sets. The optimal value of γ is again the one for which the ARV on the test set is minimum. Using these "optimal" values of the delay window size and γ, the SVM is employed to predict one step ahead in time. The flow chart for the SVM predictive model is given below.

Figure 23.5 shows predictions of European bonds made with an SVM model. The evidence for this model is approximately 14.

23.5 The Relevance Vector Machine (RVM)

The relevance vector machine (RVM) has recently been introduced as a new Bayesian alternative to the support vector machine. It is described in detail in Chapter 14.

23.5.1 Model Selection

We will describe here the method for carrying out model selection using the RVM.

As in the case of the ARMA and nearest neighbour predictive models, the first step is to smooth the raw index series using SVD (as described in Chapter 13). The return series is then constructed from this smoothed series. For the RVM we use *radial basis functions* for the kernel. Radial basis functions are of the form $\exp(-\gamma|x-y|^2)$, where γ is user-defined.

Next, a training set is created using variable delay windows, and the RVM is trained on this set. This optimal delay window size is determined from the SVD

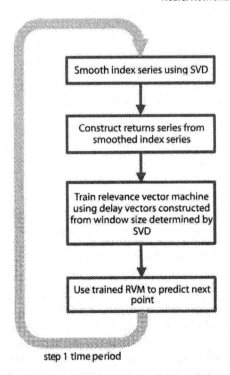

Fig. 23.6 Flow chart of the RVM prediction technique.

using the technique described in Chapter 14. Using this optimal delay window, the RVM is employed to predict one step ahead in time. The flow chart for the RVM predictive model is shown in Fig. 23.6.

Figure 23.7 shows the out-of-sample predictions obtained using this procedure to predict German bond returns.

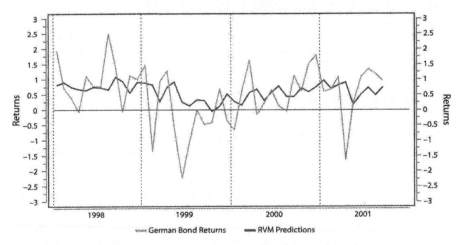

Fig. 23.7 Predictions from RVM model of German bond returns.

24. Combining Models

Neep Hazarika and John G. Taylor

24.1 Introduction

There is a large body of literature describing how best to combine models of various types of processes (Bunn, 1975; Bunn and Kappos, 1982; Bunn, 1985; Jacobs, 1995; Harrald and Kamstra, 1997; de Menezes *et al.*, 1998; Sharkey, 1998). Two such groups of methods are ensemble methods (Freund and Shapire, 1995; Breiman, 1994), and mixture of experts methods (Jacobs *et al.*, 1991; Jordan and Jacobs, 1994). Combining forecasts effectively is a non-trivial process in the case where high levels of noise exist, as can occur in the financial markets. The current trend is towards combining predictive models, rather than employing large monolithic predictors. The advantage of the former is that such a methodology could be more efficient in terms of training time (Lu and Ito, 1998). Further, it is also possible to achieve a lower generalisation error from the combiner (Krogh and Vedelsby, 1995), as well as to prevent overfitting. The models considered in this paper are of the prediction of bond returns over the next few time points, as for example for the next month for monthly data, based on the values of a range of inputs provided initially from economic analysis. We will consider how an effective solution be achieved for such a task, an important component in the overall prediction process for such time series with important financial implications

In this book a variety of modelling methodologies are described, including the multivariate approaches of linear regression (LG); linear correlation (LC); neural networks (NN); weak integration, also using neural networks (WI); and finally the adaptive lag models (AL), also based on neural networks. There are also several univariate methods based on the support vector machine (SVM), the group method of data handling (GMDH), the relevance vector machine (RVM) and a further technique based on smoothing using singular value decomposition (SVD). The problem one is faced with is how to combine the predictions of these separate models in order to make the most effective use of the knowledge that each of these models has gained from the the set of indicator variables, or the past history of the target series, that it uses to calculate the prediction. We should note here that the chosen inputs for the various models differ, so that one can assume that the different models attempt to extract different information from the total set of economically relevant inputs originally presented to them (and from which different subsets were selected by criteria natural to the different models themselves). So again the essential question remains: how can an effective combination of predictions be achieved each month?

24.2   Linear Combiners

A simple approach is to take a linear combination of the predictions of all the models for each month. Thus, we take a set of n weights $w_1, w_2, w_3, ..., w_n$ (where n is the number of models), and form the weighted sum $[w_1x_1 + w_2x_2 + ... + w_nx_n]$ where $x_1, x_2, ..., x_n$ are the predictions of the models at a given time step. We are then faced with the question: how should one choose the numerical values of the weights? It is the answer to this question that has been a central focus in prediction over the last few years, as the references already cited indicate.

In the absence of further information the correct procedure is to average the predictions. However, this method does not penalise bad models or reward good ones. As an alternative, a weighted linear combiner can be used, with weights chosen to minimise the prediction error of the weighted prediction over some period. The question then becomes that of choosing the constraints on the minimisation The obvious constraint is that the weights should sum to unity, but should we constrain the weights to be positive or allow a bias term?

In the extreme, a linear weighting can become a "winner-take-all" situation, where we simply accept the prediction from the best performing model.

24.3   A Temperature-Dependent SOFTMAX Combiner

Our experience with linear combiners, after careful and extended testing, is that they do not sufficiently penalise under-performing models. The new method described here incorporates both averaging and "winner takes all" methods. This is achieved by linearly combining all predictions such that, given the data, the "best" prediction can be determined when measured in an appropriate metric. A novel aspect is that the current combiner weights are obtained from a SOFTMAX distribution (Brindle, 1990; Jacobs *et al.*, 1991). The weights can then be interpreted as probabilities, as they lie in [0, 1] and sum to unity.

We want to derive a linear combination of all the predictions such that the "best" possible prediction can be determined given the data, when measured in an appropriate metric. Such a metric can be provided by the Average Relative Variance (ARV) of the individual models. The ARV is defined as follows.

Given a time series $x_1, x_2, ..., x_N$ the ARV for prediction values $\hat{x}_1, \hat{x}_2, ..., \hat{x}_N$ is given by:

$$\text{ARV} = \frac{1}{\sigma^2 N} \sum_{i}^{N} (x_i - \hat{x}_i)^2 \tag{24.1}$$

where x_i is the true value of the ith point of the series of length N, $\hat{x}_i$ is the predicted value and σ^2 is the variance of the true time series during the prediction interval N. In other words, ARV gives the ratio of mean squared errors of the prediction method in question and the method which predicts the mean at every step.

We also want to normalise the weights w_j given to each prediction model j such that they sum to one. The weights can thus be interpreted as *probabilities*, i.e., they must lie in the range $[0, 1]$, and they must sum to unity. Such a normalisation can be achieved by using the so-called Potts or SOFTMAX activation function (Brindle, 1990) which takes the form

$$w_j = w(ARV_1, ARV_2, \ldots, ARV_M, k, T) = \frac{e^{\alpha_j}}{\sum_{l=1}^{M} e^{\alpha_l}} \tag{24.2}$$

where $\alpha_j = -(ARV_j)^k / T$, ARV_j is the ARV of the jth prediction model and M is the number of prediction models. The term "SOFTMAX" is used because this activation function represents a smoothed version of the *winner-takes-all* model, in which the prediction with the largest "probability" is given a weight of +1 while all other weights have output zero. We incorporate two additional parameters k and T in this model. These parameters are determined each month by optimisation in order to minimise the ARV over the preceding twelve months. The parameters k and T vary dynamically with time. When T takes on large values the αs approach zero and the average of all predictions is the best that the combiner can obtain. Such a case arises, for example, when there are a large number of equally poor models, so that the combiner cannot distinguish between them. On the other hand, if some of the models outperform most other models, these are then singled out, since T tends to have a low value (as expected from the winner-takes-all strategy). Also, the winner-takes-all model is recovered in the limit $k \to \infty$ or $T \to 0$.

For $T \to \infty$, we regain the average, with no *a priori* knowledge. Since the process is dynamic, the combiner parameters adapt to the latest changes in the data, giving rise to different values of k and T over different time periods. With the passage of time, the set of (k, T) values effectively encapsulate the most recent behaviour of the market predictions. The parameters k and T can be determined by using optimisation techniques, as described in the next section.

24.4 The Combiner Algorithm

We now describe the cost function to be optimised. If the prediction window over which the ARV is calculated has length N, the current combiner requires at least $2N$ prediction values for each prediction model. The algorithm is as follows:

- Let the number of prediction models be M. Form a sequence of $N + 1$ model ARVs for each model $MARV_{ij}$, $i = 1, ..., N + 1, j = 1, ..., M$ by moving a window of length N across the data:

$$MARV_{ij} = \frac{1}{\sigma_i^2 N} \sum_{l=1}^{N} (x_{i+l-1} - \hat{x}_{i+l-1,j})^2 \qquad (24.3)$$

where x_{i+l-1} is the true value of the $(i + l - 1)$th point of the series of length N, $\hat{x}_{i+l-1,j}$ is the corresponding $(i + l - 1)$th predicted value of the jth model, and σ_i^2 is the variance of the ith segment of the true time series during the ith prediction interval.

- Compute the sequence of N combined predictions:

$$\hat{y}_i = \sum_{j=1}^{M} w_{ij} \hat{x}_{i+N,j} \quad i = 1...N \qquad (24.4)$$

where the weights w_{ij}, $j = 1 ... M$ are given by

$$w_{ij} = \frac{e^{\alpha_{ij}}}{\sum_{j=1}^{M} e^{\alpha_{ij}}} \qquad (24.5)$$

and

$$\alpha_{ij} = \frac{-(MARV_{ij})^k}{T}$$

Note that the weights w_{ij} are functions of the parameters k and T.

- Compute the combined ARV as follows

$$CARV = \frac{1}{\sigma_{N+1}^2 N} \sum_{i=1}^{N} (x_{i+N} - \hat{y}_i)^2 \qquad (24.6)$$

Note that $CARV$ is also a function of the unknown parameters k and T.

- Determine the values of k and T at the global minimum of $CARV$. The global minimisation is determined in this case via a *simulated annealing* technique (Goffe *et al.*, 1994).

- Update the weights w_{ij} in equation (24.5) using the most recent values of k and T obtained at the global minimum as follows:

$$w_{N+1,j} = \frac{e^{\beta_{N+1,j}}}{\sum_{j=1}^{M} e^{\beta_{N+1,j}}} \qquad (24.7)$$

and

$$\beta_{N+1,j} = -\frac{(MARV_{N+1,j})^k}{T} \qquad (24.8)$$

- Compute the combined prediction as follows:

$$\hat{y}_{N+1} = \sum_{j=1}^{M} w_{N+1,j} \hat{x}_{2N+1,j} \tag{24.9}$$

where $\hat{x}_{2N+1,j}$ is the prediction of the jth model for the next time step.

A word of caution regarding the computation of the parameters k and T is in order at this stage. At the first time step 1, when no previous information about the series are available, the values of k and T are computed across the entire window as k_1 and T_1. At the next step, the sliding window is moved forward one time unit, and the values k_1 and T_1 determined from the previous step are kept constant. Only the latest value is calculated as (k_2, T_2). The justification for this procedure is that changing the previous (k,T) values has the effect of modifying the prediction history of the models, which would be invalid. At the Nth time step, the set of N values of (k,T) thus obtained is an effective description of the most recent behaviour of the market predictions.

In our case, we choose $N = 12$. This value was chosen after extensive experiments. $N = 6$ gives rise to an extremely volatile regime, while $N = 24$ is too smooth, and may not take account of the noise in the data very well.

Many statistical models rely upon optimisation to estimate model parameters. However, many algorithms fail to converge in a reasonable number of steps: they may head towards infinitely large parameter values, or even loop through the same point over and over again. Further, the algorithm may have difficulty with ridges and plateaux, and even if the algorithm converges there is no assurance that it will have converged to a global, rather than a local, minimum, since conventional algorithms cannot distinguish between the two. The simulated annealing optimisation algorithm explores the function's entire surface and tries to optimise the function moving both uphill and downhill. As such, it has the advantage of being largely independent of starting values. Simulated annealing also requires less stringent conditions regarding the function than conventional algorithms, e.g. the function need not be continuous. Such relaxed assumptions make simulated annealing a natural choice for optimisation compared to conventional techniques.

24.5 Results

The general effectiveness of the combiner is determined as a process of continued testing by comparison with the trivial (average) model and minimisation of the residual squared error. Quality control is applied to the combiner by comparing the running ARV of the combined predictions, for a given market, against that for each of the model predictions used in the combiner. The effective generalisation capability of the combiner is demonstrated by a comparison of the model ARV's with that computed by the combiner. Figure 24.1 shows a number of sets of predictions for USA Bonds, along with the combiner prediction, against the actual bond

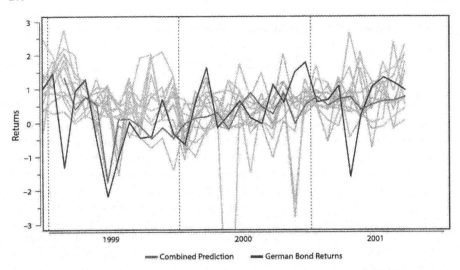

Fig. 24.1 Predictions of German Bond returns for a number of models, along with the combiner prediction, shown against the actual bond returns.

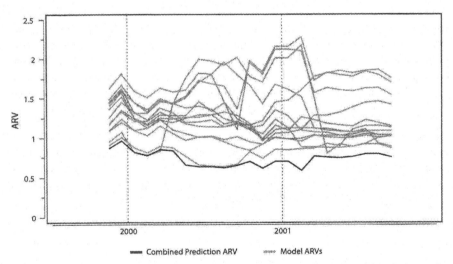

Fig. 24.2 Comparison of running ARV of combined predictions with that for each model prediction used.

returns. Figure 24.2 shows the ARVs for the same set of models, along with that of the combiner predictions. As seen from the figure, the combiner ARV tends to be as low as the lowest model ARV; it can be even lower, indicating its effective generalisation ability.

Various modifications of the combiner have been studied, e.g. fixing the values of k or T, or only allowing them to lie within a restricted range. None of these modifications appear to be beneficial, as measured by the generalisation error of the resulting combiner.

24.6 Conclusions

The temperature dependent SOFTMAX combiner leads to a highly effective way of achieving the best of the models. In some cases, it even produces a better prediction ARV than any of the separate predictive models.

PART V
Optimising and Beyond

The overall *NewQuant* process is completed when allocations are made to given markets across a given portfolio. A quadratic optimiser is developed in Chapter 25 for this allocation process. The quadratic component is equal to the cross-correlation matrix of the assets, calculated over a suitably long past history (of the order of three years). Problems arising from the allocations determined by this approach are then discussed and an ensemble approach developed to avoid some of them.

The penultimate chapter describes a recent approach to model more explicitly the dynamics of trading and various strategies and predictions which may be made by investors. We indicate how this approach should lead to a more effective inclusion of non-linear structure in the overall process, allowing non-linear modelling techniques, like neural networks, to attack the problem of unknown functionality more efficiently.

The final chapter gives a summary of the book and associated questions raised, together with a brief discussion of possible future directions to be followed. The summary covers the philosophy of the approach – that of attempting to capture as much information as possible from other financial and economic variables, at the same time not neglecting any information that may be carried by the target series itself.

The requirements of the process are:

1. The need to create a set of multivariate models involving an extensive concurrent exercise of input selection; this requires heavy use of both linear and non-linear multivariate prediction techniques.

2. The development of expertise in univariate modelling.

3. This leads further to the process of extraction of the best predictions from the two classes of modelling approaches (multi- and univariate) by the development of a combining technology. This was accomplished by the temperature-dependent combiner.

4. Last, but not least, there is a need to allocate assets by portfolio optimisation. We have used a quadratic risk–return optimiser, suitably extended so as to avoid too large a dependence on the swings of monthly asset allocations that noisy predictions can cause.

Various questions are discussed that are raised by the approach: why use monthly data? What is the value of combining models? Why avoid riskier assets?

Future work directions are discussed at the end of the book. Our overall conclusion is that our approach has been designed specifically to overcome changes in market dynamics. As such, it is therefore expected to stand up well to market changes in future years.

25. Portfolio Optimisation

C. J. Adcock

The aim of this chapter is to give an overview of the methodology and the process of portfolio optimisation and of some of the properties of portfolios built in this way. We include a discussion of alternative optimisation approaches and some of the issues that arise. The chapter is concerned with single period optimisation and omits the issue of currency hedging. The examples provided are solely for illustrative purposes.

25.1 Portfolio Optimisation

Formal methods of portfolio optimisation were introduced by Markowitz (1952) and have now been in use in finance for almost 50 years. As all who have had any exposure to these methods know, the basic idea is to construct a portfolio that (a) for a given level of volatility has the maximum expected return, or (b) has the minimum volatility for a given level of expected return. By varying the level of volatility or expected return, a family of portfolios is generated which is known as the efficient set. If the expected returns and volatilities of the portfolios in the efficient set are plotted, they lie on a parabolic curve[1], universally known as the efficient frontier. A sketch is shown in Fig. 25.1. This method of portfolio selection, frequently called mean-variance optimisation, is described in more detail in the sections below. It is based on the expected returns and volatilities of the universe of securities under consideration, together with the associated pairs of correlations. In practice, these theoretical quantities are replaced by estimated values.

Markowitz's portfolio optimisation methods are widely known, and the associated literature, which covers all aspects of the subject, is very large. The methods are set out in two celebrated texts, Markowitz (1959) and Markowitz (1987), as well as in numerous other books on portfolio theory.

Although these methods are widely known, they are not as commonly used as one might expect. This is for numerous reasons, of which the most significant is the

---

1 Strictly speaking, the curve is usually piece-wise parabolic.

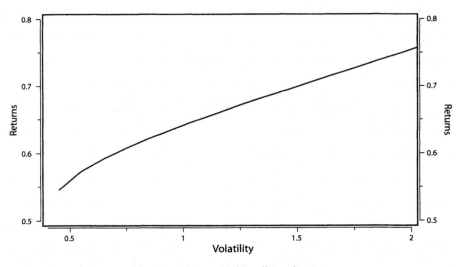

Fig. 25.1 An example of the efficient frontier.

sensitivity of the optimisation process to the quality of the input estimates. The sensitivity to input and other shortcomings, both real and perceived, have also been widely discussed in the literature. They have been summarised in the book by Richard Michaud (1998). Notwithstanding the criticisms, Markowitz's methodology, in one form or another, is the method of choice for the majority of those who construct portfolios using quantitative techniques. Furthermore, the majority of procedures for optimal portfolio construction are based directly or indirectly on mean–variance optimisation.

The aim of this chapter is to give an overview of the methodology, the process of portfolio optimisation and of some of the properties of portfolios built in this way. Included in the chapter is a discussion of alternative optimisation approaches and some of the issues that arise.

The chapter is concerned with single period optimisation. It omits the issue of currency hedging. In addition to the basic notation described in Section 25.2, other notation is introduced as required and is generally that in common use. The examples provided are solely for illustrative purposes.

25.2 Notation and Terminology

Portfolio optimisation is based on four sets of quantities:

- Expected returns
- Variances and covariances of asset returns
- Weights
- Actual returns

The first two items are inputs to the process. The weights are the principal outputs. Actual asset returns are required in order to compute the performance of portfolios based on the output weights. In practice, the true expected values, variances and covariances are unknown and estimated values are always used.

We assume an investment universe of N assets. Portfolio weights are denoted:

$$w_1, w_2, ..., w_N,$$

where $100w_i$ represents the percentage of wealth invested in asset i. The weights usually, but not always[2], add to the budget constraint:

$$w_1 + w_2 + ... + w_N = \sum_i w_i = 1$$

Actual portfolio return is weighted sum of individual returns:

$$R_{port} = w_1 R_1 + w_2 R_2 + ... + w_N R_N = \sum_{i=1}^{N} w_i R_i$$

The expected return of the portfolio is a weighted sum of individual expected returns:

$$E[R_{port}] = w_1 \mu_1 + w_2 \mu_2 + ... + w_N \mu_N = \sum_{i=1}^{N} w_i \mu_i = \mu_{port}$$

The variance of the portfolio return is:

$$V[R_{port}] = \sum_i w_i^2 \sigma_i^2 + \sum_{i \neq j} w_i w_j \sigma_{ij} = \sigma_{port}^2, \text{ say}$$

where the variance of stock i is σ_i^2 and the covariances between stock i and stock j are σ_{ij} for all pairs of stocks (i,j).

There is extensive use of matrix and vector notation in the literature. Specifically, we use the following vector notation for the weights, returns and expected returns[3]:

$$w = \begin{bmatrix} w_1 \\ w_2 \\ \vdots \\ w_N \end{bmatrix} \qquad R = \begin{bmatrix} R_1 \\ R_2 \\ \vdots \\ R_N \end{bmatrix} \qquad \mu = \begin{bmatrix} \mu_1 \\ \mu_2 \\ \vdots \\ \mu_N \end{bmatrix}$$

These are column vectors. If they are transposed or rotated through 90°, the corresponding row vectors are:

$$w^T = (w_1, w_2, ..., w_N)$$

and so on. The matrix notation for the variance–covariance (VC) matrix is:

---

2   A geared portfolio of financial futures is one exception, for example.

3   This notation is slightly ambiguous, but meanings should be clear from the context.

$$V = \begin{bmatrix} \sigma_1^2 & \sigma_{12} & \cdots & \sigma_{1N} \\ \sigma_{21} & \sigma_2^2 & \cdots & \sigma_{2N} \\ \vdots & \vdots & \ddots & \vdots \\ \sigma_{N1} & \sigma_{N2} & \cdots & \sigma_N^2 \end{bmatrix}$$

It is assumed that this matrix has full rank. The inverse matrix is:

$$V^{-1}$$

We also use a column vector of ones:

$$1 = \begin{bmatrix} 1 \\ 1 \\ \vdots \\ 1 \end{bmatrix}$$

with corresponding row vector:

$$1^T = (1, 1, \ldots, 1)$$

This means that we can write the budget constraint as:

$$w_1 + w_2 + \ldots + w_N = \sum_i w_i = 1^T w = 1$$

Portfolio expected return, μ_{port}, and portfolio variance, σ_{port}^2, are respectively expressed by $\mu^T w$ and $w^T V w$. In the rest of this chapter, it is assumed that these quantities exist and that they may be estimated consistently.

25.3   Scope of Portfolio Optimisation Methods

There are many types of users of portfolio optimisation methods. The aim of the portfolio manager, for example, is to build and manage portfolios that typically comprise stocks, bonds and cash. The investment time-scales are long and optimisation is done monthly, or perhaps less frequently. The portfolio generally has no short positions, although there are exceptions to this. A treasury manager is more concerned with risk and the emphasis is more likely to be on the control of volatility. Short positions are allowed and are essential for effective currency management. The speculator is concerned with return, even at the expense of risk: she or he might consider any asset, and very short-time scales and short positions are encouraged.

Portfolio theory and hence portfolio optimisation tend to concentrate on stocks. But, as implied above, there are many other assets that form part of portfolios. These are often handled using mean–variance optimisation methods, even though some of them, options for example, have return distributions that are substantially non-normal.

25.4 Efficient Set Mathematics and the Efficient Frontier

In its most simple form, portfolio optimisation requires the minimisation of volatility at a given level of expected return subject only to the budget constraint: the restriction that the portfolio weights add to one.

Even in an idealised situation where μ and V are assumed, this invariably results in portfolios with negative as well as positive holdings. These short positions are often prohibited. Consequently, almost all practical portfolio optimisation, and much of the related methodology, therefore imposes other constraints on portfolio weights, most notably the restriction that each weight be non-negative.

Nonetheless, efficient set mathematics, the term for study of the idealised form in which only the budget constraint is considered, offers numerous insights into the properties and behaviour of optimised portfolios. Specifically, it provides an analytical expression for the efficient frontier. This in turn gives insights into the likely behaviour of optimised portfolios and the dependence on the estimated input parameters.

Using the notation above, the idealised form of portfolio optimisation is to solve:

$$\min_w \phi = w^T V w \quad \text{such that} \quad 1^T w = 1 \quad \text{and} \quad \mu^T w = \tau$$

for a given target expected return τ. This is equivalent to assuming that investors seek to maximise the expected utility of return[4] at the end of the investment period where their utility function is the quadratic expression:

$$U(R) = \theta R_{\text{port}} - \frac{1}{2}(R_{\text{port}} - \mu_{\text{port}})^2$$

where $\theta \geq 0$ is a parameter that determines the individual investor's attitude to risk[5]. Increasing values of θ correspond to an increasing appetite for risk on the part of the investor. This utility function, although universally used, is not without problems. These, as well as some of the solutions, are discussed in Section 25.10.

Regardless of the underlying probability distribution of the assets, the expected value of the utility function is:

$$E[U(R_{\text{port}})] = \theta \mu_{\text{port}} - \frac{1}{2}\sigma^2_{\text{port}} = \theta w^T \mu - \frac{1}{2}w^T V w$$

This is a quadratic function of the unknown portfolio weights $\{w_i\}$. Maximising this quantity subject to the budget constraint $w^T 1 = 1$ is identical to performing OLS regression with a single constraint imposed on the parameter values. As is well known – see for example Roll (1977) or Best and Grauer (1991) – there is an analytic expression for the vector of portfolio weights, namely:

$$w^* = \frac{1}{1^T V^{-1} 1} V^{-1} \mu + \theta \left(V^{-1} - \frac{1}{1^T V^{-1} 1} V^{-1} 1 1^T V^{-1} \right) \mu$$

---

4   This is done by demonstrating that the two approaches give the same portfolio and that there is a relationship that links risk to the target return τ.

5   Other authors prefer to use risk aversion defined as $\rho = 1 / \theta$.

The vector:

$$\frac{1}{1^T V^{-1} 1} V^{-1} \mu = w^*_{mv}$$

is the minimum variance portfolio, with weights adding to unity, the budget constraint. The vector:

$$\left(V^{-1} - \frac{1}{1^T V^{-1} 1} V^{-1} 1 1^T V^{-1} \right) \mu = w^*_{off}$$

is a set of offsetting positions, which add exactly to zero. All efficient set portfolios consist of an investment of the budget in the minimum variance portfolio and a self-financing investment in the offsetting portfolio, with the size of individual positions being determined by risk appetite.

As the weight vector is an explicit function of μ and V, there are also analytic expressions for the mean and variance of R^*_{port}, the return on the efficient portfolio. These are:

$$E[R^*_{port}] = \alpha_0 + \theta \alpha_1 = E^*, \text{ say}$$

$$V[R^*_{port}] = \alpha_2 + \theta^2 \alpha_1 = V^*, \text{ say}$$

where the three α constants are defined in terms of μ and V as follows:

$$\alpha_0 = \frac{\mu^T V^{-1} 1}{1^T V^{-1} 1}$$

$$\alpha_1 = \mu^T \left(V^{-1} - \frac{1}{1^T V^{-1} 1} V^{-1} 1 1^T V^{-1} \right) \mu = \mu^T \left(V^{-1} - \frac{1}{\alpha_2} w_{mv} w_{mv}^T \right) \mu$$

$$\alpha_2 = \frac{1}{1^T V^{-1} 1}$$

It should be noted that whereas α_1 and α_2 are always non-negative, it is possible for α_0 to take negative as well as positive values.

25.4.1 The Efficient Frontier and Its Confidence Limits

If we use the equations for E^* and V^* to eliminate θ, we obtain the well-known equation for the efficient frontier:

$$(E^* - \alpha_0)^2 = \alpha_1 (V^* - \alpha_2)$$

or:

$$E^* - \alpha_0 = \sqrt{\alpha_1} \sqrt{V^* - \alpha_2}$$

The efficient frontier is a relationship between expected return and volatility or variance. The two quantities E^* and V^* do no more than define the first two moments of the probability distribution of return on the optimised portfolio. As everyone knows, actual returns can be very different from those expected. The corresponding confidence limits are wide. Assuming normal returns and level of risk appetite θ, the 95% limits for R_{port} are:

$$E^* \pm 1.96\sqrt{V^*}$$

The limits become wider as risk appetite increases because of the dependency of V^* on θ. It is possible for actual returns on an efficient portfolio to be both above and below the frontier. It may also be noted that it is possible, although unusual, for α_0, the expected return of the minimum variance portfolio, to be negative; generally an unsatisfactory state of affairs.

25.4.2 The CAPM and the Maximum Sharpe Ratio Portfolio

Another product of efficient set mathematics is that, for a specified risk free rate, the market portfolio in the CAPM is also the portfolio on the efficient frontier that maximises the Sharpe ratio. This has led to the popularity of Sharpe ratio maximisation as a specific criterion for portfolio optimisation.

25.4.3 Sensitivity to the Inputs

Portfolio optimisation is sensitive to the inputs. There are well-known studies due to Best and Grauer (1991) and Chopra and Ziemba (1993) and the topic of sensitivity is one the main themes of Michaud (1998). For real portfolio optimisation it is necessary to carry out investigations in portfolio sensitivity using a mixture of analytical and numerical methods. For the idealised efficient set portfolio, it is possible to gain insights using analytical methods.

It is important to note that there are two aspects of sensitivity. The first is the intrinsic sensitivity of portfolio optimisation to the parameters μ and V. Even in an ideal world where these are assumed to be known exactly, the optimised portfolio weights w^*, and consequently the mean and variance E^* and V^*, are sensitive to small changes in these parameters. This intrinsic sensitivity is not within the control of the analyst; it is a consequence of the original utility function or the original criterion for portfolio optimisation. The second aspect of sensitivity is the fact that, in practice, estimates are always used. Intrinsic sensitivity is therefore compounded by the second source, which is, to some extent at least, within the control of the analyst.

The intrinsic sensitivity of w^* to μ and V may be found by differentiation. The resulting expressions are beyond the scope of this publication. However, clear insights may be gained from looking at an example portfolio of two assets.

Example – Two Stocks From the FTA-All Share Actuaries Index

This example is based on weekly data from 13 January 1978 to 20 October 1995, 928 weeks in all, for two randomly selected stocks from the FTA-All Share Actuaries index. Each week, the latest estimate of variances and covariance are computed using exponential smoothing with a smoothing factor of 0.98. The minimum variance portfolio is built and held for one week. The gross and net returns after deducting 1% transactions costs are indexed and the two indexed series are shown

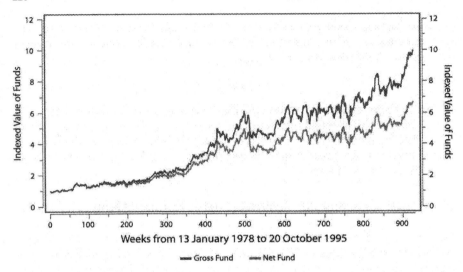

Fig. 25.2 Gross and net returns for minimum variance portfolio based on two stocks from the FTA-All Share Actuaries index; weekly data from 13 January 1978 to 20 October 1995.

in Fig. 25.2. The discrepancy between the two series is an indication of the changing weights, i.e. the sensitivity to variation in the estimates of variance and correlation.

Figure 25.3 shows the corresponding values of the weight for one of the assets. The message from the two figures is that the weights are sensitive to relatively small changes in the weekly input values of variances and correlation.

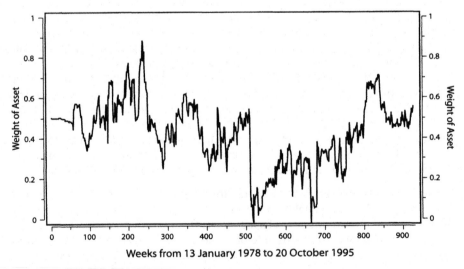

Fig. 25.3 Weight for Asset A from a two asset portfolio based on two stocks from the FTA-All Share Actuaries index; weekly data from 13 January 1978 to 20 October 1995.

25.4.4 Dependence on Estimates

The effect of estimated input parameters is, as noted above, a source of sensitivity which may be within the control of the analyst. In addition to the sensitivity of portfolio weights to estimates, users frequently observe poor portfolio performance, which is considered to be due to the use of poor estimates.

Analytical investigation of the effects of estimates is in general an open question, although the effect of estimates on the maximum Sharpe ratio portfolio has been reported in some detail by Jobson and Korkie (1980). In Adcock (2000) it is shown that, when uncertainty in estimation of the mean μ is taken into account, the expected return and variance of an efficient set portfolio are respectively:

$$E[R^*_{port}] = \alpha_0 + \theta\alpha_1 + \beta_0\theta$$

$$\text{and} \quad V[R^*_{port}] = \alpha_2 + \theta^2\alpha_1 + 2\theta\beta_1 + \theta^2\beta_2$$

The αs and θ are as defined above. The β terms are functions of the parameters of the (assumed) multivariate normal joint probability distribution of asset returns and of the estimates used in portfolio construction. The equations above indicate that, depending on the β values, expected return and variance may be less or more than that predicted by standard theory.

25.5 Construction of Optimised Portfolios Using Quadratic Programming

Construction of real optimised portfolios is conventionally based on the quadratic expected utility:

$$\theta\mu_{port} - \frac{1}{2}\sigma^2_{port}$$

which is maximised subject to the budget constraint $1^Tw = 1$ and the non-negativity restrictions:

$$w_i \geq 0, \quad i = 1, ..., N$$

For given inputs μ and V, the solution is found using quadratic programming (QP) methods. This is equivalent to minimising portfolio variance at a given level of expected return or maximising expected return at a given level of volatility, in the presence of the non-negativity restrictions as well as the budget constraint.

In the standard notation that is common in the optimisation literature, this QP may be expressed as:

$$Max_w \phi = \theta w^T \mu - \frac{1}{2}w^T Vw \quad \text{such that} \quad A^T w \geq b$$

The matrix A contains the constraint normals. For this QP, A is an $N \times (N + 1)$ matrix:

$$A = [1, I], \quad \text{with } I \text{ an } N \times N \text{ unit matrix}$$

The vector b contains the corresponding $(N + 1)$ constraint values:

$$b = \begin{bmatrix} 1 \\ 0 \\ \vdots \\ 0 \end{bmatrix}$$

An individual constraint is written:

$$a_j^T w \geq b_j$$

where a_j is the jth column of A and b_j the corresponding value of b. There are several algorithms that are suitable for solving this QP and software to carry out the computations is widely available. Further details of these methods may be read in texts like Fletcher (1987) or in the survey article by Gill *et al.* (1990). New algorithms, that may be more suitable for some types of problem, appear periodically. For example, the algorithm due to von Hohenbalken (1974) enjoyed a period of popularity. Active set methods are probably used in the majority of software, but the interior point methods associated with Karmarkar (1984) will possibly become increasingly common.

The basic QP may be solved at a specified level of risk θ. The algorithm may also be set up so that it will generate the whole of the entire efficient frontier.

An interesting application is reverse optimisation, which is the ability to take a set of weights and to apply the QP solution process in reverse to compute the implied input vector μ.

25.6 Issues in Practical Portfolio Construction

In practice, real portfolio optimisation embodies numerous other features. Generally we would include other constraints. It is also common to optimise relative to a benchmark portfolio and to include transactions costs.

25.6.1 Other Constraints

These are typically upper and lower limits on the weight for any asset. They may also encompass more complex restrictions, such as limits on sector holdings for an equity portfolio or market exposure in asset allocation.

It is normal practice to re-optimise portfolios regularly. Many users will be familiar with the substantial turnover that can arise at each re-optimisation: another manifestation of portfolio sensitivity. A common way of regulating this is to restrict turnover at each optimisation by imposing a pair of constraints for each asset[6]:

---

6   This is $100|w_i - w_{i,0}| \leq \text{TO}$.

$$w_{i,0}\left(1-\frac{\text{TO}}{100}\right) \le w_i \le w_{i,0}\left(1+\frac{\text{TO}}{100}\right)$$

where $w_{i,0}$ is the existing holding in asset i and TO is the permitted turnover at each re-optimisation expressed as a percentage.

From a technical perspective, linear constraints are usually expressed as lower bounds and the corresponding vector of normals and value added into A and b, respectively.

Constraints play two distinct roles in portfolio optimisation. First, they are included when they reflect portfolio design criteria specified by the fund manager or by another third party. As such, they are quite independent of the method of portfolio construction. Secondly, they may be included in the belief that they will improve portfolio performance in some way. There is ample empirical evidence to suggest that use of constraints can lead to improved performance as well as reduced volatility and portfolio turnover. The paper by Frost and Savarino (1988) explores this theme. However, it is also generally accepted that fine-tuning constraints to improve performance is not good practice, as it may conceal inadequacies in the estimates of m and V.

25.6.2 Optimisation Relative to a Benchmark

Optimisation to a benchmark portfolio is also widely employed. Portfolio expected return is usually replaced by excess return, i.e. portfolio return minus benchmark return. If the benchmark portfolio weights are denoted by the N vector p, this is:

$$ER_{\text{port}} = (w-p)^T R$$

The corresponding variance is:

$$(w-p)^T V(w-p)$$

and these two quantities are used in the QP formulation above. At the minimum variance point, corresponding to $\theta = 0$, the optimised portfolio will be equal to the benchmark. Exceptions occur only if there are portfolio design constraints in place which the benchmark does not meet[7].

Optimisation relative to the benchmark also often employs the types of constraints described above. However, they are usually expressed relative to the benchmark weights. For example, upper and lower limits would appear as:

$$p_i\left(1-\frac{L_i}{100}\right) \le w_i \le p_i\left(1+\frac{U_i}{100}\right)$$

where the percentages L and U define the permitted variation below and above the benchmark weight. Sometimes these are applied additively:

$$p_i - \frac{L_i}{100} \le w_i \le p_i + \frac{U_i}{100}$$

---

7   Exceptions can also occur when transaction costs are included in the optimisation – see Section 25.8.

This, however, needs to be done with care. There is the risk of serious over- or under-weighting of assets with small benchmark weights. Conversely, there is the risk of staying too close to the benchmark weight for assets for which this value is large. Sector or asset class constraints would be applied relative to the benchmark in the same way.

Another type of constraint that is used when optimising relative to a benchmark is concerned with factor models. Detailed discussion of this topic is omitted, but the basic idea is to limit the factor exposure of the portfolio relative to the benchmark. In this context, the estimated betas of securities may be regarded as factors and an optimised portfolio may be designed to have a specified beta, or a beta that lies in a pre-specified range.

It is widely accepted that it is difficult to beat the market! Optimisation relative to a benchmark portfolio, which is taken as a proxy for the market, is widespread. However, many would apply constraints to such an optimisation and regard the process as one of *"tilting modestly away from the benchmark"*[8]. Benchmark weights usually change slowly and are therefore a source of stability, particularly at low levels of risk

If the benchmark portfolio is efficient with respect to the estimates of μ and V that are used, then relative optimisation will give portfolios that lie on the efficient frontier. However, if the benchmark is inefficient, relative optimisation will produce portfolios that lie below the frontier. The discrepancy between the two frontiers reduces to zero as risk appetite increases. At low values of risk, the difference can be marked, as the sketch in Fig. 25.4 illustrates. Note that to illustrate the curvature, the horizontal axis is variance rather than volatility, which is used more conventionally.

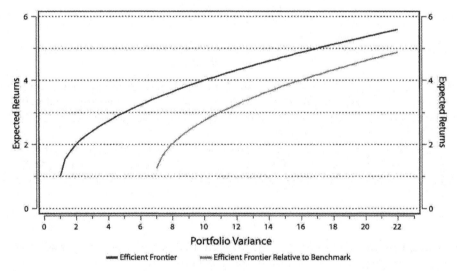

Fig. 25.4 Sketch of efficient frontiers absolute and relative to an inefficient benchmark portfolio.

---

8   This is a quotation, I think. Unfortunately the name of the speaker is long since forgotten.

25.6.3 Transactions costs

The criteria described so far are concerned with the gross return on the portfolio. Transactions costs may be regulated using the constraints described above. However, it may be preferable to consider a utility function based on net returns after the deduction of costs. This is an important issue because it is relatively common for optimised portfolios to achieve their investment objectives prior to the deduction of costs, but not when net returns are computed.

If costs are taken to be c_i for asset i, regardless of the amount transacted, the transactions costs at each optimisation are:

$$\sum_{i=1}^{N} c_i |w_i - w_{i,0}|$$

Maximisation of the expected utility of net return leads to the modified QP:

$$Max_w \phi = \theta w^T \mu - \frac{1}{2} w^T V w - \eta \sum_{i=1}^{N} c_i |w_i - w_{i,0}|$$

such that $\quad A^T w \geq b$

The additional parameter η (≥ 0) is included as a convenience to allow easy scaling of costs. This may be re-expressed as a standard QP and solved with standard methods. However, for N assets this is at the expense of including $2N$ dummy variables, which increases solution time substantially. Adcock and Meade (1995) describe a method that avoids this. It is straightforward to extend the cost model to allow for different buy/sell costs and to incorporate price breaks and quantity discounts.

Inclusion of a cost term duplicates the role of the turnover constraints described above. Although one could invoke duality to remove the duplication, the method of choice normally depends on empirical investigation. In general, formulation of the QP in terms of net return is usually to be preferred to the use of turnover constraints. However, there are exceptions to this and empirical investigation of the better approach is often needed.

25.7 What Portfolio Selection Requires

In general, portfolio selection requires good estimates of future expected returns, variances and covariances. Portfolio optimisation is sensitive to errors in expected returns, variances and covariances in that order. Further details of the relationships between the effects of errors in the three sets of parameters are in Chopra and Ziemba (1993) and Best and Grauer (1991). It is generally accepted that, of the three sets of parameters, it is most important to employ good estimates of expected returns.

However, what constitutes good estimates of expected returns is not always clear. Suppose that we have an estimate of μ, the vector of expected returns, which is correct apart from a scale factor, and a given value of risk appetite θ. The resulting optimised portfolio will still be on the efficient frontier corresponding to μ. It will just be at a different point in mean–variance space from that portfolio which would result from using μ itself. The use of scaled forecasts may produce a portfolio that meets investor objectives. If it does not, then since variation of θ generates all portfolios on the efficient frontier, a portfolio that is acceptable may be found using the same set of forecasts and just varying θ.

It is also possible to construct forecasts, which, because of their joint correlation with actual returns, have a more favourable expected return–risk trade-off than the use of μ itself. See Adcock (2000) for details of how this may arise. However, it must be noted that, although it is easy to build such forecasts for the purposes of theoretical investigation, construction of such models, which can be used to build real portfolios is a more difficult task.

25.8   The Process of Building an Optimised Portfolio

The process of building and evaluating optimised portfolios usually employs the process of back-testing. Back-testing requires a time-series database of returns on the assets in the universe, together with forecasts of expected returns, variances and covariances made at the start of each investment period. All forecasts must be constructed so that they use only information that was available at the start of the investment period in question.

Even when we go to considerable lengths to ensure compliance with the statement in the last paragraph, there is a potential problem with back-testing. It is as follows. Back-testing is based on historical data. By the time we get this history, it will generally be complete and accurate and will contain data that is available to all. If we implement an investment or trading strategy now and hold the resulting portfolio until the end of the current investment period, it is self-evident that the strategy, whatever it may be, can only depend on information that is available now and furthermore only on information that is available to us. Thus the data used in real time for real investment decisions is likely to be substantively different from the historical data used in back-testing.

If we go to considerable lengths, it is possible to build databases that approximate what our true knowledge was at each time period in the past. Nonetheless, the process of back-testing, although it is a standard methodology, inevitably contains some degree of foresight. The results of back-testing should therefore always be interpreted with caution.

With this warning in mind, the aim of back-testing is to establish that our forecasting processes and models will allow us to build optimised portfolios which meet given investment objectives. In principle, this process requires four steps.

The following notation is used. The actual returns on securities $I = 1, ..., N$ in the period which starts at time $t - 1$ and ends at time t are denoted by $\{R_{i,t}\}$. The forecasts that are made of the expected returns for the period that ends at time t are denoted by $\{F_{i,t}\}$. These forecasts are made at time t-1 and use only information that is available at time $t - 1$. There are also corresponding estimates of the variance–covariance matrix, $\{s_{i,j,t}\}$ say, which are constructed using the same principles. The weights produced by the optimisation process carried out at time $t - 1$ are denoted $\{w_{i,t}\}$. These determine the investment proportions for the period $t - 1$ through t.

The return data and the forecasts (made one period before) are available from time 1 to time T. The four steps are as follows.

25.8.1 Build the Ex-post Efficient Frontier

At each time period, we build the entire efficient frontier by solving the basic QP described in Section 25.4. This requires us to find the minimum variance portfolio and then, strictly speaking, to establish the points on the frontier that are corner solutions. Since the corner solutions can occur at different levels of risk appetite at each time period, the procedure used in practice is to construct a discrete frontier by using a pre-specified set of values of θ^9.

At each value of θ, the inputs to the optimisation are the forecasts $\{F_{i,t}\}$ and the corresponding estimates of variances and covariances. The actual return on each portfolio for the period ending at time t is:

$$R_{\text{port},t} = \sum_{i=1}^{N} w_{i,t} R_{i,t}$$

This process is carried out for all times 1 through T. At each value of θ, this data is used to compute the mean return at each level of risk and the realised volatility. The mean return per period is usually computed assuming reinvestment, i.e. as:

$$R_g = \left(\prod_{t=1}^{T} (1 + R_{\text{port},t}) \right)^{1/T} - 1$$

The volatility is computed as:

$$S = \sqrt{\frac{\sum_{t=1}^{T} (R_{\text{port},t} - \overline{R}_{\text{port}})^2}{(T-1)}}$$

where $\overline{R}_{\text{port}}$ is the sample mean of the portfolio returns.

25.8.2 Assessment of the Ex-post Efficient Frontier

Repeating this process at each of the pre-specified values of θ allows the construction of the ex-post efficient frontier, which is constructed by plotting the pairs of points (S, R_g).

This will not be a smooth curve in general, since it depends both on forecasts and on actual returns. However, if the forecasts $\{F_{i,t}\}$ and $\{s_{i,j,t}\}$ are good estimates of the corresponding population values, we may expect to see a curve which is approximately parabolic in shape and has a positive gradient. If this proves to be the case,

---

9   This set should be such that it covers the entire frontier. Its values depend on the units of measurement use for returns. Establishment of the set usually requires some experimentation.

there is then empirical evidence that the forecasting methodology used possesses some signal and contains information about the distribution of future returns.

We can then proceed to employ the forecasts to build a portfolio, which meets our specific investment objectives. This may involve use of other constraints, a benchmark portfolio, transactions costs and so on. Once these design parameters have been specified, the output from the back-test would, as above, be computed for all time periods and at several levels of risk appetite. This facilitates the construction of an ex-post frontier, which matches the precise design parameters of the portfolio.

As already noted, there is evidence that constraints can improve aspects of the performance of an optimised portfolio, but one should avoid the temptation of fine-tuning in an attempt to improve performance.

25.8.3 Ex-post Performance Analysis

As well as reporting the mean return and volatility of a back-tested strategy, it is common practice to compute other performance statistics. These typically include:

- Portfolio turnover, total transactions costs and hence net return
- Ex-post betas and Sharpe ratios
- Ex-post factor exposures
- Minimum portfolio value
- Worst performance over any 12 month period

25.8.4 The Effect of Transactions costs

The solution to the basic QP defined in Section 25.4 does not depend on the holdings at the start of the period. Given the inputs, the result of each optimisation is independent of its predecessor. This may not be true when we employ turnover constraints and is certainly not true when we incorporate transactions costs in the utility function.

Thus, starting a set of optimisations, which includes transactions costs in the objective function, in January 1990 will not produce the same sets of portfolio weights for February 1990 onwards as a strategy that starts in February 1990 itself. When transactions costs are included, it is therefore sensible to start back-testing at a number of different time periods in order to establish the robustness of the input forecasts to the starting date.

25.9   Example of an Asset Allocation Portfolio

As noted in the introduction, this example is provided solely for the purpose of illustration. It is an example of an asset allocation portfolio, based on six asset classes. These are as follows:

Table 25.1 Basic statistics for six assets and the corresponding forecasts

	US		Japan		Europe	
	Bonds	*Equities*	*Bonds*	*Equities*	*Bonds*	*Equities*
Mean actual return	0.0059	0.0100	0.0056	−0.0039	0.0065	0.0092
Volatility	0.0330	0.0484	0.0117	0.0651	0.0300	0.0444
Mean forecast return	0.0082	0.0118	0.0050	0.0076	0.0056	0.0111
Volatility	0.0041	0.0049	0.0033	0.0096	0.0025	0.0073
Sign test(%)	58.1633	52.0408	65.3061	47.9592	56.1224	61.2245
Correlation	−0.0743	0.0101	0.1410	0.0494	−0.1156	0.0932
MSE	0.0335	0.0484	0.0117	0.0660	0.0302	0.0441
U Statistic	1.0009	1.0077	0.9572	0.9852	1.0012	0.9845

Monthly data from September 1989 to October 1997 inclusive. All returns and forecasts measured in Japanese yen. Returns, forecasts and their volatilities are measured as decimals.

1. US equity index
2. US bond index
3. Japan equity index
4. Japan bond index
5. Europe equity index
6. Europe bond index

All returns are measured in Japanese yen. The data is monthly and runs from September 1989 to October 1997 inclusive. Forecasts of future expected returns are produced each month according to the convention above. Also estimated each month is the VC matrix of returns. The basic performance statistics for actual returns and for the corresponding forecasts are shown in Table 25.1.

A feature to note is that over the period the actual mean return of Japanese equities was negative, whereas the mean forecast return over the same period was positive. The four forecast evaluation statistics are as follows. The sign test measures the percentage of occasions that the forecast gets the sign of the subsequent market move right. Correlation is between forecasts and actual return. MSE is mean square error and U statistic is Theil's U[10]. The values shown in the table are typical of modelling in this area. The values are uninspiring and are close to the neutral values that one might expect if the forecasts had no signal at all. The key word is close!

The strategy is then to build the efficient frontier. The only constraints are the budget and non-negativity restrictions. The frontier is constructed for the following six values of risk appetite:

$$0, 0.001, 0.01, 0.1, 1.0, 10.0$$

The resulting portfolio performance is shown in Table 25.2.

---

10 The ratio of the MSE of the model forecast to the MSE of a naïve forecast, usually taken to be the return in the previous period.

Table 25.2 Portfolio performance along the efficient frontier

			Risk appetite			
	0	0.001	0.01	0.1	1	10
Portfolio return	0.0054	0.0055	0.0063	0.0046	0.0025	0.0028
Volatility	0.0112	0.0114	0.0139	0.0379	0.0545	0.0587
Return/volatility ratio	0.4804	0.4839	0.4545	0.1208	0.0458	0.0480
Turnover (%)	3.1014	5.8212	19.9483	51.1028	60.7918	60.6793
Corners (%)	39.1156	36.0544	35.2041	52.3810	89.9660	98.6395

Monthly data from September 1989 to October 1997 inclusive. All returns and forecasts measured in Japanese Yen. Returns and volatilities are measured as decimals.

Turnover is the average of the total absolute weight change at each optimisation expressed in percent. That is, it is the mean of:

$$100 \sum_{i=1}^{N} |w_{i,t} - w_{i,t-1}|$$

excluding the first optimisation[11]. The statistic "Corners(%)" measures the percentage of occasions on which the optimal weights are found to be an upper or lower limit. As risk appetite increases, and we move up the efficient frontier, turnover and the incidence of corner solutions increases. Increasing turnover, in particular, is a consequence of increasing dependence on the forecasts, which change each month.

Table 25.2 illustrates a feature that is common to practical portfolio optimisation. At low levels of risk, the signal contained in the forecasts is sufficient to provide portfolios that will give increasing ex-post return with increasing risk appetite. However, as risk appetite increases, the dependency on the signal becomes too great and the result is falling ex-post return. The best level of performance, in terms of ex-post average return, is at risk appetite 0.01. It may be noted that this does not have the maximum value of the average return–volatility ratio. For the six levels of θ covered, this occurs at risk appetite 0.001.

The same exercise is repeated for optimisation relative to a benchmark portfolio. For this example, the benchmark weights (per cent) are taken to be:

$$9, 6, 40, 30, 9, 6$$

for the six assets listed above. The resulting performance is shown in Table 25.3.

This gives similar results to the absolute optimisation. The best level of excess return occurs at risk 0.01. In this case, this is also the best value of the ratio of excess return to excess volatility.

It should be noted that at levels of risk that are less than or equal to 0.1, at the lower end of the efficient frontier, the performance of the absolute optimisations is superior to the performance of the relative optimisations. This is consistent with the sketch shown in Fig. 25.4 and probably reflects the inefficiency of the benchmark

---

11 This is always 100%, as a cold start from cash is assumed in the backtesting.

Table 25.3 Portfolio performance along the efficient frontier with optimisation relative to a benchmark

	Risk appetite					
	0	0.001	0.01	0.1	1	10
Portfolio return	0.0033	0.0035	0.0047	0.0041	0.0030	0.0029
Benchmark return	0.0033	0.0033	0.0033	0.0033	0.0033	0.0033
Excess return	0.0000	0.0002	0.0014	0.0008	−0.0003	−0.0004
Volatility of excess	0.0000	0.0011	0.0083	0.0268	0.0415	0.0445
Ratio	NA	0.1595	0.1666	0.0293	−0.0077	−0.0083
Turnover(%)	3.6167	9.1455	28.5460	49.7868	58.7158	60.2134
Corners(%)	0.0000	1.8707	13.0952	51.0204	78.2313	82.9932

Monthly data from September 1989 to October 1997 inclusive. All returns and forecasts measured in Japanese Yen. Returns and volatilities are measured as decimals.

portfolio. At the higher risk appetite levels, the two sets of returns are very similar. This reflects the eventual convergence of the two frontiers. Figure 25.5 shows the indexed performance of the portfolios based on absolute and relative optimisations at risk levels 0, 0.001 and 0.01. The three absolute optimisations are denoted by the prefix ABS in the chart and the relative optimisations by REL.

The chart shows quite clearly the effect of the inefficiency of the benchmark. It is true to say that the performance of the absolute optimisations is superior over the whole time period at all levels of risk. However, it may be noted that there is evidence of improved performance of the relative optimisations from 1995 onwards. This may reflect improving efficiency of the benchmark portfolio in later years.

Table 25.4 gives a comparison of the portfolio weights for absolute and relative optimisation at risk appetite 0.01. The reason for the difference in performance is clear. Absolute optimisation allows large holdings in Japanese bonds, but avoids

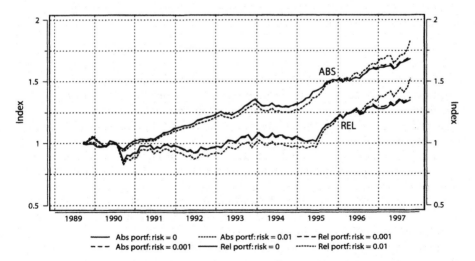

Fig. 25.5 Performance of absolute and relative optimisations. Monthly data from September 1989 to October 1997 inclusive. All returns and forecasts measured in Japanese yen. Returns and volatilities are measured as decimals.

Table 25.4 Comparison of weights for absolute and relative optimisations

		Absolute optimisation				Relative optimisation			
		Avg	Min	Max	Std.Err	Avg	Min	Max	Std.Err
US	Bonds	12.23	0	26.95	7.26	13.29	0	31.38	8.04
	Equities	2.32	0	23.61	5.55	6.59	0	34.59	9.13
Japan	Bonds	75.42	44.24	93.84	9.43	33.22	0	67.32	10.31
	Equities	2.72	0	15.05	4.18	29.94	0.8	42.32	7.59
Europe	Bonds	2.85	0	28.96	5.32	4.71	0	35.29	5.95
	Equities	4.46	0	53.11	9.89	12.27	0	69.76	12.96

Based on monthly data from September 1989 to October 1997 inclusive. All table entries are shown as percentages.

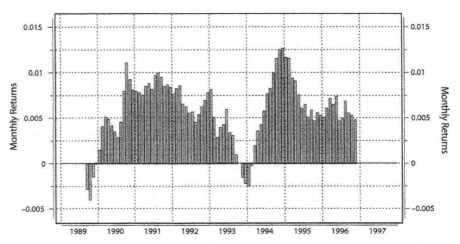

Fig. 25.6 Twelve-month holding period returns. Based on monthly data from September 1989 to October 1997 inclusive. Returns are monthly decimals.

them in Japanese equities. The relative optimisation forces holdings in Japanese equities; additional evidence of the inefficiency of the benchmark. It may be noted that both sets of weights possess comparable temporal volatility, as measured by the standard errors, although the measures for the relative optimisations are consistently slightly higher.

Figure 25.6 shows the 12-month holding period return for the absolute optimisation based on risk appetite 0.01. Out of the 87 holding periods that begin between September 1989 and November 1996, ten give 12-month holding period returns that are negative. For these 87 periods, the minimum fund value of a portfolio produced by the strategy of buy and hold for 12 months is 93.36% of the initial investment. This ignores the effect of transactions costs.

Finally, it is instructive to consider the effect of transactions costs. Table 25.5 shows the effect of such costs on optimisation relative to the benchmark at zero risk. The transactions costs used are 20 basis points for equities and 40 for bonds, for

Table 25.5 The effect of transactions costs on the minimum variance portfolio relative to the benchmark

	Ignore	Include						
		Start at						
		Sep-89	Sep-90	Sep-91	Sep-92	Sep-93	Sep-94	
Gross returns								
Portfolio	0.0033	0.0050	0.0057	0.0060	0.0064	0.0066	0.0082	
Benchmark	0.0033	0.0033	0.0045	0.0047	0.0055	0.0051	0.0064	
Excess	0.0000	0.0017	0.0012	0.0012	0.0010	0.0014	0.0018	
Net returns								
Portfolio	0.0032	0.0050	0.0057	0.0059	0.0064	0.0065	0.0081	
Excess	−0.0001	0.0017	0.0011	0.0012	0.0009	0.0014	0.0017	
Turnover(%)	3.6167	1.0206	1.1629	1.3515	1.6131	2.0001	2.6317	

Based on monthly data from September 1989 to October 1997 inclusive. Table entries are shown as decimals, except where indicated.

both sale and purchase[12]. The scaling parameter h is set to 1. When costs are ignored, the benchmark portfolio is reproduced for all months from September 1989 through October 1997. When costs are included in the optimisation, there is a positive net excess return of about 17 basis points per month. Bearing in mind the possible dependency of this result on the start date, Table 25.5 shows the same strategy started at yearly intervals until September 1994. The result is always a positive net excess return, with the minimum value being 9bp per month.

25.10 Alternative Measures of Risk and Methods of Optimisation

The basis of Markowitz's method is to find a portfolio that has the maximum expected return for a given level of volatility or to find a portfolio that has the minimum volatility for any given level of expected return. Both methods are equivalent to the use of a quadratic utility function with a specified level of risk appetite. From a statistical perspective, all versions of the method are based on parameters of the multivariate probability distribution of return, specifically the vector of expected returns, μ, and the VC matrix of returns, V. There are numerous methodologies that are used to construct estimates of these parameters.

In addition, many researchers have investigated a wide variety of alternative methods. These include other measures of risk, different utility functions or criteria for portfolio selection, and inclusion of other moments, to name but three topics.

---

12 These costs are purely illustrative. If these assets were transacted through the futures market, then actual costs would be far lower. The example has been constructed this way to demonstrate the effect of costs on portfolio selection. It should be noted that the same effect can be achieved with lower costs, but a higher value of η.

25.10.1 Other Measures of Risk

A straightforward extension to the estimation of V is to include the uncertainty due to the use of forecasts or of estimated returns. This "forecast VC matrix" will, loosely speaking, have numerically larger estimates of variance than the corresponding estimates in V. For a given level of risk appetite, it will therefore produce an optimised portfolio that is closer to the minimum variance portfolio. Assets, for which the forecasts of expected return are less accurate, will be de-weighted relative to others.

This approach will appeal greatly to any Bayesian, since it only requires the use of what is called the predictive or pre-posterior distribution of future returns to determine the appropriate matrix to estimate. From a practical perspective, use of the forecast VC matrix and the corresponding estimate of expected return are used as inputs to the standard optimisation methodology. From a theoretical point of view, it is necessary to take a different view of the utility function and the appropriate expectation to use – further details of this are given by Wagner (1998), who cites Bawa *et al.* (1979).

A second extension is to use semi-variance rather than variance. This variation to standard methodology has been fashionable in recent years. The idea is attributed to Markowitz himself and was popularised by Frank Sortino; see for example Sortino and Price (1994). Use of semi-variance should be undertaken with care, particularly if it done in conjunction with standard estimates of correlation. This is because the QP optimiser is a process that operates mechanically on the inputs. An input matrix in which variances have been replaced by semi-variances, which are usually smaller numerically, will appear to the optimiser to have high correlations. As is well known, these can cause whipsawing; weights that go up and down at successive portfolio optimisations. This is another manifestation of portfolio sensitivity.

The performance of optimised portfolios based on semi-variance and similar measures has been reported by Grootveld and Hallerbach (1998) and Eftekhari *et al.* (2000). At this stage, it is appropriate to say that an assessment of the benefits of semi-variance should be made on a case-by-case basis.

25.10.2 Ensembles of Portfolios

In each time period, the history of forecasts may be used to compute an estimate of the variance covariance matrix of the distribution of forecasts of future expected returns. In the sub-section above, this might simply be added to the VC matrix of actual returns to allow for forecasts uncertainty. A second use is to generate ensembles of portfolios each investment period. To do this, the vector of forecast expected returns and corresponding VC matrix are used to generate sets of simulated forecasts. Each set is used as inputs to the optimisation process at time $(t-1)$, generating, in the notation of Section 25.8, a matrix of portfolio weights $\{w_{i,s,t}\}$, where s indexes the simulation. The resulting sets of weights may be averaged in various ways to produce the final set of weights $\{w_{i,t}\}$. As above, this procedure will appeal to any Bayesian and is similar to the resampling procedures described in Michaud (1998).

25.10.3 Other Utility and Objective Functions

There are many who use or develop different utility or objective functions for portfolio optimisation. For example, two common approaches are to maximise the Sharpe ratio of the portfolio or to maximise the probability of the portfolio return exceeding a given target. For practitioners, the motivation for different criteria is to seek to improve some aspect of portfolio performance.

Such efforts are often ostensibly justified by the fact that the quadratic function is not a proper utility function. The function:

$$\theta R_{\text{port}} - \frac{1}{2}(R_{\text{port}} - \mu_{\text{port}})^2$$

is quadratic in R_{port} and therefore has a global maximum at the point $\mu_{\text{port}} + \theta$. It implies that for all returns greater than the global maximum, increasing return leads to lower utility. According to the well-known criticism of Pratt (1964), there are situations where we prefer less return to more return.

Very often, however, the search for a better utility function is fruitless. Maximisation of the Sharpe ratio leads to the market portfolio – a point on the efficient frontier. If returns are assumed to be normally distributed, maximisation of the probability of beating a given target return also leads to a point on the efficient frontier. In fact, the portfolio in this case is a market portfolio corresponding to a risk-free rate equal to the target.

Furthermore, if returns are normal, then any well-defined utility function will lead to a point in the efficient frontier. This important result, due in its most general form to Kallberg and Ziemba (1983), implies that, within the framework of the normal distribution, all one needs to do is to find a point on the frontier that complies with the investor's attitude to risk. Within the framework of normal returns, variations on the standard QP objective function will not produce new performance characteristics[13]. As noted in Adcock (2001), the only issue is whether a different utility function proves more effective in determining the appropriate point on the efficient frontier.

If the expected utility function is a suitable function of expected portfolio return and variance[14], this too will lead to a point on the efficient frontier regardless of the distribution of returns.

25.10.4 Non-normally Distributed Returns

When returns are not normally distributed, the most obvious weakness of mean–variance optimisation is that it does not take account of other moments of the probability distribution of returns. There are numerous papers in the literature that incorporate skewness in the utility function – see for example Levy and Markowitz (1979), Hlawitschka (1994) or Loistl (1976). The general consensus

---

13 See Van der Sar (1993) or Whittle (1990) for two examples.

14 It should be an increasing function of expected return and a decreasing function of variance.

seems to be that the effect on the structure and performance of the resulting portfolios is inconclusive.

It is widely accepted that return distributions are fat-tailed. This suggests that the utility function should also include a fourth moment term. As above, the evidence for this is believed to be inconclusive. Furthermore, if the distribution of returns is elliptically symmetric, then all higher moments are proportional to a power of the variance[15]. This suggests, although does not prove, that a quadratic utility function is likely to be as good as a quartic, at least over a specified range of returns.

25.10.5 Other Methods

There are numerous other methods. Linear programming in which the objective function is expected portfolio return is an obvious simplification. When used, this is typically accompanied by constraints that limit exposure. These generally include sector constraints, as well as upper and lower limits for each asset. Linear programming can also be used in conjunction with factors of return, which are also employed as constraints. From a technical perspective, LP is equivalent to carrying out a constrained mean–variance optimisation at a very high risk appetite[16].

There is also a robust method due to Konno and Yamazaki (1991). This does not involve a utility function. Instead the objective is to minimise a robust measure of portfolio tracking error. This may be reduced to a linear programming problem, so the previous comment applies. Grauer and Hakansson (1985) use a different utility function and compute its expected value non-parametrically.

25.10.6 Soft Constraints

When constraints are used, it is common to find that the optimiser will produce corner solutions, that is solutions in which at least one of the inequality constraints is active. For example, if all assets in an optimisation of FTSE 100 stocks are required to have a weight of at least 0.5%, we may find that several holdings equal this "corner" value. Given that 0.5% is probably an arbitrary value selected for subjective reasons, it raises the following questions What would happen if the lower limit were 0.4% or 0.6%, and would different limits improve performance?

An efficient way of investigating the effect of varying constraint values is to replace a hard constraint:

$$d_j = a_j^T w - b_j \geq 0$$

by a penalty function. In this approach, negative values of d are permitted, but increasingly large breaches attract an increasing penalty. The logarithmic barrier:

$$\tau \ln(d_j), \qquad \tau > 0$$

is an example of a possible penalty function as is the logistic function

---

15 The most common member of this class is the multivariate Student distribution.

16 That is $\theta \to \infty$, to make dependence on variance vanish.

$$\frac{1}{(1+(1/\tau)e^{-vd_j})}; \quad \tau, v > 0$$

where the parameters τ and v are set to achieve the desired degree of penalisation.

25.11 Questions about Portfolio Optimisation and Discussion

Portfolio optimisation is a sophisticated technique, which is rich in terms of the facilities that it offers to the skilled analyst. Its perceived shortcomings can be overcome by careful use and, in the right hands equipped with good estimates, it can make a highly effective contribution to portfolio management.

Effective use of the technique does, however, make demands on the time and skill of the user. There are issues that will not be apparent to the casual observer, but which will require resolution by anyone who plans to use the technique operationally. The final section covers some of these issues. The following is not, of course, an exhaustive list.

Limitations on the Types of Forecast That Can Be Used
Strictly speaking, the forecasts of expected return should follow a normal distribution. This will rarely be the case. However, it is probably sufficient to be able to appeal to the Central Limit Theorem, which implies that portfolio return is asymptotically normal even if the distribution of returns on individual assets is not. Whether this is a safe course of action for a small number of highly skewed assets is an open question.

Is it a Good Idea to Maximise Expected Utility Anyway?
Expected utility maximisation is one of the central components of the methodology of economics and hence of finance. However, in finance we are compensated for what actually happens and not what we expect to happen. The utility of return is a random variable. A strategy that maximises its expected value may result in a distribution of utility that has high variance. The actual value of utility – the basis for our compensation – may then be very different from what we expect. In short, there is always some sense in considering new criteria, even in cases where all they do is position us elsewhere on the efficient frontier.

Does it Matter if We Do not Implement the Exact Output from an Optimiser?
We rarely implement the exact output, because of lot sizes and/or the need to trade in whole numbers of securities or contracts. Whether it makes a difference to an individual strategy is easily determined empirically.

A more important question is whether the imposition of lot size or trade size constraints would lead to a significantly different optimised portfolio in the first place. This transforms QP into a mixed integer quadratic programme. Cardinality constraints – restricting the number of assets in a portfolio – are studied by Chang *et al.* (2000).

Resampling and Bootstrapping
The idea of reducing the sensitivity of an optimised portfolio by resampling has been popularised by Richard Michaud (1998). Resampling will reduce sensitivity and the incidence of corner solutions. However, as Michaud (1998, p. 62) notes, it is still necessary to have good estimates of expected return.

Computational Limitations
The time taken to solve a QP is roughly proportional to N^2. Unless N is very large, it seems unlikely that computational limitations will be a problem. However, it is important to bear the other parameters of back-testing in mind. As well as T, the length of the history, resampling can add both to time and to output storage needs. Use of non-linear modelling methods and estimation of the VC matrix using true multi-variate GARCH would also add a substantial overhead.

Estimation of the VC Matrix
A consequence of the belief in the importance of accuracy in estimates of expected return is a generally low level of effort in estimation of the VC matrix. Many use rolling historic averages or exponential smoothing. Reduced forms are also commonly used, these being convenient by-products of factor models and the market model.

There is a growing body of evidence that suggests that the use of GARCH methods will lead to improved VC matrix estimation – see for example Rossi and Zucca (2000) or Gerhard and Hess (2002).

Use of Non-quadratic Objective Functions
As long as the function is convex, then optimisation subject to the linear constraints that are found in finance is usually straight forward.

Should We Experiment with Lots of Models?
We all do this! The temptation is frequently irresistible. There is a telling analysis by Halbert White[17], which illustrates the dangers. If we have several models and built an optimised portfolio corresponding to each, the resulting returns when ranked are like a set of order statistics. Picking the best is taking something from the right-hand tail of the distribution. Future returns based on the chosen model will not always come from this tail.

---

17 Keynote address at the 24th Meeting of the Euro Working Group on Financial modelling held in 1999 in Valencia. See White (2000) and Sullivan *et al.* (1999) for more details.

26. Multi-Agent Modelling

John G. Taylor

26.1 Introduction

We discussed in Chapter 1 the manner in which effects at different time-scales play a role in the financial markets:

- For long time-scales (monthly or more) economic fundamentals are recognisably playing an influence.
- For short time-scales (daily or less) market sentiment and trading psychology are present to a much higher degree.

Such a sharp separation is not necessarily valid, however; market sentiment and psychology may also be influencing the longer-term trends. Thus if market confidence is low prices will be expected to drop and risk aversion to increase. Thus it is of value to incorporate such effects, where possible, in the longer term models. At the same time it is important to tackle extension of prediction modelling to higher frequency data. That has been attempted by a number of groups, using similar technology to our own in *NewQuant*. Yet we suggest that there is not much success in such modelling, since the problems presented by trader dynamics are highly non-linear. This leads to most of the signal looking like pure noise. It is driven by many stochastic terms, corresponding to the large number of available investor strategies. What can be said about such market dynamics?

One approach is to consider more simplified models of a market, in which only a restricted set of strategies is available to investors. This has been done recently for the minority game, and exact quantitative results (Coolen and Heimel, 2001) will be reported below on this. Beyond this rather simple model of the financial markets, a number of simulations of more realistic multi-agent models of the financial markets have become available (Ankebrand and Tomasini, 1997; Patterson, 1998; Iori, 1999). These indicate that it is possible to capture in such models certain global aspects of financial dynamics (burst in volatility, for example).

Following this work, the purpose of the main part of this chapter is to develop a non-linear framework for the creation of prediction models which includes certain general features of market forces. In this way it is hoped to include in particular a certain level of domain knowledge, and so help make the prediction process easier and more effective. Presently such domain knowledge is completely foreign to *NewQuant* methodology, which sets up models in a somewhat blind and untutored manner. This is satisfactory if the main functionality is composed of economic driving forces. The addition of agents in this context, with their completely unknown functionality, can only add a percentage of extra value. However, market sentiment has been an important feature over several years, as the "irrational exuberance" of the late 1990s and earl 2000s showed so strongly. The importance of inclusion of market sentiment has already been noted in various chapters. It is possible that some of our indicators already contain components of such market sentiment, as we noted above in the influence of market sentiment and psychology on long time-scales. We have not, however, explicitly considered indices of market confidence, such as those determined by the CBI and similar organisations in the USA and other countries. Thus for longer term data, such as that gathered monthly or quarterly, we may be able to dispense with a micro-economic approach, in which aggregates of single agents are explicitly considered. However for shorter term predictions such a framework may be essential. This is explored, but only the framework can be described. Both mathematical analysis, possibly along the lines of the statistical mechanical ideas of (Coolen and Heimel, 2001) as given for the minority game, and simulation, using *NewQuant* methodology, can expose any possible value. However, independently of that the framework has a certain natural character about it, so it deserves expression and further development.

26.2   The Minority Game

The minority game is played by a fixed set N of agents, At each time step they each have to decide whether to buy or to sell (the same amount of a given asset). Profit is made only by those traders who find themselves in the minority. The essence of the game is that each trader individually wishes to make a profit. However, the net effect of the trading strategy of each trader is relative to the bids made by the other traders: there is a high degree of frustration, since all traders cannot be successful at the same time. It is possible to allow agents to have knowledge of the past history of the market. However, it has been discovered by simulation (Coolen and Heimel, 2001, and references therein) that this does not seem to play any role in the market dynamics; no difference is observed in simulations if a random past history is provided to each trader. Each trader has available p decision strategies, each of these producing either a buy or sell signal.

For a large number N of traders it has been discovered by simulation that as the ratio p/N varies, there is a critical value dividing a situation were agents can have profitable strategies (for $p/N > 1$) from a regime in which average profitability is worse than random. This critical value corresponds to the existence of some phase transition. A similar situation turns out also to hold if decision-making by agents is not deterministic but also has a random element. These features were not expected, and show that the properties of even an apparently simple model of this form can have very complex behaviour.

26.3   A General Multi-agent Approach to the Financial Markets

We now develop a more general approach, in which there are a range of traders and investors, each with their own strategy for buying or selling, in this case a range of assets (Ankenbrand and Tomasini, 1997; Patterson, 1998; Iori, 1999). A further essential difference from the minority game is that the strategy used depends both on a set of asset predictions and on a portfolio optimisation methodology. In more detail, the basis of the approach is to assume the existence of an ensemble of agents (investors) who make trades through traders and thereby influence the markets. The level of risk assumed by each of these agents is variable, being part of the definition of the ensemble character. Each agent is assumed to run a portfolio of assets, and at the end of each period T (assumed initially the same for them all) reallocates these assets on the basis of a set of predictors the agent has constructed for the asset. We develop the details of the model in the following sub-sections.

26.3.1 Single Agent Structure

Each agent is assumed to have a predictor $p(m, t)$ for each market asset m at each time t, defined by a general function of both multivariate and univariate data:

$$p(m,t) = F(p(\text{multivariate}, t-1), p(\text{univariate}, t-1)) + \varepsilon(t) \qquad (26.1)$$

where "multivariate" in equation (26.1) denotes a set of multivariate variables at time $t - 1$ or earlier, and "univariate" denotes the target series at earlier times. The predictor may itself be a combination of predictions, obtained, for example by averaging or by more sophisticated methods. Predictions are combined in an optimiser to give allocation weights $w(m, t)$ to market m, using a mean–variance optimiser, so with assignments (modulo weight normalising to sum to unity)

$$w(t) = V(t)^{-1} p(t) \qquad (26.2)$$

in which $V(t)$ denotes the risk matrix for the various target series in the portfolio at time t. Allocations are changed at time I by the change

$$w(t-1) \rightarrow w(t)$$

with no problems assumed for liquidity, etc.

Each agent then trades by changing the allocations in each market according to the new weights, provided the changes are above a certain threshold (Θ and Θ'):

$$\text{Buy in market } m \text{ if: } w(m,t) > w(m,t-1) + \Theta$$

$$\text{Sell in market } m \text{ if: } w(m,t) < w(m,t-1) - \Theta'$$

$$\text{Hold: otherwise}$$

26.3.2 Price Changes in the Market

For an ensemble N of agents as above, the resulting price changes for each market asset are determined by the volumes of trades:

$$\text{Buy volume } B(m,t) = \sum ([w(m,t) - w(m,t-1)] | w(m,t) > w(m,t-1) + \Theta) \quad (26.3)$$

$$\text{Sell volume } S(m,t) = \sum ([w(m,t-1) - w(m,t)] | w(m,t) < w(m,t-1) - \Theta') \quad (26.4)$$

$$\text{Hold volume } H(m,t) = N - B(t) - S(t)$$

The price $P(m, t)$ is determined from that at time $t - 1$ as

$$P(m,t) = G(P(m,t-1), B(m,t), S(m,t)) \quad (26.5)$$

for some unknown function G. Various assumptions have been made for G:

$$G(x, y, z) = x + \frac{a(y-z)}{y+z} \quad (26.6)$$

$$G(x, y, z) = x \cdot e^{(a(y-z)/(y+z))} \quad (26.7)$$

That different functions have been chosen across authors is an indication of possible ambiguities; equation (26.6) has been used by Ankenbrand and Tomasini (1997) and Patterson (1998), whilst equation (26.7) has been used by Iori (1999).

26.3.3 The Iterative Process

The new prices at time t are then used in the univariate prediction models to develop further prediction models, new portfolio allocations and hence new prices at the next time point.

26.3.4 Implications for Prediction Model Creation

The process of model creation may be helped by the following features from Section 26.2:

- The return is to be modelled as an unknown function G of the buy and sell volumes, B and S, as in equation (26.5).
- B and S are determined by the non-linear equations (26.3) and (26.4) in terms of the weight allocations.
- The weights are determined by the linear equations (26.2) in terms of the predictions.
- The predictions are determined by the non-linear models (26.1).

The overall unknown functionality is thus:

The function G

The prediction model F

The unknown distributions, in the ensemble of agents, over the parameters Θ, Θ' and over those in the prediction models

It is in these places that non-linear modelling is required.

26.3.5 Overall Information Flow

This takes the form:

$$\{\{w(m,t-1), w(m,t-2),\ldots\}\} \rightarrow \{B(m,t-1), S(m,t-1)\} \rightarrow \{p(m,t-1)\}$$
$$\rightarrow \{p(m,t)\} \rightarrow \{w(m,t)\}$$

where the double bracket denotes the investors ensemble and the market ensemble respectively, and the single brackets only the market ensemble, and the various steps require knowledge of:

- averaging over the investors ensemble
- use of unknown G
- use of unknown F
- use of portfolio optimiser
- timings of individual reallocations (so leading to a stochastic process for the allocation changes in the ensemble of investors).

The total lack of knowledge can be reduced by the following assumptions:

For G, assume the values (26.4a) or (26.4b);
For the investors ensemble, assume initially that there is no variation on Θ, Θ'.
For F, assume F common to all investors, such as a linear regressor.
For the choice of the multivariate variables, take all the same.

Then all investors are identical initially; at the second stage Gaussian probability distributions can be introduced for the spread in Θ, Θ' over investors (so the investment process becomes a stochastic one), and that there is a distribution over the possible sets of prediction models.

26.4 Conclusions

A framework of an ensemble of agents can be formulated in which there are specific uncertainties (along with many simplifying assumptions). Thus it is possible to insert modelling technologies to determine the unknowns at these places using the actual target and indicator variables as part of the *NewQuant* process. This approach has already been considered for high frequency data by Iori (1999) and others referenced there. Further developments of this approach (Iori, 2000a,b) show how large fluctuations in returns in a market of interacting traders possessing powers of imitation and communication. Also, introduction of a trade friction reproduces empirically observed cross-correlations between volatility and trading volumes. Thus there is empirical support for this approach using a simplified model of the market place.

The value of this approach is still to be determined for longer term data. There are still several problems which have to be sorted out in developing the model in detail. We have already considered the uncertainty in the various non-linear functions in the model of Section 26.3. In addition, the time quantum we used in the model has not yet been specified. We can see that there are very likely a number of such time-scales. The shortest will be for high-frequency data (tick by tick). Then will come opening and close of day prices. The longest time-scales present will involve monthly figures, with associated quarterly economic data having an influence. At the same time there will be the periodic appearance of company reports and budget statements. There will thus be a complex interplay between the shorter time-scale effects and those with a longer scale.

Yet this approach, in spite of its complexity, will allow us to insert more efficiently the non-linearities which we were trying to catch with our non-linear neural network and univariate models, such as the GMDH, SVM and NNB models, in earlier chapters. Thus the non-linearities associated with the decision processing (26.3, 26.4) and the pricing formula (26.5) lead to a complex non-linear time series for the time evolution of the price P over time. It is unknown whether the methods developed successfully for the minority game (Coolen and Heimle, 2001) or for the high-frequency market data (Iori, 200a,b) can be extended to the more complex multi-time-scale model we have been describing. Large-scale simulation may be the only way forward. But a suitably careful approach should in the end be able to capture the essence of the market dynamics. It will not, however, be able to capture unexpected occurrences, such as the tragedy brought about by terrorist acts on 11 September 2001.

27. *Financial Prediction Modelling: Summary and Future Avenues*

John G. Taylor

27.1 Summary of the Results

This final chapter starts with a summary of the material of the book, and questions that arise from this, before attempting to view further avenues opened up by the work. To begin with, the philosophy of the prediction modelling approach has two main components, that determine its more detailed character:

- To attempt to capture as much information as possible from other financial and economic variables so as to improve the quality of the predictions of a given asset.
- At the same time not to neglect any information that may be carried by past values of the target time series itself.

This two-pronged approach leads to two distinct approaches to creating prediction models, and two further areas needing development.

1. On general economic grounds, predictive information on the values of a given financial asset is carried by earlier values of other financial and economic variables. This leads to the creation of a set of multivariate models, in which the other variables suspected of driving the target asset values enter on the right-hand side as inputs to the models, with the target values on the left as outputs. However, we are then faced with the question of which input variables to select from the very large number of potential driving inputs? Economic theory gives some general answers, but not a very large reduction, nor is it very specific. Therefore there is still an extensive exercise of input selection to be performed. Part of this can be done independent of detailed models, but there is still model dependence expected in finer selection detail. How to proceed to solve this problem was discussed in various parts of the book, using a general Bayesian-optimal approach as well as more detailed use of linear and non-linear multivariate prediction modelling techniques. The development of multivariate models of a range of forms was described in Part II from a theoretical point of view and in Part III from a more model-specific viewpoint. In Part IV the results of the application of these prediction model approaches to various asset were given.

2. On general dynamical systems grounds, a given financial target series should contain within its own past history information about its underlying dynamics, and so about its future. In an autonomous dynamical system this historical information would be complete; in the real world of financial markets, effects on market prices from outside the market system itself are important and cause a degradation of the value of a pure univariate approach. Thus events such as a change in the oil price or the US interest rate, or catastrophes like the 11 September 2001 terrorist attacks in the USA bring external information to bear that requires more than a dynamical systems approach. However, between such shocks there can be some value to extract from a univariate modelling approach, since the markets can expect to behave more autonomously. Therefore there also needs to be development of expertise in univariate modelling. The creation of univariate models of a range of forms was also described in Part II from a theoretical point of view, in parallel with the multivariate models, and in Part III from a more model-specific viewpoint. In Part IV (Chapter 23) the application of these univariate prediction models to various assets were described.

3. This leads on to the process of extraction of the best values of the two prediction approaches, univariate and multivariate, being optimally preserved by the development of suitable combining technology. This was accomplished by the temperature-dependent combiner, described in Chapter 24. This was shown to give added value in preserving and emphasising, in a combination of models, predictions from the best performing models over the previous period (chosen in our case to be the previous year).

4. Last, but not least, there is a need to allocate assets by portfolio optimisation. We have used a quadratic risk–return optimiser, suitably extended so as to avoid too large a dependence on the swings of monthly asset allocations caused by noisy predictions by various methods.

What, then, can we claim for the success of the overall process? There are two components to the answer to this question. Firstly we have described an overall process to solve the difficult problem of enhancing "gut feelings" of the future in the financial markets. Our advice can only be shown effective by its end product: the effectiveness of the various predictions made at the relevant future times for the appropriate assets. However, the predictive process itself that we have outlined is, we claim, a broad one, and can only help to enhance financial intuition. We accept that there are quantitative aspects not covered by our process, since we have not emphasised, for example, high-frequency data, such as foreign exchange or tick-by-tick asset values. Nor have we discussed stock picking. But we have avoided both (and other financial assets) for general economic reasons that we discussed in Chapter 1 and will discuss in more detail in the next section: the more successful areas for use of technical analysis are in the lower frequency monthly or quarterly range of time periods, and then for more secure assets. Data at this frequency has the effect of shocks, mentioned earlier, removed by suitable smoothing due to loss of market memory. Individual stocks involve very detailed data from the appropriate market sector. For that reason we expect the market data to be run mainly by other longer-term economic and financial effects, without too detailed a view of sector variation.

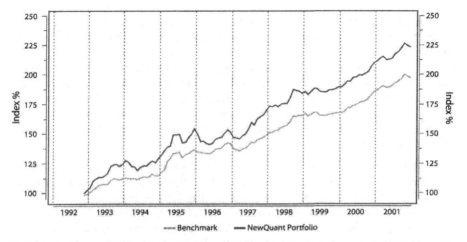

Fig. 27.1 Performance of live bond portfolio. The portfolio consists of bonds in seven markets (USA, Japan, UK, Germany, France, Canada and Australia). Allocations between the markets are adjusted monthly on the basis of predictions made by the *NewQuant* team.

Given that expectation, how well have we lived up to it for our predictions mainly of month-on-month bond and equity stock indices? To answer that, we developed various metrics to enable such estimates of prediction effectiveness to be calculated for a range of models separately, for the combined models through various combination methods, and finally for the effectiveness of the overall process including portfolio optimisation in terms of profitability. The ratios of evidences were shown to indicate that value was being added across all of these components. The bottom line are the month-on-month returns from the overall process. These are shown in Fig. 27.1, which is a plot of the outperformance of funds in a global bond portfolio measured against the Salomon Global Bond Index. This is a live history of funds managed since November 1992.

This shows a steady accumulated return over the period from 1992 to the present. It indicates that the overall process is effective. A more detailed breakdown is appropriate, but cannot be given here.

27.2 Underlying Aspects of the Approach

Let us move from assessment of the effectiveness of the *NewQuant* approach to put the methodology into a broader perspective. The world economic and financial scene has changed considerably over the period that the product has been in operation and the overall process has been in development (which is from 1992 to the present). At the time of writing (April 2002), the dotcom bubble has been and gone, the 11 September 2001 catastrophe has begun to sink into the collective unconscious, and the recession which was developing well before that has shown signs of bottoming out. In the UK and USA, manufacturing has suffered heavily, with increasingly important components being hived off to regions with cheaper manufacturing costs, such as in Eastern Europe or the Far East. Only 17% of GDP in the UK now comes from the manufacturing sector (as of 19 January 2002). The euro has also been introduced as the only legal form of currency across 12 countries in Europe (since 1 January 2002, although the process began a number of years ago). These changes all lead to alterations in the overall dynamics of the markets, and hence to increased difficulty in predicting future values of assets. Given this state of affairs, how can we explain the continued success of the *NewQuant* bond prediction process we have described and exhibited in Fig. 27.1? There are several factors we suspect are at work here:

1. We have used an assessment of only 12 months (the 12 months ARV) in determining the coefficients we use to combine predictions across models in a given market (as described in Chapter 24). This length of assessment period was tested, with comparison being made of results from 6 and 24 month choices, and even longer time periods. Twelve months was determined by our assessment metrics to be optimal for obtaining the best overall returns with relatively smooth upward slope over the period. Twelve months is a period which is roughly the time taken for interest rate and related economic statistic data to filter through the economy to affect factory products and so determine market expectations of bond values for investors.

2. Given that we are using a relatively short period over which to assess our models, we are taking a variety of models to enter the combination process. This may be important in that if there is considerable variation in market dynamics this could be catered for by the various model technologies. To illustrate this, we note that there appear to be considerable non-linearities in some of the best models. Thus for the USA, for example, recent models with greatest success have had a considerable non-linear component. Values for this can be read off from the most successful models (with evidence ratios, discussed in Chapters 15 and 24, of more than 1000) of above 90%. But at the same time in the USA successful linear models (although at a different level of evidence ratio) have also been created. In other markets multivariate and univariate models enter in combination, since both types have proved effective in the previous 12 months. Thus we suggest that our ability to weather the recent choppy weather of the financial markets is through the process of combining across a range of potential predictive models stemming from a variety of modelling technologies able to cater for a variety of dynamical structures and a variety of shocks.

3. A further feature of importance to note is that we have restricted ourselves mainly to a specific financial asset, that of global bonds with AAA rating. There are many other assets, some far more exotic, that we could have considered. In particular the darlings of the financial mathematics community are derivatives: futures, swaps etc., all with unlimited leverage but unlimited risk. The debacle with LTCM, which some commentators noted almost brought down the Western financial markets, in spite of having two Economics Nobel prizewinners at the LTCM helm, indicates the risky character of such products. At the same time, and as we noted earlier, there are many other assets, such as individual stocks, that we have not discussed at all. That is not to say that profit cannot be made from them, but information is needed to do that, as well as this being much more of a technical problem as far as we see it. But given the more general philosophy

basic to *NewQuant*, exotic or individual stock assets are more remote from our approach since they involve less in the way of a broad-brush approach to determine economic influences.

Finally, some of the comments under the previous point are relevant to the problems we have to face in prediction from changing influences and society: the increasing presence of the Web, increasing data availability, ever-growing dependence on modelling methods like ours, and competition from predictions of other assets such as the exotica we noted above. We have already answered the question about predictions of exotica: they are appropriate for risk-accepting clients with money to lose, but not for those who do not want to face up to losing considerable sums of money (but also with the chance of gaining considerable sums of money). The Web has made data far more available. That does not seem to have drastically speeded up the complex process that is involved in macro-economic changes making their way through into bond prices. This process is highly complex, but our data do not indicate any such more rapid flow of data. It is to be expected that there will be increased volatility of the markets over short periods, such as minutes to days. But the assets most affected will be foreign exchange and day-to-day bond prices. However, trends will remain being driven by longer term variations, these being exactly those arising from the macro-economic fluctuations we discussed earlier. That there is also more model prediction is not at issue; this is also expected to influence the higher frequency markets first. Ultimately the "slower" markets driven by economic data – the ones we have concentrated most on here – will succumb to even more quantitative analysis. But that has not happened yet, nor will it do so for some time to come.

27.3 Future Avenues

The point made at the end of the previous section, that of increased quantification of longer term financial and market components, is one which we tried to begin to consider in Chapter 26. There we introduced a model of the market process, in which dealers and investors interacted in a semi-realistic manner, and in which prices of assets were determined by the relative levels of supply and demand. Such a multi-agent approach is proving of interest across a broad range of areas of investigation, for example associated with the ongoing "Disappearing Computer" EC program of a range of research and development projects. These projects involve replacing the PC by a set of sensors and related intelligent agents. The latter are needed to enable useful decisions to be made about the sensor outputs, for example in the case of those from an elderly person undergoing a heart attack or a car driver falling asleep at the wheel. In the case of Chapter 26 we attempted to include in the multi-agent market model basic decision non-linearities involved in buying and selling and in price setting. Further non-linearities could then hopefully be determined by the non-linear modelling technologies we have described in this book: that is for us to test in the near future.

However, a multi-agent approach to financial markets is only one of a range of aspects still to be moved forward in our *NewQuant* process. Thus we need to:

- Constantly improve the metrics used to monitor the overall *NewQuant* process. This requires updating the evidence ratio and related measure, which is presently under way.

- Introduce and test new algorithms (such as the reinforcement algorithm of Chapters 12, 21 and 22) to try to capture an increasing range of market dynamics for the specific AAA assets under analysis. Again, this is under way.

- Extend the yield curve analysis of Chapters 4 and 16. This is an area with considerable mathematical analysis, but rather few published results for predictions across the yield curve. Again, this is under way.

- The combiner is under constant monitoring. Bayesian approaches to model combining have been popular in recent years in the information processing community, yet it has not necessarily produced an optimal method for combining model predictions in our domain of application. Model combination is thus under constant development in our approach.

- Finally, the optimiser is also under constant analysis. We have introduced an ensemble construction, so as to prevent too strong a movement of assets driven by varying predictions. This, as well as other features, have been shown by careful analysis to improve allocation effectiveness. The present methodology and parameter settings appear optimal. But we do not sleep on the job, and are constantly checking for further improvement.

Given the constant state of flux in the financial markets, and more generally in the work economy and in society at large, we expect that the material in this book will have to be modified somewhat to take account of such fluctuations. But our overall method has a strong degree of robustness built into it. That is clear from our use of many models, of a combiner picking predictions only from the few best models, and in the use of an optimiser containing features playing down strong shifts in assets across markets. We suggest that this approach holds a way of predicting the future which should be relatively immune to these changes.

Further Reading

Statistical Analyses of Data and Non-linear Dynamics

Casdagli, M. and Eubank, S. (eds) (1992) *Nonlinear Modelling and Forecasting*. Reading, Addison-Wesley.

Judge, G. G., Hill, R. C., Griffiths, W. E., Luetkepohl, H. and Lee, T.-C. (1988) *Introduction to the Theory and Practice of Econometrics*. Chichester, Wiley.

Nerlove, M., Grether, D. M. and Carvalho, J. L. (1995) *Analysis of Economic Time Series*. London, Academic Press.

Taylor, S. J. (1986) *Modelling Financial Time Series*. Chichester, Wiley.

Neural Networks in Finance

Bharati, R., Desai, V. S. and Gupta, M. (1999) Predicting real estate returns using neural networks. *Journal of Computational Intelligence in Finance*, 7, 5–15.

Donaldson, R. G. and Kamstra, M. (1996) Forecast combining with neural networks. *Journal of Finance*, 15, 49–61.

Geigle, D. S. and Aronson, J. E. (1999) An artifical neural network approach to the valuation of options and forecasting of volatility. *Journal of Computational Intelligence in Finance*, 7, 125.

Hanke, M. (1999) Neural networks v Black–Scholes. *Journal of Computational Intelligence in Finance*, 7, 26–34.

Journal of Finance: Special Issue on Neural Networks and Financial Economics, (September–November 1998), 17(5/6), 347–496.

Moshiri, S. and Cameron, N. (2000) Neural networks versus econometric models in forecasting inflation. *Journal of Finance*, 19(5), 201–218.

Refenes, A. P. N. and Zapranis, A. D. (1999) Neural model identification, variable selection and model adequacy. *Journal of Finance*, 18(5), 299–332.

Conference Proceedings

International Conference on Artificial Neural Networks, International Joint Conference on Neural Networks, Neural Information Processing

Proceedings of the International Conferences on Neural Networks in the Capital Markets, e.g. Refenes, A.-P. N., Abu-Mostafa Y., Moody, J. and Weigend, A. (eds) (1996), Singapore, World Scientific.

Books

Taylor, J. G. (1993) *The Promise of Neural Networks*. London, Springer.

Van Eyden, R. J. (1996) *The Application of Neural Networks in the Forecasting of Share prices*. Haymarket, VA, Finance and Technology Publishing.

Zapranis, A. and Refenes, A.-P. N. (1999) *Principles of Neural Model Identification, Selection and Adequacy, with Applications to Financial Econometrics*. London, Springer.

References

Abecasis, S. M., Lapenta, E. S. and Pedreira, C. E. (1999) Perfomance metrics for financial time series forecasting. *Journal of Computational Intelligence in Finance*, July/August, 5–23.

Adcock, C. J. (2000) The dynamic control of risk in optimised portfolios. *The IMA Journal of Mathematics Applied in Business and Industry*, 11, 127–138.

Adcock, C. J. (2001) In defence of mean variance optimisation. *Management*, 5(1), 109–118.

Adcock, C. J. and Meade, N. (1995) A simple algorithm to incorporate transactions costs in quadratic optimisation. *European Journal of Operational Research*, 79, 85–94.

Akaike, H. (1974) A New look at the statistical model identification. *IEEE Transactions on AC*, AC-19, 716–723.

Almon, S. (1965) The distributed lag between capital appropriations and expenditures. *Econometrica*, 33, 178–196.

Amari, S. I., Murata, N. and Ikeda, K. (1995) Learning and generalisation in neural networks. *RIKEN Review*, No. 9, April.

Ankenbrand, T. and Tomasini, M. (1997) Agent based simulation of multiple financial markets. *Neural Network World*, 4(4,5), 397–405.

Back, A. D. and Weigend, A. S. (1998) Discovering structure in finance using independent component analysis. In *Decision Technologies for Computational Finance* (eds. A.-P. Refenes *et al.*). Dordrecht, Kluwer Academic, pp. 309–322.

Banfield, J. D. and Raftery, A. E. (1993) Model-based Gaussian and non-Gaussian clustering. *Biometrics*, 49, 803–821.

Bawa, V., Brown, S. J. and Klein, R. (1979) Estimation risk and optimal portfolio choice. *Studies in Bayesian Econometrics*, 3, North Holland, Amsterdam.

Bentz, Y. (1999) Identifying and modelling conditional factor sensitivities: an application to equity investment management. *PhD Thesis*, London Business School.

Bentz, Y., Refenes, A.-P. N. and De Laulanie, J.-F. (1996) Modelling the performance of investment strategies, concepts, tools and examples. In *Neural Networks in Financial Engineering* (eds. A.-P. Refenes *et al.*). Singapore, World Scientific, pp. 241–258.

Bertsekas, D. P. (1995) *Dynamic Programming and Optimal Control*. Belmont, MA, Athena Scientific.

Bertsimas, D. and Lo, A. (1998) Optimal control of execution of costs. *Journal of Financial Markets*, 1, 1–50.

Best, M. J. and Grauer, R. R. (1991) On the sensitivity of mean–variance-efficient portfolios to changes in asset means: some analytical and computational results. *Review of Financial Studies*, 4, 315–342.

Bishop, C. M. (1995) *Neural Networks for Pattern Recognition*. Oxford, Oxford University Press.

Black, F. (1986) Noise. *Journal of Finance*, 41, 529–544.

Black, F. and Scholes, M. (1973) The pricing of options and corporate liabilities. *Journal of Political Economy*, 81, 673–654.

Box, G. E. P. and Jenkins, G. M. (1970) *Time Series Analysis: Forecasting and Control*. San Francisco, CA, Holden-Day (revised edn, 1976).

Box, G. E. P. and Pierce, D. A. (1970) Distribution of residual autocorrelations in autoregressive-integrated moving average time series models. *Journal of the American Statistical Association*, 70, 1509–1526.

Breiman, L. (1994) Bagging predictors. *Technical Report 421*, Department of Statistics, University of California, Berkeley.

Brindle, J. S. (1990) Probabilistic interpretation of feedforward classification network outputs, with relationships to statistical pattern recognition. In *Neurocomputing: Algorithms, Architectures and Applications* (eds. F. Fogelman Soulié and J. Hérault). New York, Springer-Verlag, 227–236.

Brock, W., Lakonishok, J. and LeBaron, B. (1992) Simple technical trading rules and the stochastic properties of stock returns. *Journal of Finance*, 47, 1731–1764.

Broomhead, D. S. and King, G. P. (1986) Extracting qualitative dynamics from experimental data. *Physica* 20D, 217–236.

Brown, R. G. (1963) *Smoothing, Forecasting and Prediction*. Englewood Cliffs, NJ, Prentice Hall.

Bunn, D. W. (1975) A Bayesian approach to the linear combination of forecasts. *Opinions on Research Quarterly*, 26, 325–329.

Bunn, D. W. (1985) Statistical efficiency in the linear combination of forecasts. *International Journal of Forecasting*, 1, 151–163.

Bunn, D. W. and Kappos, E. (1982) Synthesis of selection of forecasting models. *European Journal of Operational Research*, 9, 173–180.

Burgess, A. N. (1995) Non-linear model identification and statistical significance tests and their application to financial modelling. In *IEE Proceedings of the 4th International Conference on Artificial Neural Networks*, Cambridge, pp. 312–317.

Burgess, A. N. (1996) Statistical yield curve arbitrage in eurodollar futures using neural networks. In *Neural Networks in Financial Engineering* (eds. A.-P. Refenes *et al.*). Singapore, World Scientific, pp. 98–110.

Burgess, A. N. (1998) Controlling nonstationarity in statistical arbitrage using a portfolio of cointegration models. In *Decision Technologies for Computational Finance* (eds. A.-P. N. Refenes *et al.*). Dordrecht, Kluwer Academic, pp. 89–107.

Burgess, A. N. (1999) A computational methodology for modelling the dynamics of statistical arbitrage. *PhD Thesis*, Decision Technology Centre, London Business School.

Burgess, A. N. and Refenes, A.-P. N. (1995) Principled variable selection for neural network applications in financial time series. *Proc Quantitative Models for Asset Management*, London.

Burgess, A. N. and Refenes, A.-P. N. (1996) Modelling non-linear cointegration in international equity index futures. In *Neural Networks in Financial Engineering* (eds. A.-P. N. Refenes *et al.*). Singapore, World Scientific, pp. 50–63.

Campbell, J. Y., Lo, A. W. and MacKinlay, A. C. (1999) *The Econometrics of Financial Markets*. Princeton, NJ, Princeton University Press.

Carlin, B. P. and Chib, S. (1995) Bayesian model choice via Markov chain Monte Carlo methods. *Journal of the Royal Statistical Society B*, 57, 473–484.

Chang, T.-J., Meade, N., Beasley, J. E. and Sharaiha, Y. M. (2000) Heuristics for cardinality constrained portfolio optimisation. *Computers and Operations Research*, 27, 1271–1302.

Choey, M. and Weigend, A. S. (1997) Nonlinear trading models through Sharpe Ratio maximzation. In *Decision Technologies for Financial Engineering* (eds. A. S. Weigend, Y. S. Abu-Mostafa, and A.-P. N. Refenes). Singapore, World Scientific, pp. 3–22.

Chopra, V. and Ziemba, W. T. (1993) The effect of errors in means, variances and covariances on optimal portfolio choice. *Journal of Portfolio Management*, Winter, 6–11.

Cohen, K., Maier, S., Schwartz, R. and Whitcomb, D. (1986) *The Microstructure of Securities Markets*, Englewood Cliffs, NJ, Prentice Hall.

Coolen, A. C. C. and Heimel, J. A. F. (2001) *Dynamical Solution of the On-Line Minority Game* (unpublished King's College preprint).

Cootner, P. (1974) *The Random Character of Stock Market Prices*, Cambridge, MA, MIT Press.

DeBondt, W. and Thaler, R. (1985) Does the stock market overreact? *Journal of Finance*, 40, 793–805.

de La Grandville, O. (2001) *Bond Pricing and Portfolio Analysis: Protecting Investors in the Long Run*. Cambridge, MA, MIT Press.

DeLong, B., Shleifer, A., Summers, L. and Waldmann, R. (1989) *Positive Feedback Investment Strategies and Destabilising Rational Speculation*. Working Paper 2880, NBER.

de Menezes, L. M., Bunn, D. W. and Taylor, J. W. (1998) *Review of Guidelines for the Use of Combined Forecasts*. London Business School preprint, April.

Demiral, H. T., Ma, S. and Ji, C. (1995) Combined power of weak classifiers. *Proceedings of the World Congress on Neural Networks*, Washington.

Diebold, F. X. (1998) *Elements of Forecasting*. Cincinnati, OH, South-Western College Publishing.

Efron, B. and Tibshirani, R. J. (1993) *An Introduction to the Bootstrap*. New York, Chapman & Hall.

Eftekhari, B., Pedersen, C. S. and Satchell, S. E. (2000) On the volatility of measures of financial risk: an investigation using returns from European markets. *European Journal of Finance*, 6, 18–38.

Engle, R. F. and Granger, C. W. J. (1987) Cointegration and error-correction: representation, estimation and testing. *Econometrica*, 55, 251–276.

Eriksen, P. S. (1987) Proportionality of covariances. *Annals of Statistics*, 15, 732–748.

Fama, E. (1965) The behaviour of stock market prices. *Journal of Business*, 38, 34–105.

Fama, E. (1970) Efficient capital markets: a review of theory and empirical work. *Journal of Finance*, 25, 383–417.

Fama, E. (1991) Efficient capital markets II. *Journal of Finance*, 26(5), 1575–1617.

Fama, E. and Blume, M. (1966) Filter rules and stock market trading profits. *Journal of Business*, 39, 226–241.

Fama, E. and MacBeth, J. (1973) Risk, return and equilibrium tests. *Journal of Political Economy*, 81(3), 607–636.

Fama, E., Fisher, L., Jensen, M. and Roll, R. (1969) The adjustment of stock prices to new information. *International Economic Review*, 10(1), 1–21.

Fisher, L. (1966) Some new stock market indexes. *Journal of Business*, 39, 191–225.

Fletcher, R. (1987) *Practical Methods of Optimization*. New York, John Wiley & Sons.

Flury, B. (1986) Proportionality of k covariance matrices. *Statistics and Probability Letters*, 4, 29–33.

Flury, B., Schmid, M. J. and Natayanan, A. (1994) Error rates in quadratic discrimination with constraints on the covariance matrices. *Journal of Classification*, 11, 101–120.

Fogel, D. B. (1991) An information criterion for optimal neural network selection. *IEEE Transactions on Neural Networks*, 2, 490–497.

Frank, I. E. and Friedman, J. H. (1993) A statistical view of some chemometrics regression tools (with discussion). *Technometrics*, 35, 109–148.

Fraser, A. M. and Swinney, H. L. (1986) Independent coordinates for strange attractors from mutual information. *Physical Review A*, 33, 1134.

French, K. R. (1980) Stocks returns and the weekend effect. *Journal of Financial Economics*, 8, 55–70.

Freund, Y. and Shapire, R. E. (1995) A decision-theoretic generalization of on-line learning and an application to boosting. *Proceedings of the Second European Conference on Computational Learning Theory*. Berlin, Springer-Verlag, pp. 23–37.

Frost, P. and Savarino, J. (1988) For better performance constrain the weights. *Journal of Portfolio Management*, 14, 29–34.

Gardner, E. S. (1985) Exponential smoothing: The state of the art (with discussion). *Journal of Forecasting*, 4, 1–38.

George, E. I. and McCulloch, R. E. (1993) Variable selection via Gibbs sampling. *Journal of the American Statistical Association*, 85, 398–409.

George, E. I. and McCulloch, R. E. (1996) Stochastic search variable selection. In *Practical Markov Chain Monte Carlo* (eds. W. R. Gilks, S. Smith and D. J. Spiegalhalter). London, Chapman & Hall, pp. 203–214.

George, E. I., McCulloch, R. E. and Tsay, R. (1995) Two approaches to Bayesian model selection with applications. In *Bayesian Statistics and Econometrics: Essays in Honor of Arnold Zellner* (eds. D. Berry, K. Chaloner and J. Geweke). Amsterdam, North-Holland.

Gerhard, F. and Hess, D. (2002) Multivariate market risk estimators: reliability and transaction costs in the context of portfolio selection. *European Journal of Finance*, 8, 1–18.

Gibbons, M. R. and Hess, P. J. (1981) Day of the week effects and asset returns. *Journal of Business*, 54, 579–596.

Gill, P. E., Murray, W., Saunders, M. A. and Wright, M. H. (1991) Inertia-controlling methods for general quadratic programming. *SIAM Review*, 33, 1–36.

Girosi, F., Jones, M. and Poggio, T. (1995) Regularisation theory and neural network architectures. *Neural Computation*, 7, 219–269.

Goffe, W. L., Ferrier, G. D. and Rogers, J. (1994) Global optimization of statistical functions with simulated annealing. *Journal of Econometrics*, 60, 65–99.

Granger, C. W. (1969) Investigating causal relations by econometric models and cross spectral methods. *Econometrica*, 37, 424–438.

Granger, C. W. (1983) Cointegrated variables and error-correcting models. *UCSD discussion paper*.

Grauer, S. R. and Hakansson, N. H. (1985) A half-century of returns on levered and unlevered portfolios of stocks, bonds and bills with and without small stocks. *Berkeley Program in Finance Working Paper No. 153*.

Greene, W. H. (1993) *Econometric Analysis*. Englewood Cliffs, NJ, Prentice Hall.

Griliches, Z. (1967) Distributed lags: a survey. *Econometrica*, 35, 16–49.

Grimmett, G. and Welsh, D. (1981) *Probability, an Introduction*. Oxford, Oxford University Press.

Grootveld, H. and Hallerbach, W. (1998) Variance vs. Downside risk: is there really that much difference? *European Journal of Operations Research*, 114, 304–319.

Grossman, S. (1976) On the efficiency of competitive stock markets where trades have diverse information. *Journal of Finance*, 31, 573–585.

Grossman, S. and Stiglitz, J. (1980) On the possibility of informationally efficient markets. *American Economic Review*, 70, 393–408.

Gultekin, M. N. and Gultekin, N. B. (1983) Stock market seasonality: international evidence. *Journal of Financial Economics*, 12, 469–481.

Hampel, F. R., Ronchetti, E. M., Rousseeuw, P. J. and Stahel, W. A. (1986) *Robust Statistics, The Approach Based on Influence Functions*. New York, Wiley.

Harrald, P. G. and Kamstra, M. (1997) Evolving Neural Networks to Combine Financial Forecasts. *IEEE Transactions on Evolutionary Computation*, 1, 40–51.

Harris, L. (1986) A transaction data study of weekly and intra-daily patterns in stock returns. *Journal of Financial Economics*, 14, 99–117.

Harrison, P. J. and Stevens, C. F. (1976) Bayesian forecasting. *Journal of the Royal Society, Series B*, 38, 205–247.

Harvey, A. C. (1989) *Forecasting, Structural Time Series Models and the Kalman Filter*. Cambridge, Cambridge University Press.

Harvey, A. C. (1993) *Time Series Models*, 2nd edn. London, Harvester Wheatsheaf.

Hastie, T. and Mallows, C. (1993) Discussion of Frank and Friedman (1993). *Technometrics*, 35, 140–143.

Hastie, T., Buja, A. and Tibshirani, R. (1995) Penalized discriminant analysis. *Annals of Statistics*, 23, 73–102.

Hatanaka, M. (1975) On the global identification of the dynamic simultaneous equations model with stationary disturbances. *International Economic Review*, 16, 545–554.

Haugen, R. A. (1993) *Modern Investment Theory*, 3rd edn. London, Prentice Hall.

Haykin, H. (1999) *Neural Networks – a Comprehensive Foundation*, 2nd edn. London, Prentice Hall.

Hlawitschka, W. (1994) Empirical nature of Taylor series approximations to expected utility. *American Economic Review*, 84, 713–719.

Hoerl, A. E. and Kennard, R. W. (1970a) Ridge regression: biased estimation for nonorthogonal problems. *Technometrics*, 12, 55–67.

Hoerl, A. E. and Kennard, R. W. (1970b) Ridge regression: applications to nonorthogonal problems. *Technometrics*, 12, 69–82.

Hohenbalken, B. von (1974) A finite algorithm to maximise certain pseudo-concave functions on polytopes. *Mathematical Programming*, 8, 189–206.

Holt, C. C. (1957) Forecasting seasonals and trends by exponentially weighted moving averages. *ONR Research Memorandum No 52*, Carnegie Institute of Technology.

Igelnik, B. and Pao, Y. H. (1995) Stochastic choice of basis functions in adaptive function approximation and the functional-link net. *IEEE Transactions on Neural Networks*, 6, 1320–1329.

Iori, G. (1999) A microsimulation of traders' activity in the stock market: the role of heterogeneity, agents' interactions and trade frictions. In *Proceedings of the 7th Annual Symposium of the Society for Nonlinear Dynamics and Economics*. New York, New York University Press.

Iori, G. (2000a) A microsimulation of traders' activity in the stock market: the role of heterogeneity, agents' interactions and trade frictions. *Colchester University preprint* (unpublished).

Iori, G. (2000b) Avalanche dynamics and trading friction effects on stock market returns. *Colchester University preprint* (unpublished).

Ishikawa, M. (1996) Structural learning with forgetting. *Neural Networks*, 9, 509–521.

Jacobs, R. A. (1995) Methods of combining experts' probability assesments. *Neural Computation*, 7, 867–888.

Jacobs, B. I. and Levy, K. N. (1988) Disentangling equity return regularities: new insights and investment opportunities. *Financial Analysts Journal*, May–June, 18–43.

Jacobs, R. A., Jordan, I. M., Nowlan, S. J. and Hinton, G. E. (1991) Adaptive mixtures of local experts. *Neural Computation*, 3(1), 79–87.

Jennergren, R. and Korsvold, P. (1975) The non-random character of Norwegian and Swedish stock market prices. In *International Capital Markets* (eds. E. J. Elton and M. J. Gruber). Amsterdam, North-Holland.

Jobson, J. D. and Korkie, B. (1981) Estimation for Markowitz efficient portfolios. *Journal of the American Statistical Association*, 75, 544–554.

Johansen, S. (1988) Statistical analysis of cointegration vectors. *Journal of Economic Dynamics and Control*, 12, 131–154.

Jones, C. D., Pearce, O. K. and Wilson, J. W. (1987) Can tax-loss selling explain the January effect? A note. *Journal of Finance*, 42(2), 453–461.

Jordan, M. and Jacobs, R. (1994) Hierarchical mixtures of experts and the EM algorithm. *Neural Computation*, 6(2), 181–214.

Kallberg, J. G. and Ziemba, W. T. (1983) Comparison of alternative functions in portfolio selection problems. *Management Science*, 11, 1257–1276.

Kalman, R. E. (1960) A new approach to linear filtering and prediction problems. *Journal of Basic Engineering, Transactions ASME, Series D*, 82, 35–45.

Karmarkar, N. (1984) A New polynomial time algorithm for linear programming. *Combinatorica*, 4, 373–395.

Kato, K. and Shallheim, J. (1985) Seasonal and size anomalies in the Japanese stock market. *Journal of Financial and Quantitative Analysis*, 20(2), 243–260.

Kingdon, J. (1997). *Intelligent Systems and Financial Forecasting*. London, Springer-Verlag.

Konno, H. and Yamazaki, H. (1991) Mean–absolute deviation portfolio optimization model and its applications to Tokyo stock market. *Management Science*, 53(5), 519–531.

Krogh, A. and Vedelsby, J. (1995) Neural network ensembles, cross-validation, and active learning. In *Advances in Neural Information Processing Systems 7* (eds. G. Tesauro, D. Touretzky and T. Leen). Cambridge, MIT Press, pp. 231–238.

Lapedes, A. and Farber, R. (1988) How neural nets work. In *Neural Information Processing Systems* (ed. D. Z. Anderson). New York, American Institute of Physics, pp. 442–456.

LeBaron, B. (1996) Technical trading rule profitability and foreign exchange intervention. *Working Paper No. 5505*, National Bureau of Economic Research, Cambridge, MA.

Lee, T.-H., White, H. and Granger, C. W. J. (1993) Testing for neglected nonlinearity in time series models. *Journal of Econometrics*, 56, 269–290.

LeRoy, S. F. (1973) Risk aversion and the Martingale property of stock returns. *International Economic Review*, 14, 436–446.

Levy, H. and Markowitz, H. M. (1979) Approximating expected utility by a function of mean and variance. *American Economic Review*, 69, 308–317.

Levy, R. (1967) Relative strength as a criterion for investment selection. *Journal of Finance*, 22, 595–610.

Lo, A. W. and MacKinlay, A. C. (1988) Stock market prices do not follow random walks: evidence from a simple specification test. *The Review of Financial Studies*, 1(1), 41–66.

Lo, A. W. and MacKinlay, A. C. (1989) The size and power of the variance ratio test in finite samples: a Monte Carlo investigation. *Journal of Econometrics*, 40, 203–238.

Lo, A. W. and MacKinlay, A. C. (1990) Data-snooping biases in tests of financial asset pricing models. *Review of Financial Studies*, 3, 431–468.

Lo, A. W. and MacKinlay, A. C. (1995) Maximising predictability in the stock and bond markets. *Working Paper No. 5027*, National Bureau of Economic Research, Cambridge, MA.

Lo, A. W. and MacKinlay, A. C. (1999) *A Non-Random Walk Down Wall Street*. Princeton, NJ, Princeton University Press.

Loistl, O. (1976) The erroneous approximation of expected utility by means of a Taylor series expansion. *American Economic Review*, 66, 904–910.

Lowe, D. and Webb, A. R. (1994) Time series prediction by adaptive networks: a dynamical systems perspective. In *Artificial Neural Networks: Forecasting Time Series* (eds. V. Rao Vemuri and Robert D. Rogers). IEEE Computer Society Press, pp. 12–19.

Lu, B. L. and Ito, M. (1998) Task decomposition and module combination based on class relations: a modular neural network for pattern classification. *Technical Report*, Nio-Mimetic Control Research Center, The Institute of Physical and Chemical Research (RIKEN), 2271-130 Anagahora, Shimoshi-dami, Moriyama-ku, Nagoya 463-003, Japan.

Lucas, R. E. (1978) Asset prices in an exchange economy. *Econometrica*, 46, 1429–1446.

Lyung, G. M. and Box, G. E. P. (1979) On a measure of lack of fit in time series models. *Biometrika*, 66, 265–270.

MacKay, D. J. C. (1991) Bayesian methods for adaptive models. *PhD Thesis*, California Institute of Technology, Pasadena.

Madala, H. R. and Ivakhnenko, A. G. (1994) *Inductive Learning Algorithms for Complex Systems Modeling*. Boca Raton, FL, CRC Press.

Makridakis, S. and Hibon, M. (2000) The M3 competition: results, conclusions and implications. *International Journal of Forecasting*, 16, 451–476.

Makridakis, S., Anderson, A., Carbone, R., Fildes, R., Hibon, M., Lewandowski, R., Newtaon, J., Parzen, E. and Winkler, R. (1982) The accuracy of extrapolation (time series) methods: results of a forecasting competition. *Journal of Forecasting*, 1, 111–153.

Makridakis, S., Chatfield, C., Hibon, M., Lawrence, M., Mills, T., Ord, K. and Simmons, L. F. (1993) The M2 competition: a real-time judgementally based forecasting study. *International Journal of Forecasting*, 9, 5–22.

Manly, B. F. J. and Rayner, J. C. W. (1987) The comparison of sample covariance matrices using likelihood ratio tests. *Biometrik*, 74, 841–847.

Markowitz, H. M. (1952) Portfolio selection. *Journal of Finance*, 7, 77–91.

Markowitz, H. M. (1959) *Portfolio Selection: Efficient Diversification of Investments*. New York, John Wiley & Sons.

Markowitz, H. M. (1987) *Mean-Variance Analysis in Portfolio Choice and Capital Markets*. Oxford, Blackwell.

Mees, A. I., Rapp, P. E. and Jennings, L. S. (1987) Singular value decomposition and embedding dimension. *Physics Review A*, **36**, 340.

Merton, R. C. (1973) Theory of rational option pricing. *Bell Journal of Economics and Management Science*, **4**, 141-183.

Merton, R. C. (1980) On estimating the expected return on the market: an exploratory investigation. *Journal of Financial Economics*, **8**(4), 323-361.

Michaud, R. O. (1998) *Efficient Asset Management*. Boston, MA, Harvard Business School Press.

Moody, J. (1992) The effective number of parameters: an analysis of generalisation and regularisation in non-linear learning systems. *Advances in Neural Information Processing Systems*, **4**, 847-854.

Moody, J. (1997) Optimisation of trading systems and portfolios. In *Decision Technologies for Financial Engineering* (eds. A. S. Weigend, Y. S. Abu-Mostafa, and A.-P. N. Refenes). Singapore, World Scientific.

Moody, J. E., Wu, L., Liao, Y. and Saffell, M. (1998) Performance functions and reinforcement learning for trading systems and portfolios. *Journal of Forecasting*, **17**, 441-470.

Müller, J. A. and Ivakhnenko, A. G. (1984) *Selbstorganisation von Vorhersagemodellen*, Berlin, VEB Verlag Technik.

Murata, N., Yoshizawa, S. and Amari, S. (1994) Network information criterion - determining the number of hidden units for an artificial neural network model. *IEEE Transactions on Neural Networks*, **5**, 865-872.

Muth, J. F. (1960) Optimal properties of exponentially weighted forecasts. *Journal of the American Statistical Association*, **55**, 299-305.

Nabney, I. T. (1999) Efficient training of RBF networks for classification. *Proceedings of ICANN99*. London, IEE, pp. 210-215.

Neuneier, R. (1996) Optimal asset allocation using adaptive dynamic programming. In *Advances in Neural Information Processing Systems 8* (eds. K. Touretzky, M. Mozer and M. Hasselmo). Cambridge, MA, MIT Press, pp. 953-958.

Neuneier, R. (1998) Enhancing Q-learning for optimal asset allocation. In *Advances in Neural Information Processing Systems 10* (eds. M. Jordan, M. Kearns and S. Solla). Cambridge, MA, MIT Press, pp. 936-942.

Newbold, P. (1974) The exact likelihood function for a mixed autoregressive moving average process. *Biometrika*, **61**, 423-426.

Orr, M. J. L. (1997) Extrapolating uncertain bond yield predictions. *Pareto Partners internal report*.

Owen, A. (1984) A neighbourhood-based LANDSAT classifier. *Canadian Journal of Statistics*, **12**, 191-200.

Packard, N. H., Crutchfield, J. P., Farmer, J. D. and Shaw, R. S. (1980) Geometry from a time series. *Physics Review Letters*, **45**, 712-716.

Pagan, A. R. (1975) A note on the extraction of components for time series. *Econometrica*, **43**, 163-168.

Park, J. Y. (1989) Canonical cointegrating regressions. *Econometrica*, **60**, 119-143.

Pao, Y. H., Park, G. H. and Sobajic, D. J. (1994) Learning and generalization characteristics of the random vector functional-link net. *Neurocomputing*, **6**, 163-180.

Patterson, A. (1998) A Multi-agent model of volatility in the financial markets. *King's College MSc Thesis* (unpublished)

Pratt, J. W. (1964) Risk aversion in the small and in the large. *Econometrica*, **32**, 122-136.

Press, W. H., Teukolsky, S. A., Vetterling, W. T. and Flannery, B. P. (1992) *Numerical Recipes in C*, 2nd edn. Cambridge, Cambridge University Press.

Raftery, A. E., Madigan, D. and Hoeting, J. A. (1994) Bayesian model averaging for linear regression. *Technical report 94/12*, Department of Statistics, Colorado State University.

Raviv, Y. and Intrator, N. (1999) Variance reduction via noise and bias constraints. In *Combining Artificial Neural Nets: Ensemble and Modular Multi-Net Systems* (ed. A. J. C. Sharkey). London, Springer-Verlag, pp. 163-175.

Refenes, A.-P. N. (ed.) (1995) *Neural Networks in the Capital Markets*. Chichester, John Wiley & Sons.

Refenes, A.-P. N., Burgess, A. N. and Bentz, Y. (1997a) Neural networks in financial engineering: a study in methodology. *IEEE Transaction on Neural Networks*, **8**(6), 1222-1267.

Refenes, A.-P. N., Bentz, Y., Bunn, D., Burgess, A. N. and Zapranis, A. D. (1997b) Backpropagation with discounted least squares and its application to financial time series modelling. *Neurocomputing*, **14**(2), 123-138.

Reinganum, M. R. (1983) The anomalous stock market behaviour of small firms in January: empirical tests of tax-loss selling effect. *Journal of Financial Economics*, **12**, 89-104.

Ripley, B. (1996) *Pattern Recognition and Neural Networks*. Cambridge, Cambridge University Press.

Roll, R. (1977) A critique of the asset pricing theory's tests. *Journal of Financial Economics*, **4**, 349-357.

Roll, R. (1983) The turn of the year effect and the return premium of small firms. *Journal of Portfolio Management*, **9**, 18–28.

Rosen, B. E. (1996) Ensemble learning using decorrelated networks. *Connection Science*, **8**, 373–384.

Ross, S. A. (1976) The arbitrage pricing theory of capital asset pricing. *Journal of Economic Theory*, **13**, 341–360.

Rossi, E. and Zucca, C. (2000) *Multivariate GARCH for Risk Management*, Working Paper.

Samuelson, P. (1965) Proof that properly anticipated prices fluctuate randomly. *Industrial Management Review*, **6**, 41–49.

Sauer, T. (1993) Time series prediction by using delay coordinate embedding. In *Time Series Prediction: Forecasting the Future and Understanding the Past*. Reading, Addison-Wesley.

Sen, A. and Srivastava, M. (1990) *Regression Analysis, Theory, Methods and Applications*. New York, Springer-Verlag.

Sharkey, A. (1998) *Combining Models*. London, Springer-Verlag.

Sharpe, W. F. (1964) Capital asset prices: a theory of market equilibrium. *Journal of Finance*, **19**, 425–442.

Shepherd, A. (1996) *Second-Order Methods for Neural Networks*. London, Springer-Verlag.

Slutsky, E. (1927) *The summation of random causes as the source of cyclic processes*. Econometrica, **5**, 105–146

Smola, A. J. and Schölkopf, B. (1998) A Tutorial on support vector regression. *NeuroColt2 Technical Report Series, NC2-TR-1998-030*.

Sortino, F. A. and Price, L. N. (1994) Performance measurement in a downside risk framework. *Journal of Investing*, Fall, 59–72.

Steurer, E. and Hann, T. H. (1996) Exchange rate forecasting comparison: neural networks, machine learning and linear models. In *Neural Networks in Financial Engineering* (ed. A.-P. N. Refenes *et al.*). Singapore, World Scientific, pp. 113–121.

Stock, J. (1987) Asymptotic properties of least squares estimation of cointegrating vectors. *Econometrica*, **55**, 1035–1056.

Sullivan, R., Timmermann, A. and White, H. (1999) Data snooping, technical trading rule performance and the bootstrap. *Journal of Finance*, **54**, 1647–1692.

Sutton, R. S. and Barto, A. G. (1998) *Reinforcement Learning: An Introduction*. Cambridge, MA, MIT Press.

Takens, F. (1981) Detecting strange attractors in turbulence. In *Dynamical Systems and Turbulence, Warwick 1980* (eds. D. A. Rand and L. S. Young). Berlin, Springer, Lecture Notes in Mathematics 898, pp. 366–381.

Tipping, M. E. (2000) The relevance vector machine. In *Advances in Neural Information Processing Systems 12* (eds. S. A. Solla, T. K. Leen and K.-R. Muller). Cambridge, MA, MIT Press, pp. 652–658.

Towers, N. and Burgess, A. N. (1999) Implementing trading strategies for forecasting models. In *Proceedings of the 6th International Conference on Computational Finance* (eds. Y. S. Abu-Mostafa, B. LeBaron, A. W. Lo and A. S. Weigend). Cambridge, MA, MIT Press.

Towers, N. (2000) Decision technologies for trading predictability in financial markets. *Unpublished PhD thesis submission*, Decision Technology Centre, London Business School.

Ueda, N. and Nakano, R. (1996) Generalization error of ensemble estimators. In *Proceedings of the International Conference on Neural Networks 1996*. Piscataway, NJ, IEEE Press, pp. 90–95.

Van der Sar, N. L. (1993) Asset allocation and the investor's relative risk aversion. In *Modelling Reality and Personal Modelling* (ed. R. Flavell). Heidelberg, Physica-Verlag.

Vapnik, V. N. (1982) *Estimation of Dependencies Based on Empirical Data*. Berlin, Springer-Verlag.

Vapnik, V. N. (1995) *The Nature of Statistical Learning Theory*. New York, Springer-Verlag.

Wagner, N. F. (1998) Portfolio optimisation with cap weight restrictions. In *Decision Technologies for Computational Finance* (eds. A.-P. N. Refenes, J. Moody and N. Burgess). Dordrecht, Kluwer.

Wallis, K. F. (1977) Multiple time series analysis and the final form of econometric models. *Econometrika*, **45**, 1481–1497.

Watkins, C. J. (1989) Learning with delayed rewards. *PhD Thesis*, Psychology Department, Cambridge University.

Weigend, A. S. and Gershenfeld, N. A. (1993) *Time Series Prediction: Forecasting the Future and Understanding the Past*. Reading, MA, Addison-Wesley.

Weisberg, S. (1985) *Applied Linear Regression*. New York, John Wiley & Sons.

White, H. (1988) Economic prediction using neural networks: the case of IBM daily stock returns. *Proc. IEEE International Conference on Neural Networks*, July 1988, reprinted in Trippi, R. and Turban, E. (eds.) (1996) *Neural Networks in Finbance and Investing: Using AI to Improve Real-World Performance*. New Yor, McGraw-Hill.

White, H. (2000) A Reality check for data snooping. *Econometrica*, **68**, 1097–1127.

Whittle, P. (1990) *Risk-Sensitive Optimal Control*. New York, John Wiley & Sons.

Williams, D. (1991) *Probability with Martingales*. Cambridge, Cambridge University Press.

Winkler, R. C. and Makridakis, S. (1983) The combination of forecasts. *Journal of the Royal Statistical Society A*, **146**, 150–157.

Winters, P. R. (1960) Forecasting sales by exponentially weighted moving averages. *Management Science*, **6**, 324–342.

Wolpert, D. H. (1997) On bias plus variance. *Neural Computation*, **9**, 1211–1243.

Yule, G. U. (1921) On the time-correlation problem with special reference to the variate-difference correlation method. *Journal of the Royal Statistical Society*, **84**, 497–526.

Zapranis, A. and Refenes, A.-P. N. (1999) *Principles of Neural Model Identification, Selection and Adequacy, with Applications to Financial Economics*. Springer, London.

Index

ACF   *see* autocorrelation function
activation function   157, 158, 160, 213
activity   89
adaptive lag
  kernel function   168
  kernel function derivatives   169
  networks   167*ff*
APT   181
arbitrage   181, 183*ff*, 193*ff*
ARIMA   31, 70, 72, 195
ARMA   72, 195, 204, 207, 209
ARMAX   72
ARV   *see* average relative variance
asset returns   23
attracting subspace   109
attractors   13, 14, 109
autocorrelation   104
autocorrelation function   19, 20, 73
Autocorrelation Test   30
average relative variance   50, 129, 153,
        154, 212, 214
axon   89

backpropagation   104, 160, 169
bagging   61, 63, 65, 67
Bayes   57, 118, 123*ff*, 145, 176
  evidence ratio   127
  integration   128
  theorem   125, 176
bias   62
bias variance trade-off   61
biased estimates   74
Black–Scholes–Merton   52
bonds
  pricing   35, 37, 39
  maturity   133
  yield curve   133
  zero-coupon   36, 134
bootstrap   61, 63, 65, 67, 78, 162, 246
  with noise   65
Box–Pierce test   27
breakthrough barrier trading   27
budget constraint   226

canonical correlation   181
CAPM   27, 33, 181, 227
central limit theorem   245
chaos   14
charting   30
cointegrating vector   183
cointegration   31, 43, 70, 73, 181*ff*, 194
combinations of assets   32, 73, 182–4, 194
  time-series   181
combiners   9, 211*ff*
  linear   212
  temperature-dependent SOFTMAX   212
  winner takes all   212
complexity   112–13
conditional entropy   81
conditional expectation   61
conditional probability   175
conditional statistical arbitrage   185
confidence   56, 62, 74, 78, 226
connection weights   87, 89, 92, 104, 111,
        158*ff*
control system   99
correlation   27, 30, 43, 66, 78, 113, 183,
        193, 228
cost function   49–51, 55, 58, 66, 103, 197, 213
covariance   44, 62, 65, 73, 223, 227, 233–5,
        243
cross-correlation   28, 251
cross-validation   56, 162, 171, 206, 207
cycles   28, 70, 75, 167

data
  analysis   6, 8
  economic   6, 11*ff*
  financial   15, 16
  frequency   7
  input data analysis   17
  selection   9, 41*ff*
  smoothing   16, 70, 71, 114, 167, 195*ff*
  statistical features   17
  temporal characteristics   16
data sampling   63, 110, 124, 125, 145, 206,
        242, 246

data selection   41*ff*, 253
decision making   96*ff*
decorrelated models   66
degrees of freedom   30, 109, 112–14, 186, 204
delay reconstruction   109
delay co-ordinate map   110, 112
delay embedding   111
delay vector   204
dendrites   89
Dickey–Fuller test   27, 73, 194
diffeomorphism   110
dimensionality   13, 43, 81, 109*ff*, 117, 121, 146, 147, 179, 203
directional symmetry   50
discount factor   35–6, 99
discounted least squares   71
distributed lag models   72, 167
dynamic trading strategies   29, 95, 97
dynamical systems   13, 93, 109*ff*, 254

early stopping   56, 162
economic environment   3, 5
economic influences   42
economists   41
efficient frontier   221, 222, 225*ff*
efficient markets hypothesis   7, 17, 23–6, 95
   random walk   26
   relative   25
   semi-strong   26
   strong   26
   weak   26
efficient set mathematics   225
eigenvalues   44, 113
eigenvectors   44
embedding   109, 111, 113, 115, 147
   delay coordinate   111
   dimension   82, 110–11, 147
   vector   110
ensembles   61*ff*, 175, 211
   agents   250, 251
   portfolio   242
entropy   81
   conditional   81
   joint   81
error correction models   70, 73–4, 184, 194
evidence   57, 120, 123*ff*
   ratio   127
example models
   Australian Bond Returns   149
   European bond returns   209
   German bond returns   173
   Japan Topix returns   173

UK Bond Returns   207
USA bond returns   165, 177, 216
exchange rates   7, 42
exponential smoothing   70–1

factor models   181, 232, 246
fair price   183
feedback   92, 163
feedforward networks   90, 91, 163, 177
financial markets   3–4, 23, 25, 27, 29, 31, 33
Fourier transform   19
free parameters   56, 135, 164
FTSE   4, 31, 185*ff*, 193*ff*
fundamentals   7–9, 11, 15, 17, 69, 183, 247
futures   4

GARCH   246
general economic model   42
generalisation   55, 57, 59, 101, 108, 117, 118, 158, 162, 172, 185, 205, 211, 216
generator   112
Gibbs sampling   145
global demand   42
GMDH *see* group method of data handling
government bonds   4
gradient descent   52, 92, 160, 178
group method of data handling   22, 140, 203, 205
   combinatorial   206
   iterative multilayered   207

head and shoulders   27, 203
hyperparameters   118, 120, 146
hypothesis testing   30, 73, 123, 125*ff*, 186

independent component analysis   181
indicator variables   147
   fundamentals   8, 11, 17–22
Industrial Revolution   4
inefficient traders   24
inflation   35
information content   109, 112, 113
information criteria   57
   AIC   57
   final information statistic   57
   FIS   57
   mutual information   81, 82
   network information criterion   57
   NIC   57
   processing   87, 157
input relevance detection   78

input selection   15, 74, 77ff, 145, 148, 177, 186
interest rates   5, 35ff, 42, 52
interpolation   6
irrelevant inputs   77, 145, 148, 149

January effect   26
joint entropy   81
joint optimisation   193ff

Kalman filter   75-6
kernels   117ff, 146, 147, 167ff, 207, 209
kernel regression   118
Kolmogorov–Gabor polynomial   206

lags   5, 8, 12, 13, 30, 49, 52, 72, 77, 81, 82, 109, 146, 167ff, 206
leverage   4, 256
likelihood   73, 119, 125, 126
linear models   19, 69ff
linear regression   78
linear relevance vector machine   145ff

markets   5
   confidence   248
   degeneracy   24
   efficiency   23
   impact   97, 103
   models   see example models
   general form of models   49, 51, 53
   price changes   38, 250
   psychology   6
   sentiment   6, 42
Markov   5, 99
Markowitz   95, 221
mean reversion   183, 194
mean square error   49–51, 61, 71, 128, 146, 154, 206, 213
Merton Measure of Market Timing   29
Michaud   242, 246
minority game   247, 248
mispricing   104, 183ff, 193ff
MLP   145
modelling methods
   Black–Scholes–Merton   52
   ensemble methods   211
   GMDH see group method of data handling
   linear RVM see relevance vector machine
   mixture of experts   211
   multivariate   11, 15, 31, 56, 67, 72, 74, 146, 171, 181, 211
   nearest neighbour   203–5
   neural networks   87ff, 157ff, 167ff, 175ff, 186

RVM see relevance vector machine
SVM see support vector machine
univariate   11ff
models
   ARV12   50
   benchmark   129
   building   9
   combining   211ff
   complexity   56
   econometric   52
   generalisation   55ff, 211
   overfitting   55ff, 211
   parameterisation   51
   parameters   56
   predictive   49
momentum   161
monetary policy   5
money
   time value of   35
   supply   5, 42–3
moving average   19, 70, 71, 196
multi-agent systems   43, 247ff
multi-period trading   104
multivariate modelling   11ff, 146, 172
mutual information   81
mutual self-information   82

nearest neighbour   203–5
network ensembles   175
network integration   145, 175–7, 179
neural networks   87, 89, 91, 93, 111, 157ff, 176
   activation function   158
   architectures   90
   auto-association   90
   backpropagation   160
   classification   91
   feedforward   90, 91
   hetero-association   91
   MLP   159
   recurrent   91, 163
neurons   87, 158
   spiking   90
noise   14, 15, 62, 112, 148
noise traders   24
noisy data   205
nonstationarity   112

options   4
overfitting   55ff, 101, 135, 161, 205, 211
oversampling   112
overtraining   62, 162, 176

PACF   19, 73
pairs trading   183

parameters, effective number of   57
Pareto   135
pattern recognition   87, 117, 146, 159
PCA *see* principal component analysis
penalty function   58, 66, 244
perceptron   92
perceptron learning   92
phase space   112
polynomial lag models   72
polynomial model   206
portfolio allocation   9
portfolio theory   97, 221*ff*
   benchmark tracking   231
   constraints   230
   transaction costs   233, 236
   turnover   230
power spectra   19, 20
predictability   17, 120, 123*ff*, 175, 182
prediction
   multivariate   11*ff*
   univariate   11*ff*
predictions, combining   9, 221*ff*
principal component analysis   43–5, 181
prior knowledge   41, 110, 123, 124
probability   175
   a posteriori   126
   a priori   71, 112,123, 124, 126, 205, 214
   conditional   125
   distribution   125, 175
profitability   96
proxies   42, 184
pruning   118, 145, 206

Q-learning   96, 99
Q-statistic   30
quadratic programming   229

radial basis functions   207
random vector functional link   145, 178
random walk   15, 23*ff*, 69, 75, 96, 194
recurrent networks   92, 163
regression   51, 70, 73*ff*, 77, 78, 117, 120,
   147, 160, 184, 194
regularisation   55, 57, 59, 186
reinforcement learning   96, 99
relevance vector machine   118, 146, 148,
   203, 209
   linear   145*ff*
   multivariate   146
   prediction   146
return predictability   194
ridge regression   58, 74, 78
risk appetite   225*ff*
risk matrix
forecast VC matrix   242

semi-variance   242
   VC matrix   223, 242
Runs Test   27
RVFL *see* random vector functional link
RVM *see* relevance vector machine

S&P   4
seasonal component   19
seasonality   26, 75
Sharpe Ratio   190, 197, 199, 200, 227, 243
shrinkage   145
sigmoid   89
signal to noise ratio   181
simple moving average   70
singular value decomposition   114, 204,
   207, 211
smoothing   16, 70, 71, 114, 168, 185, 195,
   196
smoothing models   71
soft constraints   244
SOFTMAX   213
Sortino   242
spectrum
   singular   113, 204
   eigen   114
spiking neurons   90
state space models   70, 75, 109
statistical arbitrage   95*ff*, 183*ff*, 193*ff*
statistical learning
   networks   207
   learning theory   117
statistical mispricing   104, 183*ff*, 193ff
stepwise regression   78, 186, 194
stochastic modelling   75, 112
stochastic search variable selection   145
stock indices   7
stock market overreaction   28
stock markets   4
subspace decomposition   113
support vector machine   117, 203, 207
SVD   *see* singular value decomposition
SVM   *see* support vector machine
synapse   88, 89, 157
synthetic asset   99, 183, 184

Takens' theorem   110
technical analysis   30
technical trading   26, 203
time domain   112
time series analysis   12
trading
   actions   100
   environments   96
   restrictions   97
   pairs trading   183

path-dependent rules   196
strategies   24*ff*, 95*ff*, 184, 193*ff*
systems   95*ff*, 193*ff*
training rules   92
transaction cost models   98ff
transaction costs   27, 96*ff*, 193, 233, 236
transition equation   75
trends   16*ff*, 31, 70, 75, 104, 163, 183, 184,
   247

univariate models   11–13, 146, 147, 171,
   203*ff*
universal approximation theorem   93,
   176
utility function, portfolio optimisation
   225*ff*

VAR   *see* vector autoregressive model
variable ranking   78, 80, 145, 148
variance
   bias–variance tradeoff   61*ff*
   coefficient estimates   74, 78
   data   18, 27, 29, 43, 44, 69, 182, 186
   noise   58, 75, 148

target   62
Variance Ratio
   statistic   194
   test   27, 31
VC (variance–covariance) matrix   223,
   242, 246
vector autoregressive model   73, 74
vector machines
   relevance VM   118, 203
   support VM   117, 203
Volterra function   206
VR   *see* Variance Ratio

weak classifier   177
weight decay   58, 71, 118
Willner   135
window length   16–18, 70, 110–12, 196,
   209, 214

yield curve   35, 37, 39, 133
   convexity   39
   modelling   133*ff*
   parameterisation   135